FOUNDATIONS FOR A LOW-CARBON ENERGY SYSTEM IN CHINA

Climate change is a key problem of the twenty-first century. China, as the largest emitter of greenhouse gases, has committed to stabilize its current emissions and dramatically increase the share of electricity production from non-fossil fuels by 2030. However, this is only a first step: in the longer term, China has committed to reaching net-zero emissions by 2060. Through detailed discussions of electricity pricing, electric vehicle policies, nuclear energy policies, and renewable energy policies, this book reviews how near-term climate and energy policies can affect long-term decarbonization pathways beyond 2030, building the foundations for decarbonization in advance of its realization. Focusing primarily on the electricity sector in China – the main battleground for decarbonization over the next century – it provides a valuable resource for researchers and policymakers, as well as energy and climate experts.

HENRY LEE is the Jassim M. Jaidah Director of the Environment and Natural Resources Program in the Belfer Center for Science and International Affairs at Harvard University's Kennedy School of Government. He is also a senior lecturer in Public Policy at the Kennedy School. For the past three decades, he has written and taught about climate policy, electric vehicles, power markets, and China's energy and environmental policies. Before joining the Kennedy School, Lee spent nine years in Massachusetts state government as Director of the state's Energy Office and Special Assistant to the governor for environmental policy. Lee's recent research interests focus on energy and transportation, China's energy policy, and public infrastructure projects in developing nations.

DANIEL P. SCHRAG is the Sturgis Hooper Professor of Geology and Professor of Environmental Science and Engineering at Harvard University. He is Director of the Harvard University Center for the Environment. He also co-directs the Program on Science, Technology and Public Policy at the Belfer Center for Science and International Affairs at the Harvard Kennedy School. His research interests include climate change, energy technology, energy policy, and digital technology policy. From 2009 to 2017, he served on President Obama's Council of Advisors for Science and Technology, contributing on reports to the president on a variety of topics, including energy technology and national energy policy, agricultural preparedness, and climate change.

MATTHEW BUNN is the Faculty Lead of Harvard University's Managing the Atom research project. He is the author or co-author of over 25 books or major technical reports and over

150 articles in publications ranging from the journal *Science* to *The Washington Post*. His most recent co-edited book is *Preventing Black Market Trade in Nuclear Weapons Technology* (Cambridge University Press, 2018).

MICHAEL R. DAVIDSON is Assistant Professor in the School of Global Policy and Strategy and the Department of Mechanical and Aerospace Engineering at the University of California at San Diego. His research focuses on engineering implications and institutional conflicts of deploying low-carbon energy in China, India, and the United States.

WEI PENG is an assistant professor at the Penn State University, with a joint appointment between the School of International Affairs and the Department of Civil and Environmental Engineering. She is also an associate director of the Initiative for Sustainable Energy Policy in the School of Advanced International Studies at Johns Hopkins University.

PU WANG is an associate professor at the Chinese Academy of Sciences. His research involves climate and energy policies and sustainable development strategies, particularly the comprehensive environmental impacts of China's energy transition on air, water, and land use.

ZHIMIN MAO is a specialist at the World Bank focusing on the Western Balkan region's resources management and climate adaptation challenges. Previously, she was a Postdoctoral Fellow at the Harvard Kennedy School, Belfer Center for Science and International Affairs' Environment and Natural Resources Program, with a focus on China's low-carbon development.

FOUNDATIONS FOR A LOW-CARBON ENERGY SYSTEM IN CHINA

HENRY LEE
Harvard University

DANIEL P. SCHRAG
Harvard University

MATTHEW BUNN
Harvard University

MICHAEL R. DAVIDSON
University of California at San Diego

WEI PENG
Penn State University

PU WANG
Chinese Academy of Sciences

ZHIMIN MAO
Harvard University

CAMBRIDGE
UNIVERSITY PRESS

University Printing House, Cambridge CB2 8BS, United Kingdom

One Liberty Plaza, 20th Floor, New York, NY 10006, USA

477 Williamstown Road, Port Melbourne, VIC 3207, Australia

314–321, 3rd Floor, Plot 3, Splendor Forum, Jasola District Centre, New Delhi – 110025, India

103 Penang Road, #05–06/07, Visioncrest Commercial, Singapore 238467

Cambridge University Press is part of the University of Cambridge.

It furthers the University's mission by disseminating knowledge in the pursuit of education, learning, and research at the highest international levels of excellence.

www.cambridge.org
Information on this title: www.cambridge.org/9781108842389
DOI: 10.1017/9781108903103

© Cambridge University Press 2021

This publication is in copyright. Subject to statutory exception and to the provisions of relevant collective licensing agreements, no reproduction of any part may take place without the written permission of Cambridge University Press.

First published 2021

A catalogue record for this publication is available from the British Library.
Library of Congress Cataloging-in-Publication Data
Names: Lee, Henry (Lecturer in public policy), author.
Title: Foundations for a low-carbon energy system in China / Henry Lee, Harvard University, [and six others].
Description: Cambridge, United Kingdom ; New York, NY : Cambridge University Press, 2021. |
Includes bibliographical references and index.
Identifiers: LCCN 2021024596 (print) | LCCN 2021024597 (ebook) | ISBN 9781108842389 (hardback) |
ISBN 9781108828840 (paperback) | ISBN 9781108903103 (epub)
Subjects: LCSH: Energy policy–Environmental aspects–China.|
Environmental policy–China. | Climatic changes–Government policy–China. | Greenhouse gases–Government policy–China. | Carbon dioxide mitigation–China. | BISAC: POLITICAL SCIENCE / Public Policy / Environmental Policy | POLITICAL SCIENCE / Public Policy / Environmental Policy
Classification: LCC HD9502.C62 L4395 2021 (print) | LCC HD9502.C62 (ebook) | DDC 333.790951–dc23
LC record available at https://lccn.loc.gov/2021024596
LC ebook record available at https://lccn.loc.gov/2021024597

ISBN 978-1-108-84238-9 Hardback

Cambridge University Press has no responsibility for the persistence or accuracy of URLs for external or third-party internet websites referred to in this publication and does not guarantee that any content on such websites is, or will remain, accurate or appropriate.

Contents

Acknowledgments   *page* viii

1   Introduction   1

    DANIEL P. SCHRAG AND HENRY LEE

    1.1   Background   3

    1.2   Chapters Overview   7

    1.3   Conclusions   14

2   Reforming China's Electricity Market to Facilitate Low-Carbon Transition   15

    PU WANG

    2.1   Introduction   15

    2.2   Future Trends and Challenges in China's Electricity System   17

    2.3   Power Sector Governance   21

    2.4   Key Policy Questions   23

    2.5   Policy Recommendations   32

    2.6   Conclusions   36

3   Promoting Large-Scale Deployment and Integration of Renewable Electricity   39

    WEI PENG, ZHIMIN MAO, AND MICHAEL R. DAVIDSON

    3.1   Introduction   39

    3.2   Current Governance Structure and Policies   41

    3.3   Key Considerations for Integrating Large-Scale Renewables into China's Power System   42

    3.4   Elements of Foundations for a High-Renewable System in China   50

    3.5   Conclusions   57

Contents

4 Enabling a Significant Nuclear Role in China's Decarbonization: Loosening Constraints, Mitigating Risks 65

MATTHEW BUNN

4.1 Introduction 65
4.2 China's Current Nuclear Energy Picture and the Scale of the Challenge 67
4.3 Avoiding Catastrophe: Safety and Security 70
4.4 Building Public Trust: Siting and Public Acceptance 77
4.5 Improving Economics 81
4.6 More Modest Constraints 85
4.7 Unlikely to Be a Major Constraint: Uranium Supply 87
4.8 China's Investments in Advanced Nuclear Systems 88
4.9 Conclusions 91

5 Transitioning to Electric Vehicles 101

HENRY LEE

5.1 Introduction 101
5.2 Energy Security 103
5.3 Traffic Congestion 103
5.4 Air Pollution 103
5.5 Trade and Manufacturing 104
5.6 Deploying Electric Vehicles 104
5.7 What about CO_2? 104
5.8 Magnitude of Transition 105
5.9 Is Electrification of China's Vehicle Fleet the Optimal Path for China? 105
5.10 Will Electrification of the Vehicle Fleet Result in CO_2 Emission Reductions? 106
5.11 Realizing Deeper Deployment of EVs 108
5.12 EVs: The Vehicle of Choice? 108
5.13 Freight Transport 110
5.14 What Are the Economic Challenges to Passenger EV Penetration? 111
5.15 Charging Infrastructure 112
5.16 Home Charging 113
5.17 Will the Growth in Renewables Affect the Economics of Electric Cars? 115
5.18 Are There Reasonable Scenarios in Which Electrifying the Transportation Sector Fails? 116
5.19 Conclusions 117

6	From Barrier to Bridge: The Role of Coal in China's Decarbonization	121
	MICHAEL R. DAVIDSON	
	6.1 Introduction	121
	6.2 Rise of China's Coal Industry	122
	6.3 Politics of Coal and the Grid	127
	6.4 Rewiring the Coal Generation Fleet	132
	6.5 Direct Coal Use: The Other Half of the Challenge	137
	6.6 Conclusions: Opportunities for the Coal "Bridge"	141
7	Coordinating Strategies to Reduce Air Pollution and Carbon Emissions in China	157
	WEI PENG AND ZHIMIN MAO	
	7.1 Introduction	157
	7.2 Background	158
	7.3 Synergies and Trade-offs between Air Pollution and Carbon Mitigation Strategies	160
	7.4 Foundations for Long-Term Decarbonization	163
	7.5 Conclusion	165
8	Conclusion	168
	HENRY LEE AND DANIEL P. SCHRAG	
	Index	175

Acknowledgments

This book is the output of a yearlong Harvard Kennedy School (HKS) research seminar on China and the challenges of decarbonizing its economy and its energy mix. The seminar group met biweekly to discuss the topics outlined in this book and to critique resulting research produced by the group's members.

The seminar participants included the seven contributors to this volume, in addition to other faculty and postdoctoral research fellows at the Belfer Center for Science and International Affairs' Environment and Natural Resources Program and Science, Technology, and Public Policy Program. The group also included predoctoral research fellows Qinyu Qiao and Ren Tao.

We would like to thank our colleagues in China, who have hosted us in the past and given us unique insights into the complexities of the Chinese energy system; this includes Professors Su Jun, Xue Lan, and He Jiankun at Tsinghua University and Wang Yi at the Chinese Academy of Sciences.

We would like to thank Frank White, who edited multiple versions of the volume; Louisa Lund and Karin Vander-Schaff, who coordinated the HKS seminar; and Isabel Feinstein and Julie Gardella, who edited and prepared the volume's manuscript and publication materials.

We were also fortunate to have terrific graduate research assistants, including HKS students Bonnie Cao and Yihao Li.

Financial support for this project came from the Environment and Natural Resources Program's Roy Family Fund; the Italian Ministry of Environment, Land, and Sea; Harvard University's Center for the Environment; Harvard University's Climate Change Solutions Fund; and bp.

1

Introduction

DANIEL P. SCHRAG AND HENRY LEE

In the struggle to mitigate the worst impacts of global climate change, China's energy transformation will be a critical example for the rest of the world. As the world's largest emitter of greenhouse gases and the world's second-largest economy, China's strategies for blending economic growth with decarbonization will be watched carefully, particularly by rapidly-growing countries at earlier stages of development. China has made it clear to the world that it takes climate change seriously, and it is investing in multiple decarbonization strategies, from widespread deployment of wind and solar, to a growing nuclear program, to electrification of transportation. Indeed, China now leads the world in all three major forms of nonfossil energy deployment: wind, solar, and nuclear. China's bilateral agreement with the United States in 2014 was critical to energizing the Paris Agreement. China agreed to stabilize current emissions by 2030, and to increase its share of nonfossil primary energy (i.e., hydro, nuclear, wind, and solar) to 20 percent of total primary energy. But beyond 2030, China will need to start reducing emissions, joining most other developed countries in a steady march toward zero emissions, if it is to make good on its pledge to reach carbon neutrality by 2060.

The zero-emissions target seems distant, particularly for a country responsible for more than 25 percent of global fossil fuel–related CO_2 emissions. But zero emissions must remain the ultimate goal. Climate-modeling studies have demonstrated that the climate system responds above all to cumulative emissions of CO_2, the longest-lived major greenhouse gas, and is remarkably insensitive to the specific emissions trajectory [1]. This means that the long-term objective of reducing global carbon dioxide emissions to near zero as quickly as possible should be the primary focus of climate policy. And yet until recently, nearly all international climate negotiations – including the Paris treaty and the bilateral US–China agreement – have focused on near-term emissions targets.

Near-term targets can be important, particularly for the largest economies, because progress can be more easily monitored and verified. Moreover, such targets encourage the growth of low-carbon technologies, particularly those that are already competitively priced, such as low-penetration wind and solar. But the development of critical technologies needed to achieve deeper reductions in the long run – such as next-generation nuclear power, advanced biofuels, or economical strategies for managing high penetration of intermittent energy sources such as solar and wind – is crucial. Such technologies must receive attention now to allow them to become options for the future. A balance is needed between investments that will lower emissions in the near term and investments that may have only a small effect on emissions over the next few years but will be critical to achieving success in the long run. The latter can be neglected if the sole focus is on near-term emissions targets.

In China, most energy policy analysis has focused on how to achieve the 2030 targets, although attention to longer-term emissions reductions is beginning. One of the biggest challenges for Chinese decarbonization efforts is to find a substitute for the more than 1,000 GW of coal-fired power plants that currently dominate the electricity sector and the additional 200 GW under construction as of the end of 2020. Currently, there is no plan for how to achieve this transition, and very little discussion about what might happen beyond 2030. Rapidly-growing wind and solar deployments in China are leading the world, with nearly half of global wind and nearly a third of global solar photovoltaic (PV) capacity. Renewable electricity is now nearly 40 percent of the total generation capacity with wind and solar each representing more than 10 percent of electricity generation. Will expanding wind and solar capacity be able to displace coal in the electricity sector? The answer may depend on critical decisions made today related to siting of generating capacity and transmission. Most importantly, it is likely to depend heavily on smart energy policy, which will set the stage for decarbonization in China beyond 2030. Carbon pricing, electricity market reform, and infrastructure policy, for example, will all play important roles in constraining various technological pathways for decarbonization, and may affect how easy it will be to achieve high levels of penetration of wind and solar capacity.

Another example of near-term policies likely to affect future energy systems is the strategic deployment of electric vehicles. Policies that encourage electric vehicles in China are primarily motivated by concerns about air pollution and energy security, as China is now the world's largest importer of oil. Electric vehicles in China are likely to have limited impact on CO_2 emissions over the next two decades due to the electricity sector's heavy dependence on coal. So, if one were concerned only with near-term emissions targets, electric vehicles would not be a major priority. If one considers decarbonization beyond 2030, however, investment in electric vehicles today may be the only way to lower greenhouse gas emissions from vehicles in the future, as decarbonization of the electricity sector proceeds.

In this book, we consider how a long-term perspective on decarbonization can affect current energy and climate policy choices. It would be naïve to think that decisions about energy policy in China today will be dominated by long-term concerns several decades into the future. Moreover, the advance of multiple energy technologies, from batteries to nuclear power plants, makes it difficult to predict what technologies are likely to be deployed in the future. If one evaluates energy policies and electricity market reforms in China today purely based on the near-term emissions targets over the next decade, some important opportunities for long-term technology development may be lost. Through detailed discussions of electricity pricing, electric vehicle policies, nuclear energy policies, and renewable energy policies, this book considers how near-term climate and energy policies can affect long-term decarbonization pathways beyond 2030, building the foundations for decarbonization in advance of its realization. The book focuses primarily on the electricity sector, simply because electricity will be the main battleground for decarbonization over the next century. There are certainly important efforts to decarbonize other parts of the energy system beyond electricity, such as biofuels or low-carbon fuels for heavy freight transport and air travel. But such technological changes are likely to occur later in the sequence of decarbonization steps, as their current costs are much higher than those discussed in this book.

China shows no sign of shrinking from its new position as a global leader in addressing climate change, as indicated by the EU–China climate discussions. As China continues down the path of decarbonization, the reforms discussed in this book will be important to allowing long-term decarbonization goals to be achieved more smoothly and with reduced long-term costs.

1.1 Background

1.1.1 China's Climate Progress Prior to the Paris Agreement

China's carbon emissions experienced rapid growth due to its fast-growing economy. In 1990, energy-related carbon emissions from China were 2.2 billion tons of CO_2, accounting for roughly one-tenth of the world's total, while US emissions were more than 5 billion tons, close to a quarter of the world's total. By 2019, China's energy-related emissions had increased to almost 10 billion tons, nearly 4 times its 1990 level, while the United States had added only 5 percent. In 2008, China surpassed the United States, becoming the largest carbon emitter in the world. In 1990, China's per capita carbon emissions were less than half the world average; in 2007, China's per capita carbon emissions exceeded the world average and are now quickly approaching the level of the 28 EU Member States.

In 2009, China set its 2020 carbon management target under the Copenhagen Accord, reducing its carbon intensity – measured as carbon emissions per unit of GDP – by 40–45 percent, as compared to the 2005 level. By the end of 2014, China's carbon intensity was 33 percent lower than it had been in 2005, well on track to deliver its Copenhagen pledge. Meanwhile, China's energy-related carbon emissions continued to grow, from 5.5 billion tons in 2005 to nearly 10 billion tons in 2014.

Despite the continued increase in total carbon emissions, the growth rate of Chinese emissions has decreased since 2005. Several different government policies have played key roles in bringing down the carbon growth rate. First, energy efficiency in all major sectors has been improving. Coal-fired power plants now use less than 290 grams of coal per kWh of electricity. The best coal-fired power plants in China are now the global leader in energy efficiency, and the national average efficiency of all Chinese power plants is rising to be among the best in the world.

A second factor in slowing the growth rate in emissions is the development of renewable energy. China is now leading the world in investing in renewable energy, contributing to more than a quarter of the world total. Nearly 50 percent of installed wind generation capacity is now in China. The installed capacity of solar power generation in 2005 was 700 MW and grew to more than 280 GW by the end of 2020, a 400-fold increase in 15 years.

A third factor in reducing the growth in emissions has been a concern for air pollution, which has helped to set a cap for coal consumption in key regions, which will eventually extend to the whole country. However, it is unclear whether air quality will remain a major pressure on decarbonization as improvements in scrubbing of conventional air pollutants threatens to sever the relationship between CO_2 and air quality.

Fourth, some provincial and municipal governments have taken on leadership roles in exploring low-carbon development paths. From 2009 to 2012, 42 provinces or cities entered into a national pilot program for low-carbon development. These pilots seem to be making an impact on other subnational and local governments on choosing an alternative pathway for addressing economic growth and climate change.

Finally, China has made a deliberate decision to launch a nationwide carbon market for the electricity sector. When fully deployed, this market will be the largest carbon market in the world, more than twice the size of the EU cap-and-trade program.

In the context of this progress, on November 12, 2014, China and the United States signed a bilateral agreement on climate change and clean energy cooperation. Under the joint agreement, "China intends to achieve the peaking of CO_2 emissions around 2030 and to make best efforts to peak early, and intends to increase the share of nonfossil fuels in primary energy consumption to around 20% by 2030" [2]. This was the first time that China committed itself to a target for total carbon emissions. Assuming that these goals are achieved, China's carbon emissions will continue to increase by roughly one-third to one-half of the current level before it stabilizes or declines, reaching per capita carbon emissions of approximately 10 tons. Much of this progress will come from reductions in coal use in the industrial sector, outside of electricity generation. But perhaps the most important component of the joint China–US agreement is China's commitment to increase the share of nonfossil fuels in primary energy consumption to 20 percent. Reaching this target will not be easy, as it requires the addition of 800–1,000 GW of new electricity generation capacity based on wind, water, solar, and nuclear sources. If these goals are achieved, it opens the possibility that these nonfossil technologies will be used in the rest of the developing world as rapidly-developing countries make their own energy choices in the decades ahead.

1.1.2 How Will China Actually Reduce Emissions beyond 2030, Given Their Current Dependence on Coal for Electricity Generation?

The challenge of deep decarbonization in China is more difficult than in the United States because of China's enormous dependence on coal-fired power plants for electricity generation, as well as rapidly growing demand for oil in the transportation sector. In addition, based on current estimates of its natural gas resource base, China cannot follow the path of the United States and much of Europe in reducing emissions by substituting natural gas for coal. The capacity of coal-fired plants in China is currently more than 1,000 GW and growing, which makes longer-term progress on reducing carbon emissions especially challenging. Emissions from the transportation sector are roughly 15 percent of China's total emissions, in contrast to 32 percent in the United States. But as the largest automobile market in the world since 2009, emissions from the transportation sector are likely to grow without a major shift in technology. Hence, efforts to drive decarbonization will have to tackle emissions from both the electricity and transportation sectors. This will prove more difficult with a lower rate of economic growth than that experienced over the past two decades. Investments in infrastructure, including new electricity generation capacity and new transmission, will be more difficult to finance for a post-2030 China that may be growing at less than 5 percent per year.

1.1.3 Three Pathways

There are three main technological strategies for decarbonization beyond 2030, and China is likely to require a combination of all of them. One pathway is deeper penetration of renewable electricity, in particular wind and solar, as hydroelectric power has already expanded closer to its maximum. This is a large part of China's current energy strategy, as China led the world in 2018 in new solar (45 percent) and wind (44 percent) generation and has more than 32 percent of global wind and solar cumulative installed capacity. But China has not yet faced the daunting challenge of managing high penetration of intermittent renewable energy sources. Much of China's current wind capacity is in the north, and solar capacity is mostly in the northwest, but adequate transmission to bring power to the large demand centers does not yet exist. As deployment of wind and solar continues beyond 2030, China will need to explore storage and demand management among strategies to stabilize their grid. There is also a strong provincial component of this problem, as current electricity policy in China is heavily influenced by provincial decision-making, which can create obstacles for managing the intermittency of renewables by restricting interprovincial energy trade. In particular, current electricity pricing and electricity markets are not optimized to encourage the best investments, especially not in consideration of the system operation as a whole, rather than the needs of individual provinces.

A second pathway for decarbonization is the Chinese nuclear effort, with plans to add 150 GW of new nuclear capacity by 2030. Expanding this effort to the scale required to make a significant substitution for coal-fired power plants (currently more than 1,000 GW) seems daunting. Moreover, the current nuclear program is facing various challenges, including cost and local acceptance. Investments in nuclear engineering, both in research and development of new reactor designs and in institutional knowledge and experience in building reactors more cheaply, are best understood in terms of creating an option for a decarbonization pathway, if it becomes difficult to incorporate greater levels of intermittent wind and solar resources.

A third pathway is the electrification of the transportation and industrial sectors. Due to the rising standards of living and large-scale infrastructure development over the past two decades, passenger cars are gaining penetration in China at an unprecedented rate. Emissions from transportation, previously a fraction of those from manufacturing and electricity, will see the fastest growth among all sectors. A long-term plan to fundamentally transform the transportation sector should be an integral part of China's odyssey down the path of decarbonization. But such efforts can only be viewed in the long term, as rapid substitution of electric cars for petroleum-fueled vehicles raises overall carbon emissions in the short term, due to the high carbon footprint of the electricity sector.

All of these decarbonization pathways depend on China's ability to reduce, and eventually eliminate, the inflexibilities and inefficiencies that characterize its current electricity system. These rigidities extend the life of the most inefficient and carbon-intensive generators at the same time that China is actively promoting their replacement by nonfossil-fuel alternatives. The basic structure of China's grid system was designed more than 30 years ago to provide low-cost coal-fired baseload power to a rapidly growing industrial sector. The challenge at the time was to construct new baseload generation fast enough to keep up with the rapid growth in heavy industry and manufacturing. Approximately 70 percent of China's power in 2005 was consumed by industrial facilities, most of which operated 24 hours per day.

In a decarbonized energy system, the challenges will be different. Supplies from renewable generators – such as wind and solar – will be intermittent, while the demand will vary throughout the day. The growth in service industries, transportation, and the commercial sectors will increase daily fluctuations in demand. China will need to simultaneously increase the total capacity of its grid, while improving the flexibility of the system to account for changing supply and demand patterns. Structures that met China's energy needs 30 years ago will be impediments to its ability to decarbonize.

1.2 Chapters Overview

1.2.1 Electric Utilities

In Chapter 2 of this book, Pu Wang identifies many of these structural rigidities and provides suggestions for actions that China can take to fix them. Wang focuses on three problems: (1) Outdated governance structures lead to responsibilities that are inadequately delineated and often result in internal tensions and conflict; (2) The current dispatch protocol creates perverse investment and operation incentives, resulting in the overuse of the least efficient power plants, the curtailment of renewable capacity, and additional investment in carbon-emitting coal facilities and (3) Pricing policies disincentivize investments in needed ancillary services, such as peaking generators, demand-side management, and solar and wind capacity.

Most of China's electricity generators are state-owned monopolies, two grid companies transmit all the power, operate all the regional grids, and retail almost all of the country's electricity. Financing is provided by state-owned banks and almost every aspect of this industry is regulated by either central or provincial government agencies. Hence, governance has a greater impact on the shape of this industry than it would in a system more reliant on markets and private companies.

Multiple agencies and departments oversee various parts of the investment and operation processes at both the central and provincial levels. There is a lack of formal coordinating mechanisms to improve the interface between these agencies, and, as a result, they often embrace different priorities and act inadvertently counter to each other's intentions. As regional energy markets emerge, coordination among provinces will become more important, especially if China modernizes its national grid, allowing the country to move power efficiently between regions. To be able to decarbonize successfully, China will have to improve its governance structures at all levels and create institutional structures that will encourage agencies to work together.

Most power systems in North America and Europe have adopted a least-cost dispatch protocol in which generators with the lowest operating costs access the grid before those with higher operating costs, as long as the security of the grid is maintained. Since renewable generators have almost zero marginal operating costs, they are dispatched whenever they are available. Least-cost dispatch protocols maximize the efficiency of the grid and, by favoring renewable generators, advance low-carbon options. Wang points out that China uses an "equal-share" dispatch rule in which generators are guaranteed an equal number of operating hours regardless of operating costs. This system leads to greater inefficiencies, curtailments of renewables, and excess generating capacity. In 2018, for example, although China had a surplus of generating capacity, it still proceeded to build new coal-fired plants. The driver in creating these inefficient incentives was the equal-share dispatch system. Such policies may have made sense in the past when China was attempting to accelerate investment in baseload plants, but in today's market it is retarding China's ability to accelerate the development of a less carbonized grid.

As mentioned earlier, an electric grid with substantial renewable generation will need to maximize the flexibility of the system to account for fluctuations in supply and demand. This means that the coal and nuclear assets must be able to supply power in tandem with changes in demand. It also means that the government will need to stimulate investments in facilities that provide generation capacity for only those few hours when the demand is highest. Building flexible systems requires regulators to price power at its actual value, which is constantly changing throughout the day. As the energy system transitions to greater use of electricity and less direct fuel use, pressures on government regulators to amend tariffs to reflect the real-time value of electricity will grow. A decarbonized energy grid is almost certainly one in which electricity pricing reflects the value of power across time.

1.2.2 Coal

The greatest challenge facing any effort by China to decarbonize will be to reduce its use of coal, which is comparatively inexpensive and widely available. In Chapter 6 of this book, Michael Davidson points out that the difficulty of reducing coal use is compounded by two factors. First, China has embarked on an effort to close coal-fired stations around its eastern cities, build new facilities near coal mines and then transport the power to the eastern population centers through a network of high-voltage transmission lines. Second, many of these new facilities are among the most efficient coal-fired plants in the world, reaching efficiency levels previously thought to be unattainable. As a result, China has a large fleet of very efficient generating plants, and more than half of these have a useful life that extends beyond 2050. Any effort to prematurely close these plants will result in stranding a large asset base and forfeiting billions of dollars.

Hence, China has not only a strong financial disincentive to retire its coal plants, but strong incentives to build more of them as well. Many of the same incentives discussed in Wang's chapter on electric utilities, such as average cost pricing and equal shares dispatching, encourages investors – both public and private – to develop new coal facilities. Davidson identifies additional incentives, such as an array of tax and fee subsidies, less onerous permitting processes, and lower transmission costs, that favor the construction of new coal plants and protect the operation of older and less-efficient facilities. As a result, it will be difficult and expensive for China to reduce its dependence on coal for electricity prior to 2050.

In most countries, the vast majority of coal consumption is for electricity generation. Even in India, where direct use of coal for heating remains high, 75 percent of coal consumption is in the power sector. China is an exception. In 2017, 54 percent of China's consumption of coal was for industrial, district heating, and residential uses. Thus, any long-term plan to reduce coal consumption must include strategies to transition industries, such as steel and cement, to electricity, and eliminate coal-fired district heating, either by switching the plants to natural gas or developing other sources for heating, such as direct use of natural gas or more efficient heat pumps. Coal use for home heating remains common in rural communities in northern China. The government is committed to reducing and eventually eliminating such use in order to meet local and national health standards. Direct use in small heating systems is the least efficient use of coal, and eliminating it fits not only with the country's health goals but also its commitment to improved energy efficiency.

The move away from coal is likely to be fraught with political resistance, and also raises serious social issues. Coal mining employs four million people and hundreds of thousands more work in coal-intensive sectors, such as electricity generation, steel, or cement. Davidson argues that any effort to reduce China's coal production and consumption must be accompanied by a strategy on how to manage worker displacement and the social issues that go with it. These include environmental inequities in that the localities that bear the environmental costs are not necessarily the same as those that reap the benefits. Income disparities between provinces and cities may grow larger, as some flourish in a decarbonized economy and others struggle. If there are no programmatic or policy options readily available to manage this transition, governments are likely to slow the progress to a lower-carbon energy system.

1.2.3 Renewables

Deep decarbonization will require China to dramatically increase the rate at which renewable options, such as wind and solar, are deployed. In the period 2012–2018, China has been the largest producer and consumer of renewables. Annual growth rates exceed those of any other country in the world by large margins. Yet to actually reduce emissions, China will have to increase these growth rates much faster while reducing curtailments (wind and solar generators hooked up to the grid, but not dispatched).

In Chapter 3 of this book, Wei Peng, Zhimin Mao, and Michael R. Davidson describe the magnitude of the investments that will be needed in the renewable energy sector. If the challenge could be reduced to the singular task of increasing growth in renewable generation, China would likely meet whatever schedule it sets for itself. But the task is complicated by the same system deficiencies – a grid system that is too rigid, pricing policies that protect existing conventional generators and discriminate against renewables, and the need to replace a transmission and distribution system that was established to support local baseload plants with one that supports distant intermittent sources – discussed in the earlier chapters.

China is building nine major high voltage lines to move power from western provinces that have greater amounts of solar and wind resources to eastern provinces with fewer resources and large populations. More are in the planning stage. However, long-distance transmission lines face three challenges. First, they must be sited and receive approval from multiple agencies in each province they cross. Obtaining approvals from multiple agencies may be less of a problem in China than it would be in countries like the United States, but given the governance problems discussed earlier, the challenges in China are real. Second, moving electricity through multiple provinces is only economical if utilities and consumers in one province are willing to purchase power generated in another. In the past, each province has protected its higher-cost generators, mostly state-owned enterprises, from competition from lower-cost generators in other provinces. As long as provinces receive a portion of their annual revenues from local coal plants, this barrier to trading electricity remains. Third, the economics of transmission depend critically on using power lines at a high capacity. Lines that transmit electricity from baseload facilities that operate 7 days per week and 24 hours per day will cost less per unit of electricity than lines that carry intermittent power that is only available half the time or less. A hybrid line that carries both is ideal, but not always feasible. These factors may stimulate planners to look at locating renewables closer to load centers and to consider distributive power options in some areas.

The challenge of integrating intermittent renewables increases the value of storage technologies, generation options that can follow load fluctuations, and technologies to spread out demand across larger temporal ranges and manage consumption. While advances have occurred in the development of these technologies, they are not ready for deployment at a scale that would be commercially significant. Greater investment in research and development in each of these technologies has the potential to significantly increase the available pathways to decarbonizing China's energy mix and improving the economics of reforming the grid.

1.2.4 Local Air Pollution

China has embarked on an aggressive campaign to reduce local air pollution that has plagued its larger cities, increasing mortality and morbidity rates. Initiatives include reducing coal burning in five eastern provinces, establishing stringent standards for both mobile and stationary sources, and meeting China's ever-improving energy intensity goals. Many of these efforts reduce both conventional pollutants, such as particles and sulfur emissions, and carbon emissions. However, as Zhimin Mao and Wei Peng point out in Chapter 7 of this book, not every effort to reduce air pollution will have an equivalent impact on carbon emissions. For example, using scrubbers to remove sulfur emissions can measurably benefit local health, but will result in higher CO_2 emissions, since scrubbers consume substantial amounts of incremental power. Similarly, instead of burning coal directly, gasification technologies can turn the coal into synthetic gas that can be burned in a power plant or by industry. The substitution of syngas for coal benefits local pollution levels, but the gasification process emits significantly more carbon. Even improved efficiency, which one might think would have positive abatement results for both types of emissions, can have a negative impact on efforts to reduce carbon. Persuading generators to retire superefficient coal plants will be a politically challenging task.

Many people have written about potential co-benefits of conventional air pollution abatement for reducing greenhouse gas emissions. Mao and Peng argue that the largest co-benefits may come from establishing market and institutional reforms essential to reducing conventional emissions. For example, any policies that result in rapid deployment of renewable technologies will have both carbon and air pollution benefits. China should not pull back from its goal to clean up its air, but it should consider its longer-term carbon vision in designing the programs and policies to meet those goals.

1.2.5 Nuclear Power

Nuclear power is trumpeted as a major component of a deep decarbonization strategy in China but faces major obstacles. At the end of 2017, China had 33.7 GWe of nuclear capacity. The industry's goal is to increase this fivefold by 2030 and to have 240 GWe of capacity in place by 2050 – or about 2.5 times the nuclear capacity in the United States in 2018. While this sounds impressive, it is likely to be no more than 10 percent of China's total electricity generating capacity in 2050. For nuclear power to play a significant role in decarbonizing the electricity sector, the total capacity installed will have to be much higher than what is currently forecast by the Chinese Nuclear Energy Association – a daunting task!

In Chapter 4 of this book, Matt Bunn argues that, whatever role nuclear power may have in China's decarbonized future, a fundamental emphasis must be placed on avoiding a large-scale accident, similar to those at Fukushima or Chernobyl, which would make any expansion of nuclear power politically impossible. Bunn proposes that China must also develop better communication strategies to gain greater public acceptance of the nuclear option. Such strategies require (1) Engaging with the population around the proposed sites and addressing their concerns and (2) Committing to a level of transparency much greater than currently exists, either within the Chinese nuclear industry or within the Chinese government.

Bunn assesses the challenges confronting the nuclear option and concludes that scaling the existing nuclear technologies will be difficult. On the other hand, developing, demonstrating, and eventually commercializing new, safer, and more efficient nuclear technologies may be the most promising pathway, if nuclear is to play an important role in a decarbonized energy mix. Among the more interesting technologies are sodium-cooled fast reactors, high-temperature pebble bed facilities, and molten salt reactors. All of these technologies are in the development stage, but if they realize their potential, they will herald a new generation of much safer nuclear plants, which in turn may transform the anxiety surrounding nuclear power to public support for it.

Bunn suggests that China should develop a menu of new nuclear technologies. Such a strategy does not mean stopping investment in existing nuclear technologies, as the current deployment of two to five plants per year allows the industry to expand the pool of trained nuclear engineers. But to succeed in long-term expansion of nuclear power, the Chinese government must address key issues, including improving the quality of regulation and oversight.

1.2.6 Electric Vehicles

In the last three five-year plans, China has set ambitious goals for the development of an electric vehicle industry. Despite generous subsidies, these efforts have been slow to blossom. This situation may be changing, as China's auto manufacturers are refocusing their production strategy from selling large electric vehicles (EVs) to the global marketplace to selling smaller EVs to domestic consumers. Smaller electric vehicles with more limited range may not sell well in the United States, but in China, with its world-class intercity rail system, range anxiety is less of a concern. As a result, smaller, less expensive electric vehicles sold well in China in 2017 and 2018, reaching nearly one million vehicles, not including plug-in hybrid vehicles.

The rapid commercialization of electric vehicles gives rise to two concerns. First, with China's heavy reliance on coal-fired electricity, greater penetration of electric cars will result in higher carbon emissions, particularly in the north where reliance on coal for electricity generation is greater. In Chapter 5 of this book, Henry Lee argues that China should not place much emphasis on the implications of EVs for near-term CO_2 emissions. Lee suggests that the benefits of establishing knowledgeable regulatory institutions, increasing consumer confidence, and building an infrastructure to support greater penetration of EVs will far outweigh the costs of additional carbon emissions in the short term. Moreover, the expansion of EVs in China, when coupled with decarbonization of the electricity sector over the mid- and long term, may be the only way for China to reduce emissions from the transportation sector. Lee proposes that China should not delay its aggressive policies and programs, continuing its effort to deploy greater numbers of EVs in the coming decade, regardless of the near-term impact on the 2030 emissions target.

A challenge facing electric vehicles is establishing a charging infrastructure to support 200–300 million vehicles. This challenge will require sustained government support. It will also require some of the same changes in the grid system and the structure of electricity tariffs discussed in earlier chapters. Just like transmission lines, the capital and operating costs of fast-charging stations will make it very difficult for such stations to generate sufficient revenue to cover the capital and maintenance costs. Parking lot and garage charging will be more cost-effective than fast-charging stations in the short term, but having an increasing number of cars, all plugging into the local electric grid, will require the adoption of smart grid technologies to sequence the charging and avoid disrupting local distribution systems. Whatever the choices, developing an affordable and efficient charging infrastructure will require a partnership between the Chinese government, industry (including the automobile manufacturers), the electricity sector, building owners, and consumers.

1.3 Conclusions

Decarbonizing China's energy mix will be a challenge, but China has repeatedly shown its ability to focus its resources and its commitment to meet large challenges. China will have to accelerate the deployment of renewable energy, even beyond its world-leading efforts, develop the next generation of nuclear technologies, and manage the transition of its transportation sector to electricity. Our conclusion is that all of these steps will require a focused effort to reform the country's electric grid, improve governance to encourage greater cooperation at all levels of government, and create a system of incentives that will induce governments, industry, and consumers to invest in a decarbonized energy mix. Such reforms will require China to move away from a system dominated by carbon intensive and heavily polluting industries – a system that has contributed substantially to the country's unprecedented rate of growth and one that has strong incumbent stakeholders who will resist such changes. However, the grid that worked well in the 1990s and the first decade of this century is not the grid that will support the decarbonized economy that China is likely to seek in the post-2030 period. The action that China takes over the next 10 years will have a major impact on its ability to decarbonize its energy mix over the following 30 years.

References

[1] M. R. Allen, D. J. Frame, C. Huntingford et al., "Warming caused by cumulative carbon emissions towards the trillionth tonne." *Nature* **458**(7242) (2009), pp. 1163–1166.

[2] The White House, Office of the Press Secretary, "U.S.–China Joint Anouncement on Climate Change" (November 11, 2014). Available at: www.whitehouse.gov/the-press-office/2014/11/11/us-china-joint-announcement-climate-change

2

Reforming China's Electricity Market to Facilitate Low-Carbon Transition

PU WANG

2.1 Introduction

The electric power sector constitutes the largest source of carbon emissions in China, accounting for roughly half of the country's total emissions in 2016 [1]. Meanwhile, it has also played a central role in China's response to global climate change, facilitating a series of low-carbon policies ranging from reducing coal use and integrating renewable energy sources to instituting carbon pricing mechanisms. In the coming decades, there are several trends that will dramatically affect electricity demand and supply. The first is the movement of large portions of the population from rural areas to cities as China's urbanization and industrialization continues; the second is the rising standards of living that will lead to higher electricity consumption in residential and service sectors; the third is the growth in renewable energy supplies, which have high variability both temporally and spatially; and the fourth is the potential electrification of the economy, particularly the electrification of transport and heating systems, which has gained momentum in recent years because of air pollution concerns.

One of the most fundamental challenges in decarbonizing China's electricity sector is that, on the one hand, renewable energy and electric vehicles are variable and require a highly flexible system, but on the other hand, China's electricity system is highly inflexible structurally and operationally. In the past decade, technological improvements and economies of scale have significantly reduced the costs of wind and solar energy production, making China the global champion in wind and solar deployment [2, 3]. Meanwhile, China is investing substantially in research, development, and deployment of various technologies related to power systems, such as energy storage systems, carbon capturing and storage (CCS), electric cars, and fast-charging stations. However, these new technologies also pose significant challenges to the stability and reliability of the existing system. Renewable energy sources are inherently intermittent and less predictable, and high penetration of renewables will require the power system to have sufficient reserve capacity and high flexibility to meet the changing supply [4]. In addition, renewable energy sources in China are geographically dispersed, and the locations with best resources are usually far away from load centers, requiring long-distance transmission lines to connect them to major electric grids [5, 6]. The rise of electric vehicles, if not coordinated properly, could also pose significant stress to the capacity and stability of the grid [7].

But the structure and operation of the power sector are not flexible enough to cope with the fast-changing trends. China has enormous dependence on coal for electricity generation. Total generation capacity of coal-fired plants in China is currently around 950 GW, accounting for approximately 57 percent of total capacity and 71 percent of total generation [8]. In contrast to the United States and Europe, China does not have the option to substitute natural gas for coal, due to limited natural gas resources. This makes emissions reduction more difficult, and coal-fired plants are also less flexible than gas-fired plants in backing up renewable energy sources because of slow ramp-up rates. In addition, the operation of the electricity system is both inflexible and inefficient, because of the existing policies in generation quotas, fixed prices, and infrastructure planning. To address these challenges effectively, a series of policy changes are needed to (1) facilitate deployments of low-carbon energy sources, including renewables, nuclear, and hydropower, while maintaining system reliability; (2) provide the right economic incentives to align the interests of investors and consumers with low-carbon energy transition and (3) promote wise infrastructure planning.

If China wants to achieve deeper emissions reductions beyond 2030, the power sector will need to be the most important target in any long-term decarbonization plan, not only because of its share of emissions, but also because it is the infrastructure for most other low-carbon policies. One of the key features of an electricity system is its long-term nature in system planning. The average lifetime of a coal-fired plant is about 40 years. If China's current policies encourage more coal-fired plant construction, these plants will be in service until after 2050. Also, once completed, the siting and structure of the grid system (e.g., long-distance, high-voltage transmission lines versus distributed systems) are difficult to change for decades. Thus, policy making now will affect China's ability to reduce carbon emissions several decades into the future. If the country wants to make renewable energy and emissions reduction policies work over the long term, it needs to begin correcting the problems in the electricity system now.

In this chapter, we aim to evaluate the impacts of China's current electricity policies and reform initiatives on carbon emissions reduction from a long-term perspective. We first discuss the major trends and challenges in China's power system in Section 2.2, and the governance of the power sector in Section 2.3; then

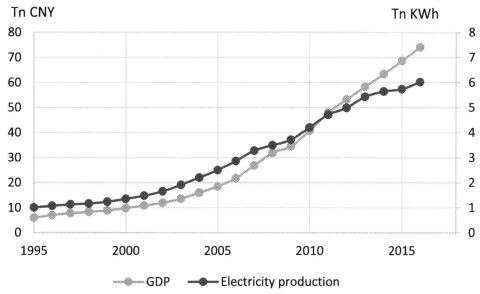

Figure 2.1 GDP growth and electricity production in China 1995–2016.
(© 2021 Pu Wang. All rights reserved)

we identify the main policy questions in system operation, electricity pricing, and infrastructure planning in Section 2.4, we evaluate different policy alternatives in terms of their potential contributions to long-term decarbonization, and provide policy recommendations in Section 2.5. Finally, we provide our concluding remarks in Section 2.6.

2.2 Future Trends and Challenges in China's Electricity System

China's electric power sector has grown rapidly in the past two decades, largely keeping pace with the country's fast economic growth (Figure 2.1). During this time, electricity production increased more than sixfold, and the power sector experienced significant structural and regulatory changes, but electricity generation remained reliable and affordable to meet residential, commercial, and industrial needs, which was a remarkable accomplishment.

But China's electric power development in the past was largely focused on expanding generation to ensure supply; the concept of low-carbon development was rarely emphasized until very recently (i.e., the past five years). In 2016, China's total generating capacity was 1,651 GW, and total electricity production was 6,023 billion kWh. The current generation fleet is dominated by coal-fired power plants, which account for 57 percent of total capacity and about 71 percent of total generation (Figure 2.2). Gas-fired plants accounted for only 4 percent of

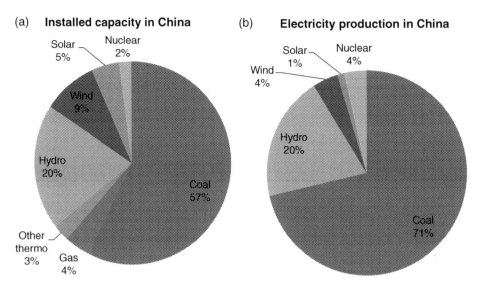

Figure 2.2 Electricity capacity (a) and generation (b) in China in 2016.
(© 2021 Pu Wang. All rights reserved)

capacity, significantly lower than the levels in the United States and Europe. Hydropower has expanded significantly since the 1980s and now accounts for about 20 percent in both capacity and generation. Wind, solar, and nuclear combined represented about 16 percent of capacity and 9 percent of generation.

Heavy reliance on coal is the main reason for China's rapid carbon emissions growth in the past decades and is also the major contributor to its recent air pollution crisis. This trend has begun to shift over the past several years, when the Chinese economy entered a critical period of structural transition. The traditional growth model, driven by large-scale infrastructure construction, real estate development, and low-end manufacturing, is nearing its end. The government began to cut excessive capacities in heavy industries and invested significantly in addressing air pollution and other environmental problems.

These changes led to China's commitments in the 2015 Paris Climate Conference to peak its total greenhouse gas emissions around 2030 and increase the share of nonfossil fuels in the primary energy mix to 20 percent by the same time. The shift of focus to low-carbon development will lead to a series of fundamental changes in the future development of the power sector and pose novel challenges to the operation and regulation of the sector.

First, on the demand side, more than 70 percent of electricity was consumed by the industrial sector in 2016, while the residential and commercial sectors each used about 13 percent (Figure 2.3). In contrast, industrial, residential, and

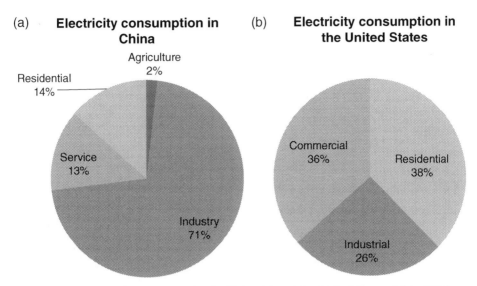

Figure 2.3 Electricity consumption in China (a) and the United States (b) in 2016. (© 2021 Pu Wang. All rights reserved)

commercial sectors each made up roughly one-third of the electricity demand in the United States. An average Chinese household consumed 1,044 kWh of electricity in 2014, compared with 10,800 kWh for its American counterpart. During China's economic structural transition, electricity demand in the industrial sector will stabilize, if not decrease; residential and commercial electricity demand will increase dramatically, due to increased penetration of air conditioners, refrigerators, electrification of heating, and the expanding service sectors. Studies have shown that industrial demand tends to be stable over the course of the day and successive months, since many industrial facilities are usually kept on around the clock; while residential and commercial consumptions are more susceptible to changes in weather, work, and life patterns. Thus, China's current load profiles are flatter than those in post-industrialized countries. But as China's consumption structure shifts toward the US pattern, the loads are likely to become more fluctuating and unpredictable, requiring the system to significantly increase its flexibility. Furthermore, the rise of electric vehicles will not only increase the magnitude of demand, but will also put pressure on system stability and reliability due to vast deployment of fast-charging stations (though some studies have suggested that electric vehicles could improve system reliability if coordinated).

On the supply side, the government began to restrict new construction of coal-fired power plants, while promoting other low-carbon energy sources. Even though the National 13th Five Year Plan for Energy Development [9] (referred to as 13th FYP hereafter) still predicts a 4 percent annual growth of coal-fired power plant capacity from 2015 to 2020 and outlines plans to build 9 mega coal-fired power bases, the actual approval of new plants has decreased because of concerns about overcapacity, particularly in eastern provinces where air pollution is a major concern. But most of the coal-fired plants were built after 2000, and it is predicted that 95 percent of these will stay in service through 2030. Hence, the issue of stranded costs will become a major challenge if China wants to reduce the coal power fleet. Hydropower has experienced fast growth since 1990, and it has many advantages over other energy sources, such as low carbon emissions, low operational costs, and high flexibility (fast ramp rates) to back up renewable energy sources. However, hydropower resources are mostly concentrated in the southwestern provinces, which are far from the load centers in coastal regions, as well as the major wind and solar installations in northern provinces. Moreover, most of the major rivers with high hydropower potentials have already been dammed, and the increasing opposition from relocated people and environmental groups makes new dam construction increasingly difficult. The hydropower capacity in operation was about 332 GW in 2016, and the 13th FYP predicts just about 1 percent of annual growth in the next 5 years.

Renewable energy sources, particularly solar and wind, had the fastest growth among all energy sources and enjoyed strong policy support in the past five years. China has already become a global leader in renewable energy facilities manufacturing and deployment. Solar- and wind-generating capacities increased by 177 percent and 34.6 percent annually from 2010 to 2015, and China plans to double the capacities of solar and wind by 2020 through substantial programmatic and financial support, according to the 13th FYP. However, integration of renewable energy sources faces significant challenges. Solar and wind are intermittent; hence the electricity system needs to develop adequate flexibility to balance the fluctuating outputs. Fast-responding units, such as gas combustion turbines, are relatively scarce in China, so a certain number of coal-fired plants need to be kept spinning and prepared to ramp up and back up renewables, which significantly reduces their capacity utilization and energy efficiency. The system also needs enough reserve capacity to meet peak loads when solar and wind are not available, which could further reduce capacity utilization. Moreover, the best wind and solar resources are concentrated in north, northeast, and west China, far from established industrial and residential centers. Costly long-distance transmission lines are needed to connect renewable energy capacity in these regions to the demand centers. The high capital cost/energy cost ratio will dramatically affect investment incentives, but at the moment there is no clear cost allocation mechanism. As the share of renewable energy sources reaches a higher level, these problems will become more prominent, and China will need to significantly enhance the capacity, flexibility, and infrastructure of its electricity system to cope.

Nuclear power is a promising, though highly controversial, candidate in the low-carbon energy portfolio. China's current nuclear power fleet consists of 32 operating units, with a total of 30 GW of generating capacity, producing about 3 percent of the country's electricity in 2015. China's target for 2020 is to have 58 GW of generating capacity in operation, and another 30 GW under construction. Given the low ebb of nuclear power in most other major countries, China's nuclear plan is very ambitious. But the current pace of development is far from that needed for nuclear to play a major role in global climate mitigation. Based on current projections, even a high-growth scenario for nuclear power would only fill a relatively small gap in emissions reduction by 2050. But scaling up nuclear power would face substantial constraints and risks, including public opposition, cost control, safety (safe operation) and security (terrorists, proliferation, etc.) risks, and the government and industry capacities. Nevertheless, China and other countries should continue to invest in research, development, and deployment of nuclear power technologies in order to keep open the option of scaling up for the future. (See Chapter 4 for more details about the potential role of nuclear energy in deep decarbonization.)

2.3 Power Sector Governance

In a country such as China, where most of the key segments of the power industry are owned and operated by the state, investments are developed and financed by the state, and government regulation of prices and production dominate, how the system of governance operates and is structured becomes an issue of paramount importance. Ideally, one would want a governance structure in which key agencies have clearly demarcated responsibilities, and there is limited duplication or overlap among them. Such a structure creates accountability, which in turn provides government officials with the incentives to improve their performance. Further, decisions should be made by those jurisdictions in which the costs are borne by the beneficiaries. For example, local populations benefit from the operation of garbage collection and therefore they should pay for that service. Alternatively, the products of energy R&D investments will benefit the whole country. Thus, R&D should be the responsibility of the national government. Each level of government should complement the capabilities of those levels directly above and below it. The interfaces among different levels of government should be efficient and cooperative as opposed to being competitive and inefficient. Where there are overlaps in responsibilities, there should be clear mechanisms to resolve any resulting conflicts.

In the area of sector power, China's electricity governance structure is far from the ideal [10]. As electricity systems become more complex, these structural problems will become more acute and costly. At the central government level, multiple ministries responsible for one aspect of electricity or another are as likely to compete with one another as they are to cooperate. The lead energy ministry is the National Development and Reform Commission, but its responsibilities are spread over several departments, three of which have substantial authority. The National Energy Administration (NEA) is in charge of generation and transmission planning and approval; the Bureau of Pricing is in charge of establishing retail and wholesale tariffs; the Bureau of Economic Operations is in charge of setting the amount of power each plant is expected to produce. Hence, one part of the NDRC controls the prices that can be charged and another controls the volume that is expected to be produced. Coordinating among these departments is challenging, as is illustrated by the ongoing tension between the deregulation of coal prices and the regulation of the prices charged by coal-fired power plants. In addition, the responsibility for operating the electric system is in the hands of two large state companies that manage the grid and all purchases and resale of power. The interface between the state-owned enterprises (SOE) in the power sector and government ministries responsible for overseeing those companies is not always smooth and harmonious. The SOE management is often well-connected politically and given a modicum of independence.

To make the governance problem more complex, the provincial and local governments retain responsibility for some energy decisions, while others are made in Beijing. For example, provincial governments supervise the construction of transmission lines above 220 KV and local governments are responsible for lower voltages. On the other hand, the central government has the final say on most generating plants. However, even in these cases, local and provincial governments have a voice on siting, diversion of some water resources, and land use – all of which affect the construction of electricity generation capacity [11]. Not only is there a need for coordination among central government agencies but also between them and local and provincial ministries officials. While China has the reputation of a very hierarchical governance structure, in reality most policy issues are addressed through the establishment of ad hoc committees that include all of the relevant national and subnational official players.

The complexities of emerging intermittent low-carbon technologies, smart meters and grids, and new storage technologies will make it much more difficult for regulators and policymakers in Beijing to keep up with these changes. The pressure will grow to transfer ever more regulatory and investment decisions to subnational levels of governance. Central government ministries will have to rely more heavily on guidelines, in lieu of direct intervention, as a means to obtain subnational compliance with national goals. They will have to thoughtfully decide where their intervention will have the greatest value and where it will only duplicate or complicate local government structures. In systems characterized by distributed power, investments will often not take the form of large power plants, but rather hundreds of small generators, storage options, voltage enhancers, and demand-side opportunities. It is hard to see how these decisions can be made centrally without a significant loss of value in the form of inefficiencies and less economic investment. Many subnational governments do not presently possess the institutional capacity to provide the regulatory, operational, and planning services needed. Again, China should use its ability to pilot different reforms in different regions and use the results of these efforts to shape longer-term policies. Ultimately, the optimal answers may very well be quite different for one province as compared with another. The traditional scenario in which there is one optimal solution for all of China may be an anachronism in a world of decarbonized energy systems.

2.4 Key Policy Questions

Electricity policies play a critical role in energy transition and decarbonization. Integration of renewable energy sources largely relies on wise design of grid systems and a dispatch mechanism that prioritizes low-carbon sources. A transparent and efficient electricity market is also essential for phasing out inefficient coal-fired plants. But China's current electricity system, featuring "equal shares dispatch" and fixed prices (both explained later in this section), is not well suited to the transition to low-carbon energy sources, and the planning of transmission grids and power plants is not coordinated by either the government or the market. Moreover, the current dispatch and pricing policies create perverse incentives that discourage R&D and investments in low-carbon technologies. Consensus has emerged recently that electricity market reforms are critically needed to improve the economic and environmental performances of the power system. However, significant questions remain regarding the proper direction of these reforms. This section aims to provide a new perspective that focuses on the long-term impacts of electricity policies on carbon emissions reduction. We identify the main challenges facing China's power sector and evaluate the current policies in terms of their potential contributions to decarbonization. Policy recommendations for these questions are discussed in the following section.

2.4.1 System Operation

China's current electric power system has evolved from a centrally-planned and vertically-integrated state monopoly [12, 13]. Before the 1980s, the development and management of the entire power system, from generation to distribution, were under the control of the Ministry of Electric Power, which became the State Power Corporation in 1997. After the onset of "the Reform and Opening-up" policy in 1978, the old power system could not meet the surge in electricity demand. Thus, in the 1980s, the central government opened up generation to investors, including provincial/municipal governments, as well as private and foreign investors. In the 2002 reform [14], which was by far the most important, the State Power Corporation was divided into five state-owned generation companies and two grid companies. The generation companies currently control 45 percent of power plants, and the rest belong to other central SOEs and the aforementioned various types of investors, which are aligned with the intention of the reform to create competing players on the generation side. However, the two grid companies became the new monopolies, which control most of the transmission and distribution lines within their jurisdiction, serving as the only wholesale buyers on the generation side and the only retailers on the demand side. Moreover, the grid companies are also the system operators, deciding which generators will be dispatched and when.

In most parts of the world, system operators adopt the principle of "economic dispatch," meaning that the generator providing an additional unit of electricity at the lowest price is dispatched first, subject to safety constraints. In contrast, China's grid companies adopt a unique "equal shares dispatch" rule. Under this regime, generators of a given technology type are guaranteed a roughly equal number of operating hours, regardless of their production costs. The historical reason for "equal shares dispatch" was to ensure reasonable returns for generators. However, this policy has many detrimental economic and environmental consequences, among which are the effects on carbon emissions from power generation.

First, since the less energy-efficient generators receive the same operating hours as the more advanced ones, there is no market incentive to phase out or reduce the use of the dirtiest plants. The generation quotas not only significantly reduce economic efficiency, but also increase carbon emissions per unit of electricity, because the most efficient plants are not optimally utilized. More importantly, the use of renewable energy sources could be depressed due to the generation quotas, even though the marginal operation costs of solar and wind power are close to zero with desirable weather.

Second, the equal shares dispatch policy has encouraged overinvestment in coal-fired power plants in provinces because the construction can boost local GDP growth and employment and investors are confident they will recover their investments. This effect has emerged repeatedly in history. Before 2000, construction of large power plants needed approval from central government agencies, but plants smaller than 50 MW were waived from the requirement.

Consequently, the provincial and municipal governments built a large number of small, energy-inefficient coal plants. Even though most of these small plants were closed after 2005 for environmental and energy conservation reasons, they had already caused significant economic and environmental losses. Then, in November 2014, as part of a national reform to streamline bureaucratic procedures, the central government decided to delegate the approval rights for thermal power plants to the provincial governments. As a result, the number of newly approved coal-fired plants surged in 2015, despite the economic slowdown and overcapacity. The central government had to intervene by canceling construction of 15 projects in September 2016, and another 101 projects in January 2017. Unless the rule for capital recovery is changed, the tendency of local government to overinvest is unlikely to disappear, and this will continue to cause economic welfare losses to the society. Moreover, due to the long lifespan of coal-fired power plants (the average life is 40 years), this high-carbon "technology lock-in" could significantly postpone the transition to cleaner energy sources.

Third, the provincial grid companies (subsidiaries of the State Grid and the Southern Power Grid) are at the same time the in-province system operators. Since there is no merit-based order in the dispatch processes, the grid companies are inclined to give priority to generators in the same province, even if electricity generated in other provinces is less costly or less carbon-intensive. This type of local protectionism has contributed to high wind and solar curtailment rates in some renewable energy-rich provinces. The central government has recognized the substantial barriers to intraregional trade and cooperation and tried to reduce or eliminate them, but to date these efforts have been unsuccessful.

2.4.2 Electricity Pricing

China's electricity prices are highly regulated by the government [15, 16]. Before 2004, the wholesale prices to the grid companies were determined by a "cost plus reasonable return" model on a case-by-case basis for generators. Starting in 2004, the NDRC began to assign "on-grid electricity tariffs" based on technology type and geographic location, and these prices are adjusted infrequently (the exception was the "coal electricity prices co-movement" rule, which was in effect for several years). The current national average tariffs are around 0.4 CNY/kWh for thermal electricity, 0.5 CNY/kWh for wind power, 0.75 CNY/kWh for solar, and nuclear and hydropower are still priced on a case-by-case basis. More specifically, the NDRC sets different thermal electricity prices for each province (Table 2.1), and different wind and solar tariffs according to regional resources quality (Tables 2.2 and 2.3).

On the retail side, the prices are, in principle, determined by the formula "on-grid price + transmission/distribution costs + government surcharges." But the

26 *Foundations for a Low-Carbon Energy System in China*

Table 2.1 *On-grid tariffs for thermal electricity in 2017 (unit: CNY/kwh)*

Province	Price (CNY/ kWh)	Province	Price (CNY/ kWh)	Province	Price (CNY/ kWh)
Beijing	0.3515	Jiangsu	0.378	Hainan	0.4198
Tianjin	0.3514	Zhejiang	0.4153	Chongqing	0.3796
Northern Hebei	0.3634	Anhui	0.3693	Sichuan	0.4012
Southern Hebei	0.3497	Fujian	0.3737	Guizhou	0.3363
Shanxi	0.3205	Jiangxi	0.3993	Yunnan	0.3358
Western Inner Mongolia	0.2772	Shandong	0.3729	Tibet	——
Liaoning	0.3685	Henan	0.3551	Shaanxi	0.3346
Jilin	0.3717	Hubei	0.3981	Gansu	0.2978
Heilongjiang	0.3723	Hunan	0.4471	Qinghai	0.3247
Eastern Inner Mongolia	0.3035	Guangdong	0.4505	Ningxia	0.2595
Shanghai	0.4048	Guangxi	0.414	Xinjiang	——

Table 2.2 *National onshore wind power on-grid tariffs in 2017 (unit: CNY/kwh)*

Regions	Price (CNY/kWh)	Specific regions in each type
Type I region	0.4	Inner Mongolia Autonomous Region, except Chifeng, Tongliao, Xing'an League and Hulun Buir; Urumqi, Karamay, and Shihezi in Xinjiang Uygur Autonomous Region
Type II region	0.45	Zhangjiakou City and Chengde City in Hebei Province; Chifeng City, Tongliao City, Xing'an League, and Hulun Buir City in Inner Mongolia Autonomous Region; Gansu Jiayuguan City, Jiuquan City; Yunnan Province
Type III region	0.49	Jilin Province Baicheng City, Songyuan City; Heilongjiang Jixi City, Shuangyashan City, Qitaihe City, Suihua City, Yichun City, Daxinganling area; Gansu Province except Jiayuguan City and Jiuquan City; Xinjiang Uygur Autonomous Region except Urumqi, Ili Kazakh Autonomous Prefecture, Karamay City, and Shihezi Shi; Ningxia Hui Autonomous Region
Type IV region	0.57	Any other regions not included in Types I, II, and III.

calculation of transmission and distribution costs lacks transparency because of the monopoly power of the grid companies. In practice, the grid companies' revenue comes from the difference between retail and wholesale prices; thus they are motivated to exploit both the generators and consumers. Due to the problem of

Table 2.3 *National solar power on-grid tariffs in 2017 (unit: CNY/kwh)*

Regions	Price (CNY/kWh)	Specific regions in each type
Type I region	0.65	Ningxia; Qinghai Hercynian; Gansu Jiayuguan, Wuwei, Zhangye, Jiuquan, Dunhuang, Jinchang; Xinjiang Hami, Tacheng, Altay, Karamay; Inner Mongolia except Chifeng, Tongliao, Xing'an League, and Hulun Buir
Type II region	0.75	Inner Mongolia Chifeng, Tongliao, Xing'an League, Hulunbeier; Hebei Chengde, Zhangjiakou, Tangshan, Qinhuangdao; Shanxi Datong, Shuozhou, Xinzhou, Yangquan; Shaanxi Yulin, Yan'an; Qinghai; Gansu; Xinjiang except type I regions;
Type III region	0.85	Any other regions not included in Types I and II

Table 2.4 *The structure of retail prices in Heilongjiang province (unit: CNY/kwh)*

User types	Per kWh charge						Lump-sum charge	
	Below 1 kV	1– 10 kV	20 kV	35– 66 kV	110– 220 kV	Above 220 kV	Maximum need (¥/kW/ month)	Transformer capacity (¥/ kVA/month)
Residential	0.510	0.500	0.500	0.490				
Ordinary commercial and industrial	0.873	0.863	0.861	0.853				
Energy-intensive industry		0.593	0.590	0.578	0.568	0.558	33	22
Agricultural	0.489	0.479	0.477	0.469				

"cross-subsidies," meaning that the residential electricity prices are set low deliberately and subsidized by industrial and commercial users, the price signals are distorted for both residential and the large industrial and commercial users (the 2015 reform aimed to change this situation by allowing large users to sign bilateral contracts directly with generators or brokers, but the effect of this reform remains to be seen). Table 2.4 gives an example of retail electricity prices in Heilongjiang province, where the regulating agency needs to determine more than a dozen prices for different types of users. (Note that Heilongjiang has the simplest retail price structure among all provinces.) In places such as Beijing and Shanghai, where there are peak/off-peak and tiered prices, the retail price structures are much more complicated. Like the "equal shares dispatch," the current pricing mechanisms have several potentially negative impacts on long-term carbon emissions reduction and renewable energy integration.

First, to accelerate penetration of solar and wind generation, the electricity market needs to provide accurate price signals, encouraging investments that can enhance backup capacity and system flexibility, and to incentivize flexible operation of the backup generators. The current fixed on-grid tariffs cannot provide an economic incentive to build natural gas "peaker" plants or more flexible coal plants, which have higher operation costs, but are quick to start and ideal to meet demand surges and back up renewables. Instead, most of the new power plants under construction or planned are still large, inflexible coal-fired plants, even in the renewable-rich provinces. In most cases, the peak load must be served by coal-fired plants, which are slow to start and need to be kept spinning. This practice is not only energy-inefficient in the short run, but also will "lock-in" more coal-fired power plants in the long run.

Second, on the consumer side, as penetration of solar and wind increases, demand response will become critical to coping with varying energy output. Empowered by advanced metering technologies, flexible retail prices, reflecting the real-time costs of electricity, could shift the time patterns of consumption to better match the output. The large industrial users would adjust their production schedules, and EV owners would charge their vehicles during off-peak hours. Government regulators are unlikely to be able to determine such highly flexible prices, so prices need to be set by market-based rules.

Third, it is difficult to align the regulated electricity market with the goals of many low-carbon initiatives, particularly carbon pricing policies such as cap-and-trade or carbon tax systems. The current policy supports to renewable energy are through feed-in tariffs or renewable portfolio standards. To date, these have been effective to date in encouraging renewables deployment, but they are unlikely to sustain in the long term, when the shares of renewables reach significant levels of penetration. Moreover, policies based on subsidies and standards could distort the market signals and lead to irrational investments. Carbon pricing policies can provide accurate economic incentives to low-carbon technologies in the long run. They are premised on the participants' rational market behaviors, which are responsive to price signals. But under the current pricing mechanisms, a carbon price becomes "infra-marginal" to the generators, meaning that it would not change the marginal cost of electricity production. As a result, the generators would not change their output, and the price signal could not be passed through to the final consumers in a timely fashion. Thus, the effectiveness of a cap-and-trade system or carbon tax would be greatly undermined. And without strong price signals, R&D and investment in storage, CCS, and other game-changing technologies are likely to be discouraged, diminishing future emissions reduction capacities.

2.4.3 Design and Planning of Transmission Networks

Most of China's transmission networks are owned by two SOEs, the State Grid Corporation of China and China Southern Power Grid. These two SOEs are also responsible for the design and construction of new transmission lines. In the past decade, these two, particularly the State Grid Corporation of China, have made remarkable progress in building ultra-high-voltage AC (1,000 kV) and DC (± 800 kV) transmission lines for regional interconnection and renewable energy integration (Table 2.5) [17]. Since the SOEs are not profit-maximizing entities, and they have received substantial financial transfers from the central government, the costs of developing the transmission lines are largely socialized, and there is no clear mechanism for cost allocation. While this development model has its merits, particularly for the integration of renewable energy sources in remote areas, there are significant concerns about its economic efficiency and coordination with other parts of the power system.

Renewable energy sources are geographically dispersed, and the best wind, solar, and hydropower resources are located far from consumption centers. There are tradeoffs between two alternative strategies to address this issue. The first involves constructing long-distance and high-voltage transmission lines to connect the consumption centers with the resource-rich regions. But this strategy incurs substantially higher costs for infrastructure construction and grid system upgrade. The second strategy is to build wind and solar plants close to consumption centers, which might have suboptimal resources endowment, but this approach would reduce the pressure on the national grids, as well as the costs in infrastructure construction. When the costs of long-distance transmission lines are mostly socialized, generation developers will tend to build too much capacity in uneconomical regions. There is no effective mechanism, either in the government or in the market, to coordinate the siting of long-distance transmission lines and the siting of renewable generation. In recent years, high curtailment rates have been pervasive in provinces rich in wind and solar resources, and part of the reason is the lack of coordination between transmission and generation developments.

2.4.4 Pricing Externalities: Cap-and-Trade and Carbon Tax Policies

Carbon pricing policies, including cap-and-trade and carbon tax, have been regarded by scholars and policymakers as cost-effective approaches to achieving

30 Foundations for a Low-Carbon Energy System in China

Table 2.5 *Ultra-high-voltage AC (1,000 kV) and DC (±800 kV) transmission lines in China*

Name of Line	Type	Voltage (kV)	Length (km)	Power rating (GW)	Year completed	Total investments (100 mn CNY)
Jindongnan–Nanyang–Jingmen	UHVAC	1,000	640	5.0	2009	57
Huainan–Zhejiang North–Shanghai	UHVAC	1,000	2 × 649	8.0	2013	185.36
Zhejiang North – Fuzhou	UHVAC	1,000	2 × 603	6.8	2014	200
Xilingol League – Shandong	UHVAC	1,000	2 × 730	9	2016	178.2
Huainan-Nanjing-Shanghai	UHVAC	1,000	2 × 779.5	NA	2016	268
West Inner Mongolia – Tianjin south	UHVAC	1,000	2 × 608	NA	2016	175
Yuheng – Weifang	UHVAC	1,000	2 × 1,050	NA	2017	241.8
Xilingol League – Shengli	UHVAC	1,000	2 × 240	NA	2017	49.56
Yunnan – Guangdong	UHVDC	±800	1,373	5	2017	222
Xiangjiaba–Shanghai	UHVDC	±800	1,907	6.4	2010	232.74
Jinping – Sunan	UHVDC	±800	2,059	7.2	2012	220
Nuozadu – Guangdong	UHVDC	±800	1,413	5	2013	187
Hami – Zhengzhou	UHVDC	±800	2,192	8	2014	233.9
Xiluodu - Zhejiang West	UHVDC	±800	1,653	8	2014	238.55
Lingzhou - Shaoxing	UHVDC	±800	1,720	8	2016	211

* Information not available.

emission reduction goals. China has favored cap-and-trade systems over a carbon tax for various political and practical reasons. In 2013, the NDRC launched seven cap-and-trade pilot programs in five cities (Beijing, Shanghai, Tianjin, Chongqing, Shenzhen) and two provinces (Guangdong and Hubei). A national cap-and-trade system, which was launched in late 2017, is widely seen as a key strategy for China to meet its mitigation goals. Also, China's cap-and-trade programs are praised as the transition of governing philosophy from the traditional command-and-control policies to market-based approaches [18].

In December 2017, the first phase of China's national program focused on building a national emissions reporting framework. This was followed by a "trial run" that was intended to initially cover the power sector, with later phases expanding coverage to include other carbon-intensive sectors. However, the design details of the national program are still unclear to the public, except for a few general principles: it will cover facilities with annual energy consumption of more than 10,000 tons of coal equivalent, and the majority of allowances will be allocated for free based on subsectoral performance standards.

Once fully established, the national cap-and-trade program will have the potential to become a key feature of China's climate governance, and the primary policy instrument of its emission reduction goals, particularly for changing the coal-dominant energy structure. A price on carbon will "internalize" the externalities of CO_2 emission from thermal power plants and make renewable sources more economically competitive.

In principle, carbon pricing is also more cost-effective than subsidy- or standard-based policies, such as feed-in tariffs and renewable portfolio standards. That is because it allows the market players to choose the optimal low-carbon options based on their specific situations, rather than relying on a government agency to make one-size-fits-all standards. A carbon price in the long term will also encourage development of various low-carbon technologies, such as CCS.

However, because of the existing policies in the electricity sector, the effectiveness of the cap-and-trade systems will be greatly undermined because emissions trading is a market-based policy tool, which is most effective when there are well-functioning market mechanisms. But China is a market economy that still contains many features of a central planning system. In particular, the SOEs, many of which evolved from former central government agencies, have nearly monopolistic control over energy supply and strong influence on national policy making. Since the SOEs do not act as conventional profit-maximizing entities, their behaviors could undermine the efficiency of the cap-and-trade program. Moreover, due to the "equal shares" dispatch rule and fixed electricity prices, the electricity sector, the largest emissions source, will not be able to respond in a timely manner to the changing carbon price. The "test run" of the national ETS, which covers only the electricity sector, will largely be a tradable performance standard system. One of the distinctive features of China's ETS pilots is that they cover both direct emissions, such as those from power plants, and indirect emissions, such as those embodied in the consumption of heat and electricity, in order to solve the issue of fixed electricity prices. But this method leads to double counting for some emission sources and could distort the price signals. To ensure the effectiveness of the cap-and-trade program, China will need to deepen its market-oriented reforms for SOEs, particularly in the energy and electricity sectors.

Besides the regulations in the electricity sector, China's cap-and-trade programs also face other significant challenges, most prominently the lack of legal foundations, institutional capacities, and reliable, verifiable emissions data at facility level. But China's cap-and-trade programs (both pilots and national) should be evaluated from a farsighted perspective. If China wants to keep the cap-and-trade system as a policy option in 2030, it needs to start building it now, even if the programs are likely to have limited accomplishments in the near term. After accumulating experiences and building institutional capacities over many years, the cap-and-trade programs could become an effective and efficient tool to usher in energy investments and optimize utilization of different low-carbon alternatives.

2.5 Policy Recommendations

2.5.1 Competitive Wholesale Market with Nondiscriminatory System Operators

The generation quotas, or "equal shares" dispatch, have been the target of China's electricity market reforms for almost two decades. The 2002 reform (often referred to as "Document No. 5") had two major goals: separating generation from transmission and establishing market-based competitive pricing mechanisms. The first goal was achieved in the same year when the State Power Corporation was divided into five state-owned generation companies and two grid companies. But progress on the second goal stalled, partly due to the rapid increase in demand in the following years, which shifted the focus from implementing reform to ensuring adequate supply.

Since 2015, overcapacity in power generation has become a notable issue as economic growth has slowed down and coal-fired plants have been assigned operating hours significantly lower than their optimal levels. Meanwhile, the imperatives to reduce air pollution and carbon emissions require limiting coal-fired plants. The situation provides the opportunity to establish a competitive market for generation and use economic forces to phase out inefficient power plants. In March

2015, the State Council published "Guidelines on deepening power sector reform" (often referred to as "Document No. 9"), which initiated a new round of reforms. Several provinces were selected as pilots, with each conducting different experiments. The idea was to accumulate abundant lessons and experiences for future national reforms. For example, the pilot in Yunnan focused on independent calculation of transmission and distribution costs, while the focus of Guangdong was on locational marginal prices and spot market. So far, however, the details of the national reforms are still opaque.

Among all reform initiatives, replacing the current generation quotas with a competitive wholesale market is arguably the most important task. One of the structural barriers to the market-oriented reform, as studies have pointed out, is that the grid companies have monopoly power in both wholesale and retail markets, and they are at the same time the system operators. Moreover, the revenue of the grid companies is determined by the difference in wholesale and retail prices, which creates conflicts of interest for dispatch. In order to establish a competitive wholesale market, China can introduce system operating agencies that are independent of network ownership (independent system operators, or the ISO model). An alternative is going in the direction of the TSO model (TSO stands for transmission system operators), which separates market from dispatch, while it keeps dispatch operations with grid owners. With either path, it is important to make the transmission lines nondiscriminatory to all generators. The core idea in the system operation reform is to "regulate the grids, and deregulate the wholesale and retail markets," rather than the current model, which "regulates the wholesale and retail markets but leaves the grid companies alone." The grid companies should be responsible for developing and maintaining the transmission lines and should hand over their wholesale and retail functions to decentralized market participants. The transmission and distribution charges should be based on the "cost plus" model, which relies on transparent calculation of transmission costs, subject to public hearings and scrutiny of regulatory agencies. Also, to accelerate the rate of decarbonization, the dispatch rules need to be merit-based and low-carbon minded, which ensures that renewable energy plants with low marginal costs will be dispatched first. It should be acknowledged that this transition is likely to encounter significant difficulties and induce massive losses, which will likely require subsidies to pay down at least part of those losses.

2.5.2 Devising Pricing Mechanisms to Facilitate Decarbonization

To have the option of accelerating the rate of decarbonization, China needs a regulatory system that provides accurate price signals to both investors and consumers. The competitive wholesale markets and transparent transmission prices discussed previously are integral components of the pricing mechanisms. In addition, in a renewable-intensive grid, intermittency will affect load curve and system reliability, which necessitates adequate backup services. Incentives are needed to enhance system flexibility, through encouraging investments in flexible reserve capacities and involving demand responses.

First, as penetration of renewable sources increases, investments in backup units, such as fast-responding gas-fired combustion turbines, as well as flexible operation of coal-fired plants, should be encouraged. At the same time, new construction of inflexible coal-fired plants should be discouraged. Premium prices are required for reserve/ancillary services provided by the gas-fired combustion turbines, as well as the existing power fleet that can be operated flexibly. In principle, an efficient electricity market, with features such as locational marginal prices and congestion charges should be able to provide the right incentives by itself. But in reality, due to incomplete information and uncertainties in long-term investments, spot prices might not be sufficient, and some government policies are needed to guide the investments, such as subsidies, tax breaks, or low-interest loans.

Second, development of flexible retail pricing, combined with advanced metering technologies, will be important to incentivizing flexibility on the demand side. The large industrial and commercial users, accounting for 70 percent of electricity consumption, are critical in demand response. The current cross-subsidies need to be removed and flexible prices that can reflect the real-time supply costs will help flatten the load curve and use electricity in a more economically efficient way. For residential consumers, the current tiered prices used in some cities serve as a good starting point. As electric vehicles become more widespread, real-time prices will be important to encouraging owners to charge their vehicles during off-peak hours.

2.5.3 Integrated Planning in Transmission and Generation Construction

While market-oriented reforms are critical in system operation and electricity pricing, market mechanisms are not sufficient in long-term planning due to long capital return time, high market uncertainties, and the myopia of short-term profit-driven investments. In the case of national energy planning, long-distance transmission lines typically involve high costs that take years to recover, and usually need to be planned ahead of generator construction, thus they face high uncertainties. It is difficult for individual market players to take all the risks, so strong state intervention and financial supports are needed to promote such large-scale infrastructure projects. China's political ability to make consistent long-term planning could be a great advantage in grid development. Also, compared to the

United States and Europe, China faces less local opposition in cross-regional projects. As a result, over the past decade China has become a world leader in building ultra-high-voltage (UHV) transmission lines. As of June 2017, China had eight UHV AC transmission lines (1,000 kV) and seven UHV DC transmission lines (± 800 kV) to connect large power bases to load centers and build large-scale synchronous networks. There are additional UHV AC and UHV DC transmission lines under construction, with the purpose of promoting renewable energy integration and mitigating air pollution in the east.

Nevertheless, there is noticeable opposition to the UHV transmission projects, particularly concerning their economic efficiencies compared with other alternatives. The costs of most of the projects are socialized, meaning that they are either passed to the end users, or are covered by the central government budget. The consequence is that generation investors usually lack considerations in the costs of transmission construction when they choose the plant locations. China's current strategy is to build large-scale renewable energy bases in the remote areas with the best resource quality, such as the nine 10-GW wind power bases that are sited mostly in remote areas. But these areas are far from the demand centers and require long-distance transmission lines to connect supply with demand centers, which will significantly increase the implicit social costs of renewables.

From a perspective of long-term decarbonization, the current state investments in UHV transmission lines are necessary and can significantly enhance the future potential of large-scale renewable integration. But at the same time, completely ignoring market signals could cause expensive consequences. A clearer cost allocation mechanism will promote renewable energy investments in more economically sensible locations and improve overall economic efficiency. A wholesale transmission tariff for the generators, for example, could motivate the investors to make more socially rational decisions. This is particularly true for UHV DC lines, which are used mostly for connecting remotely located generators and contribute little to system interconnection and reliability. In other words, even in a model ideally dominated by government planning, the integration of market information is critical and can substantially improve coordination and efficiency.

2.5.4 Coordinating Electricity Policies with Low-Carbon Policies

The electric power system is the most important sector in the low-carbon transition. To facilitate long-term decarbonization, electricity policies need to be coordinated with low-carbon policies in all stages, from system operation to pricing to transmission planning. First, system operation should give priority to renewable sources during dispatching, and provide incentives for backup and storage services to address intermittency concerns. Second, carbon pricing policies, specifically the cap-and-trade programs, need to be developed shoulder to shoulder with electricity market reforms. Both initiatives are the highlights of the national efforts to "deepen the comprehensive reforms" and "let market play a fundamental role in resources allocation." The market-based carbon pricing policies will not be effective without well-functioning price signals in the electricity market. The electricity generation quotas need to be replaced by a competitive wholesale market, and electricity prices need to be determined by that market, so that carbon prices can be reflected in a timely manner in electricity tariffs. Third, some current policies, such as feed-in tariffs and renewable portfolio standards, cannot be enforced due to limits of the transmission system. Thus, two-way communications are needed between renewable energy policies and transmission infrastructure planning.

2.6 Conclusions

As the focus of China's energy development shifts from ensuring supply to making a low-carbon transition, the country needs to undertake a series of reforms to address challenges in enhancing low-carbon energy penetration and reducing the coal-fired power fleet. System operation, electricity pricing, and transmission and generation planning are the three primary policy questions, but each one requires different approaches based on the nature of the issues.

In the cases of system operation and pricing, there is a theoretically optimal solution: independent system operators, nondiscriminatory access to the grids, complete market information, and accurate locational marginal prices. If all of these conditions can be satisfied, the electricity market should become efficient. But due to China's historical and political realities, such an optimal state is unlikely to be achieved. Still, it is helpful to use the ideal scenario as a benchmark to guide China's power sector reforms. The issue of market-oriented reforms in the power sector has many layers: competition on the generation side, flexible choices on the consumer side, accurate prices that reflect real-time generation and transmission costs, exchange and dispatch agencies independent of grid companies, and privatization. For China's decarbonization, the first three, particularly accurate price signals, are necessary for a cost-effective low-carbon power system. The latter two are more controversial, but also have lesser significance. Specifically, privatization may not be a desirable model for long-term planning, as discussed in Section 2.5.3. Replacing "equal shares dispatch" with merit-based dispatch and allowing wholesale and retail prices to be determined by market competition should be essential components in the reforms. Overall, the power sector should create market signals that can optimize electricity production among generators and guide consumer behaviors, as well as facilitate other low-carbon policies such as carbon pricing and renewable energy integration.

In the case of infrastructure planning, a central challenge is to reconcile the relationship of state planning and market mechanisms. Because of the long-term nature of energy system planning, natural monopoly in the grid system, and myopia of corporate investment behaviors, the market by itself is insufficient to stimulate farsighted policy making that can enhance the capacity of decarbonization several decades later. Here, China's ability to make consistent long-term planning is an advantage. In transmission grid development, wise state planning that integrates market information as much as possible is likely to yield the best outcome.

In summary, reducing emissions from electricity generation, particularly coal-fired power plants, is the most important target in China's decarbonization process beyond 2030. Moreover, the electricity system is at the center of most low-carbon policies, including carbon pricing, solar, wind, nuclear, and hydropower development, as well as use of electric vehicles. Thus, it is critical for China to form an effective and efficient electricity system in order to provide the infrastructure for long-term decarbonization.

References

[1] International Energy Agency, "CO_2 Emissions from Fuel Combustion 2018" (Paris: International Energy Agency, 2018).

[2] REN21, "Renewables 2015 Global Status Report" (Paris: REN21, 2015).

[3] W. Dong and Y. Qi, "Government behaviors and PPP model in clean energy industry development in China." In Y. Qi and X. Zhang, eds., *Annual Review of Low Carbon Development in China (2015–2016)* (Beijing: Social Science Academic Press, 2016), pp. 182–218.

[4] MIT Energy Initiative, "The Future of the Electric Grid" (Cambridge, MA: MIT Energy Initiative, 2011).

[5] M. R. Davidson, V. Karplus, W. Xiong et al., "Modelling the potential for wind energy integration on China's coal-heavy electricity grid." *Nature Energy* **1**(7) (2016), pp. 1–7.

[6] F. Kahrl, D. Jianhua, H. Junfeng et al., "Challenges to China's transition to a low carbon electricity system." *Energy Policy* **39**(7) (2011), pp. 4032–4041.

[7] O. Van Vliet, A. S. Brouwer, A. P. C. Faaij et al., "Energy use, cost and CO_2 emissions of electric cars." *Journal of Power Sources* **196**(4) (2011), pp. 2298–2310.

[8] China Electricity Association, "China's Electricity Sector Status and Prospects" (Beijing: People's Republic of China, 2017).

[9] National Development and Reform Commission, "National 13th Five-Year Plan for Energy Development" (Beijing: People's Republic of China, 2016).

[10] J. H. Williams and F. Kahrl, "Electricity reform and sustainable development in China." *Environmental Research Letters* **3**(4) (2008), pp. 1–14.

[11] National Energy Administration, "Guidelines on the Management of Electric Power Planning" (Beijing: People's Republic of China, 2016).

[12] F. Kahrl, J. H. Williams, and J. Hu, "The political economy of electricity dispatch reform in China." *Energy Policy* **53** (2013), pp. 361–369.

[13] P. Andrews-Speed, "Reform postponed: The evolution of China's electricity markets." In F. P. Sioshansi, ed., *Evolution of Global Electricity Markets. New Paradigms, New Challenges, New Approaches* (Waltham, MA: Elsevier, 2013), pp. 531–569.

[14] M. Zeng, J. Sun, L. Wang et al., "The power industry reform in China 2015: Policies, evaluations and solutions." *Renewable and Sustainable Energy Reviews* **57** (2016), pp. 94–110.

[15] L. Zhang, "Electricity pricing in a partial reformed plan system: The case of China." *Energy Policy* **43** (2012), pp. 214–225.

[16] J. Ma, "On-grid electricity tariffs in China: Development, reform and prospects." *Energy Policy* **39**(5) (2011), pp. 2633–2645.

[17] Z. Xu, H. Dong, and H. Huang, "Debates on ultra-high-voltage synchronous power grid: The future super grid in China?" *IET Generation, Transmission & Distribution* **9** (8) (2015), pp. 740–747.

[18] P. Wang, L. Liu, and T. Wu, "A review of China's climate governance: State, market and civil society." *Climate Policy* **18**(5) (2018), pp. 664–679.

3

Promoting Large-Scale Deployment and Integration of Renewable Electricity

WEI PENG, ZHIMIN MAO, AND MICHAEL R. DAVIDSON

3.1 Introduction

Renewable energy will play a central role in China's deep decarbonization strategy. Decarbonizing the power system by scaling up renewable capacity, coupled with electrification efforts in the demand sector (especially the transport sector), is a common feature for the exploratory future scenarios designed for China to achieve substantial reductions in carbon emissions [1, 2]. In the past decade, China has invested significantly in renewable capacity, especially wind and solar. The total investment increased from US$2 billion in 2004 to more than US$120 billion in 2016 [3]. By the end of 2018, the total grid-connected wind capacity has increased from 2 GW to more than 180 GW [4], and the installed capacity of solar from less than 1 GW to more than 170 GW [5]. To date, China is already the world's top investor and installer of renewable energy [6].

In addition, the country has ambitious plans to further expand domestic renewable energy use in the coming 10–15 years. Overall, China aims to increase the share of nonfossil energy in its total energy mix to 15 percent by 2020 and 20 percent by 2030. In the 13th Five-Year Plan (2015–2020), it aims to increase the total grid-connected wind capacity to 210 GW by 2020 (including 5 GW offshore wind), which will contribute 6 percent of total electricity generation [7]. The solar installation goal for 2020 (110 GW) set in the 13th FYP [8] was achieved by the end of 2017. Recently, China also proposed a province-level renewable quota system for 2020 [9], and an indicative 2030 national target of achieving 35 percent electricity from renewable resources [10]. Such a strong push is driven partly by the need to shift away from coal to curb conventional air pollution, as well as to strengthen domestic manufacturing capacity.

Despite the success in rapidly scaling up renewable installations, the integration of renewable electricity into China's coal-dominated power system has become challenging in recent years. Nationally, curtailment of wind, i.e., when the resource

39

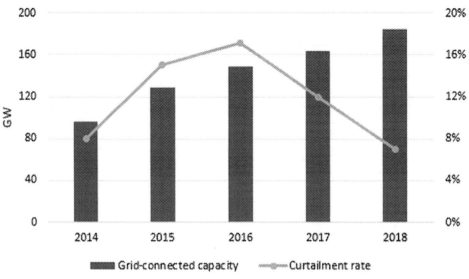

Figure 3.1 National total grid-connected wind capacity and national average wind curtailment rate.
(*Data source*: National Energy Administration) [20–24]

is available but the generator is instructed to lower its output, has been high, ranging from 7 to 17 percent over the period 2014–2018 (see Figure 3.1) [11–15]. In 2018 for instance, 28 TWh of wind power was curtailed [16]. In some major wind-producing regions in northern China, the curtailment rate was extremely high, e.g., 10 percent in Inner Mongolia (7 TWh), 23 percent in Xinjiang (11 TWh) and 19 percent in Gansu (5 TWh) [17]. Besides wind, the curtailment of solar power has also become a concern (curtailment rate: 7 percent in 2017 [18] and 3 percent in 2018) [19]. Such high curtailment rates are driven by a combination of factors, such as the inflexibility of the coal fleet to accommodate intermittent renewables, lack of incentives for grid and generation companies to integrate nondispatchable sources, and inadequate transmission capacity (see Chapter 6 for more details).

Integration of renewable energy poses challenges to the traditional operation of the power system due to its variability and limited predictability. Wind and solar resources can vary substantially over short time periods, and it is challenging to predict the availability of these renewable resources greater than a day or so in advance. As a result, when sudden changes of renewable generation occur, system operators must make rapid and substantial adjustments to balance electricity supply and load, which include adjusting the output from nonrenewable plants (including start-ups or shutdowns) as well as curtailing renewable energy.

Furthermore, the impacts of renewable penetration, as well as the solutions to manage intermittent renewable contributions to the grid, greatly depend on system configuration and the scale of penetration. For instance, in contrast to natural gas power plants, which are abundant in the United States, China relies heavily on coal-fired power plants, which are less flexible in their ability to change output over short periods of time. In addition, a review of deep decarbonization modeling studies reveals that high penetrations of renewable generation (e.g., greater than 50 percent) pose significantly different impacts than those at low penetration (e.g., 10 percent) [25–27]. For instance, with larger-scale renewable penetration, the variation in the net load is much greater. Net load is the amount of electricity that nonintermittent renewable generation plants must produce after the amount of intermittent renewable generation is subtracted from the total demand, which would require new technologies (e.g., energy storage) and operational practices. Therefore, it is critical to plan for high penetration while sufficiently addressing medium-term challenges by combining a wide range of technical solutions, including flexible generation, improved transmission, storage, and demand-side measures.

In this chapter, we first summarize the current governance structure and policies for renewable energy in China. We then combine short-term and long-term perspectives to discuss:

(1) What are key considerations for China to transition toward a power system with large-scale penetration of renewables?
(2) What strategies could serve as foundations for large-scale renewable integration and deep decarbonization in the future?

3.2 Current Governance Structure and Policies

As the central planning agency, the National Development and Reform Commission (NDRC), together with the National Energy Administration (NEA), continues to introduce ambitious renewable energy development goals through medium- and long-term plans at the national level. The overall renewable energy development and implementation were also undertaken by several other agencies. The State Council, the NDRC, the NEA, the Ministry of Finance, and the Ministry of Science and Technology (and the former State Electricity Regulatory Commission) all have a role to play at the central level on renewable energy policy.

A series of key policies have been implemented to support renewable energy development in China. Most notably, the renewable energy sector has experienced rapid growth since the introduction of the Renewable Energy Law in 2005. The initial development focused mainly on the expansion of China's renewable technology manufacturing industry. As the manufacturing capacity strengthened, which resulted in an overcapacity of domestically produced wind turbines and solar panels, China started to encourage more installations in the domestic market since the 12th Five-Year-Plan period (2005–2010).

Following on the Renewable Energy Law, China introduced feed-in tariff systems to support investments in wind and solar. The purchase prices are set by the NDRC, and are determined by considerations of the characteristics of renewable energy technologies, geographical location, and grade of local renewable energy sources. The feed-in tariff rates have been adjusted downward gradually as the cost of renewable energy has declined. In 2018, the feed-in tariff for onshore wind power was lowered to 0.4–0.57 CNY/kWh for four types of regions, based on local wind resource potential [28]. The feed-in tariff for PV generators has been reduced to 0.5, 0.6, and 0.7 CNY/kWh for resource type I, II, and III regions respectively, and China's regulators plan to adjust it every year [29]. Initially, there were complaints from generators about the delay in receiving payments, which created significant revenue uncertainty for project developers. However, such complaints have been decreasing in recent years.

Given the high curtailment rates in major renewable-producing regions, the Chinese government has taken serious measures to slow down the construction of new installations in regions with integration difficulties and to accelerate transmission grid connections. For instance, the NEA evaluates the wind investments and integration conditions in each province on a yearly basis, and imposes different levels of restrictions on new projects based on the province's current integration levels. Provinces with "red alerts" (e.g., in 2017, Heilongjiang, Gansu, Xinjiang, Jilin, Inner Mongolia, and Ningxia; the ban was lifted in 2018 for Heilongjiang, Inner Mongolia, and Ningxia based on a new assessment) [30] are required to postpone the construction of approved wind projects, and no new projects will be approved until the curtailment rate is lowered.

In addition, in 2019 China launched a renewable energy obligation policy that assigns province-level quotas for renewable electricity use. Based on the announcement, the 2020 quota for nonhydro renewable electricity was scheduled to range from 2.5 percent (e.g., Chongqing) to higher than 20 percent in the major renewable-producing regions in northwestern and northeastern China (e.g., Ningxia, Qinghai, Heilongjiang) [31]. Grid companies, electricity retail companies, and large end-users will participate in direct purchasing a percentage quota of their electricity from renewable sources.

3.3 Key Considerations for Integrating Large-Scale Renewables into China's Power System

3.3.1 Geographic Mismatch between Renewable Resources and Demand Centers

China has abundant wind and solar resources, but there are huge regional variations. The best wind and solar resources are concentrated in the north, northeast, and west of China, where local population density and electricity demand is typically low. The country's industrial and urban centers, however, are mainly located in eastern and southern China. This geographic mismatch creates a challenge to utilizing renewable electricity. Although offshore wind is gradually taking off, the scale of current deployment as well as near-term targets is much smaller for offshore than onshore wind capacity. For instance, the 2020 target of 210 GW grid-connected wind capacity includes only 5 GW of offshore wind [32].

3.3.2 Current Pattern: Concentrated Renewable Development in Resource-Rich Regions

During the past decade, renewable energy capacity development has focused mainly on resource-rich regions (Figure 3.2). For instance, since 2009 China has planned and developed seven GW-scale wind production bases in selected provinces that have good wind resources. However, many of these regions have relatively low local energy demand and thus limited ability to consume renewable-generated electricity. Given the geographic mismatch of production and demand activities, inadequate interregional electricity transmission has been one of the key barriers to using renewable electricity.

Since the approval and construction process for renewable capacity is much less time-consuming than that for long-distance transmission lines, the development of transmission capacity has fallen behind that of renewable energy production capacity. The approval and construction of interregional transmission capacity has always been under the jurisdiction of the central government, and often requires a long lead time. Wind and solar projects are approved by provincial governments (except for 2011–2012, when the central government took back the approval right for wind projects smaller than 50 MW). Given the local incentives to attract new investment, improve local GDP, and create jobs, many small wind projects were approved by the provincial governments regardless of whether these projects could be connected to the grid or not. Responding to these issues, the central government in 2016 started to set provincial installation targets and/or caps, and then let the provincial governments approve new projects within these targets [33].

In recent years, the government has explicitly considered transmission needs in its renewable development plans. It also accelerated the construction of long-distance transmission lines. Such a transmission expansion is partly driven by air pollution concerns in eastern provinces and the urgent need to reduce local coal-fired power generation. For instance, in 2014, 12 west-to-east long-distance electricity transmission lines were approved as "electricity transmission corridors for air pollution control" [34]. China is also the leading country in designing, researching, and deploying ultra-high voltage (UHV) transmission lines (i.e., direct

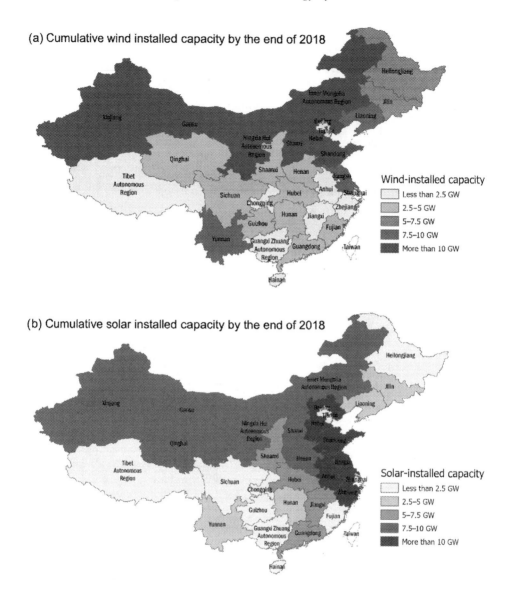

Figure 3.2 Regional variations in cumulative wind (a) and solar (b) installations in China.
(*Source*: China's National Energy Administration)

current lines higher than 800 KV, and alternative current lines higher than 1,000 kV). UHV lines can be a key technology to allowing electricity transmission over long distances. As of 2021, the State Grid Corporation of China (SGCC), a state-owned electricity grid company, had constructed 14 UHV-AC and 12 UHV-DC lines, with 2 UHV-AC line and 3 UHV-DC lines currently under construction. The total length of the finished projects reaches 41,000 km [35]. However, while some of these projects

Promoting Large-Scale Deployment and Integration of Renewable Electricity   45

aim to transmit hydropower from the southwest or a hybrid of wind and coal power from the west, a majority of these UHV lines still plan to transmit coal-fired power from north and northwest China, where three-quarters of China's coal resources are located. Relocating coal-fired power generation to inland provinces allows for continued coal use while also addressing the air pollution problems in eastern China [36]. As a result, it does not contribute directly to decarbonizing the electricity sector and the country's long-term carbon mitigation goals.

In addition, there are economic concerns around the low utilization rate of the transmission assets due to the intermittent output from renewables. A low utilization rate of transmission capacity reduces the amount of electricity being transmitted and sold to the end users, which reduces revenue. Since wind and solar generation are variable with a relatively low capacity factor, a transmission line dedicated to renewable power transmission will necessarily have a low utilization rate and hence lower revenue. Potential near-term solutions with which China is currently experimenting include transmitting a "hybrid" of renewable and other electricity sources from the production areas, which leads to a higher and more stable loading factor. For example, two UHV-DC lines are piloting a hybrid of wind and coal power from western to eastern China, though in practice it is challenging to quantify the relative contribution of wind versus coal, since the transmitted electricity cannot easily be attributed to its source. Although coal is not the best candidate to accommodate intermittent wind output, such efforts move in the right direction as test cases of a technical and economic model for long-distance renewable power transmission. Despite an ambitious plan to expand interregional transmission capacity, large-scale electricity trade between regions remains challenging for institutional reasons (see more discussions about incentives for grid companies and coal generators in Chapter 6, and on electricity sector reform in Chapter 2). Traditionally, the electricity trade between regions is based on yearly contracts with negotiated quantities. It thus leaves little flexibility for transmitting renewable electricity that has variable output.

3.3.3 Recent Trend: Increased Renewable Development Closer to Demand Centers

The difficulty of integrating renewables into the grid in major production regions has resulted in low annual average operating hours in resource-rich provinces. For example, despite great wind resources, the lowest annual average operating hours in 2018 for wind projects were found in Qinghai (1,524 hours, or 17 percent capacity factor). Yunnan, in comparison, has the highest operating hours of 2,654 hours (30 percent capacity factor), even though the local wind resource potential is among the lowest in the country.

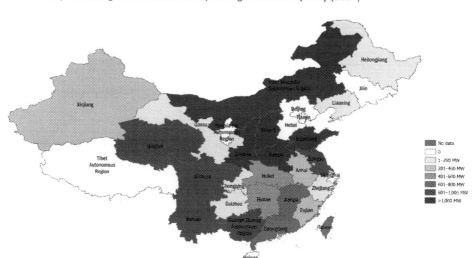

Figure 3.3 New wind installations in 2017.
(Source: China Energy Portal. Available at: https://chinaenergyportal.org/en/2017-wind-power-installations-production-province/)

Driven by the regional differences in current integration challenges, the government started to slow down new installations in regions that are already experiencing difficulties in renewable integration (as discussed earlier, new installations are completely banned in "red-alert" regions where curtailment rates are high). As a result, many southern provinces, such as Yunnan, Sichuan, and Guangxi have become important wind regions (Figure 3.3). Meanwhile, many wind-abundant regions, such as Jilin and Ningxia, have slowed the pace of new installations. In addition, the government created policy incentives to encourage renewable energy development in areas that have suboptimal resource endowments but are close to demand centers. For example, the central government has set up targets for distributed PV generation in eastern China, which does not depend on long-distance transmission across regions. While the initial development pace fell behind the original target, the expansion of distributed solar systems has picked up since 2013. However, there is still great uncertainty as to whether such a distributed system can scale to meet China's decarbonization challenge.

3.3.4 Experience in Other Countries to Deal with the Geographic Mismatch

Many other countries have experienced similar mismatches of renewable energy resources regions and demand centers. The solution boiled down to whether countries could address both short-term and long-term mismatches between electric supply and demand with fast-ramping generation, demand response, storage, adjusting the balancing area, expansion of transmission systems, and other technologies. In February 2017, the Southwest Power Pool in the United States became the first regional transmission organization in North America to reach a wind penetration level of more than 50 percent. The milestone (probably more accurately characterized as penetration levels of 10–20 percent on average and at times above 50 percent) was made possible by its geographic footprint (550,000 square miles) and a robust transmission system that connects rural, isolated wind farms to population centers [37]. In the Electric Reliability Council of Texas (ERCOT), the curtailment level was reduced from 17 percent in 2009 to 1.6 percent in 2013 by expanding transmission capacity and redesigning the market, e.g., reducing dispatch intervals from 15 minutes to 5 minutes [38].

Chile, on the other hand, already faces integration challenges after rapidly increasing its solar and wind power generation share to 6 percent in 2016,[1] in line to achieve its longer-term targets of 60 percent of renewables by 2035 and 70 percent by 2050.[2] Initial installation of solar power is concentrated in the north of Chile in remote parts of the system where solar resources are abundant. However, adding transmission was challenging, especially in the Norte Chico region. By the end of 2017, around 3,100 MW of solar and wind capacity were installed, but demand was only 1,000 MW [39]. On the other hand, Chile did make improvements on renewable resources forecasting and the interconnection between the Greater Northern Interconnected System (SING) and the Central Interconnected System (SIC), the two previously independent grid systems.

Germany has experienced a rapid increase in renewable curtailment since 2014, though at a relatively low percentage, with roughly 1.2 percent curtailed in 2014 [40]. The curtailment resulted from the fact that wind power generated in the north could not reach the demand centers in the south. While earlier development focused on the resources-rich northern plains and coastal regions, technological advancement may enable windmills to operate in regions with weaker wind conditions. Wind energy expansion thus became more even across Germany, thanks to the development of wind turbines that can operate in low-wind-speed regions [41].

3.3.5 System Flexibility Concerns

Intermittent generation from wind and solar resources poses new challenges for the power system. They are highly intermittent and nondispatchable. Integrating intermittent renewable resources into the grid at the currently low levels (less than 5 percent nationally) is already challenging China's dispatch, pricing, and trading practices, which were mainly designed for a coal-dominated system. As variable

48   *Foundations for a Low-Carbon Energy System in China*

renewable sources reach increasingly high penetration levels in line with deep decarbonization targets, these issues will become even more pronounced.

3.3.6 *Greater Demands on Conventional Generators*

From an engineering perspective, in order to maintain instantaneous balance of supply and demand and to ensure grid reliability, the variability of renewable energy will create greater challenges for other generators. Coal currently accounts for more than 70 percent of total generation nationally, and even more in the north, where wind and solar facilities are concentrated, and thus will be the predominant balancing resource in the medium term [42].

However, coal power plants have limits to how fast they can start up, shut down, and change output (see more discussions in Chapter 6 of this book). For example, coal-fired units can typically change their output at up to 1.5–3.0 percent per minute, and the efficiency of coal-fired plants also degrades at low outputs and when frequently ramped [43].

Hydropower can potentially provide greater flexibility than coal, depending on its location and technology type. Where generators are built with large reservoirs, hydropower can be highly dispatchable over days and even months. These hydropower facilities, such as Three Gorges, are limited primarily at the seasonal level as a function of rainfall, and typically have less availability in winter. Where hydropower does not have a reservoir, known as "run-of-river," it is nondispatchable, similar to wind and solar, though with less short-term variability. Currently, the main barrier to more effectively using these hydropower resources is their geographic mismatch with respect to wind and solar: hydro is largest in the center and south, while wind and solar generators are dominant in the north.

Pumped hydropower storage (PHS) consists of more than one reservoir and an additional pumping capability that allows for the storage of water at higher elevations to generate at a later time. Roundtrip efficiencies of PHS are around 75 percent – meaning that 25 percent of the energy is lost in the process of pumping and generating – comparable to batteries [44]. In China, PHS capacity reached 22 GW by the end of 2014, ranking first in the world, and 27 more PHS plants are currently under construction [45]. Existing and planned PHS plants are mostly located in eastern China, with greater expansion planned in the north. In the 13th Five-Year Plan, China aims to increase the total PHS capacity to 40 GW by 2020, of which 11 GW are slated to locate in the 3 northern regions where wind curtailment rates have been high [46].

Natural gas generators are more flexible than coal and thus more amenable to integrating renewable energy: for example, they can ramp up to approximately 8 percent per minute, or three to five times faster than coal [47]. However, most of

China's natural gas supply is currently prioritized for sectors other than electricity generation, such as industrial processes, residential uses, and heating [48]. China does aim to add 50 GW of gas plants in the 13th Five-Year Plan (2016–2020) as peaking units. As the country seeks to aggressively expand gas supply through domestic production, international pipelines and liquified natural gas (LNG), the price will remain a key obstacle to greater utilization in the power sector [49].

3.3.7 Flexibility of the Network

The flexibility of the network is also an important determinant of integration: in general, increasing the size of the area over which generating resources are managed will reduce total balancing and reliability requirements and hence the costs to manage renewable energy variability [50]. In the case of China, this means that interconnected grid regions will be more effective than separately managed provinces.

Determinants of flexibility relate to the configuration of the network in terms of physical transmission assets as well as the operation of these assets through, e.g., market-based trading. As described in Section 3.3.2, China is massively expanding its transmission network through UHV lines. However, current operational practice largely fixes the flows and/or daily profiles over these lines months or even a year in advance [51]. In this mode, they provide access to additional demand but do not contribute to network flexibility.

Besides UHV lines, China has also expanded its conventional high-voltage lines (500 kV AC) that provide connections within provinces and between neighboring provinces. To the extent that these flows are allowed to vary over the course of the day, they will also provide greater network flexibility.

3.3.8 Experience in Other Countries to Improve System Flexibility

As mentioned in Section 3.3.4, ERCOT was able to integrate a high share of wind without significant curtailment in the United States largely because it uses efficient grid operating procedures and has access to large grid operating areas, which enables access to other flexible resources [52]. The day-ahead and real-time energy markets enable the market to respond to wind output variability more effectively and at a lower cost [53].

In recent years, renewable energy supplied more than 90 percent of gross consumption for 20 percent of the time in western Denmark. Low curtailment despite high penetration of wind is made possible by increasing interconnection with neighboring countries and by switching thermal capacity from heat supply to system flexibility provision [54]. The establishment of the Nordpool regional market allows Swedish and Norwegian hydropower reservoirs to provide cost-efficient short-term flexibility [55].

In Germany, 22 percent of electricity production in 2017 came from wind and solar. During the same period, the electricity system remained reliable, with less than 15 minutes of interrupted service per customer [56]. Such a status was achieved with sufficient dispatchable capacity from conventional energy sources such as nuclear, coal, gas, and hydro, expanded regional balancing area, and system flexibility provided by conventional energy generation units [57].

3.4 Elements of Foundations for a High-Renewable System in China

3.4.1 Flexible Conventional Generators

3.4.1.1 Designs and Retrofits for Flexible Operation

China's coal-fired power plant designs were based on assumptions of high loading and stable baseload output that do not exist in a decarbonizing system. While comprehensive recent statistics are unavailable, the percentage of time an ultra-supercritical plant is operating at peak ultra-supercritical conditions is likely already small and decreasing, making peak efficiency less important even at current low levels of renewable energy. The industry should consider implementing a variety of changes that trade off performance improvements at peak efficiency for better part-load operation and cycling [58]. Experiences in Germany, Denmark, and the United States demonstrate how even aging coal-fired plants can accommodate more variable dispatch in response to renewable energy and economic drivers, with fuel savings more than compensating for reduced component lifetimes (see Chapter 6). China has targeted flexibility retrofits for 220 GW of coal plants in the 13th FYP, though without precise specification of technologies or desired performance metrics [59].

Nuclear power is currently a small fraction of total capacity and is operated at a relatively flat baseload output. However, China's nuclear expansion targets, including in northern regions, will create additional demands on this resource to operate flexibly as well. Here, there are both hardware and operational changes to substantially increase flexibility, building on operational experience in France, where nuclear provides roughly 75 percent of total generation [60, 61].

3.4.1.2 Improved Integration and Flexibility of Coupled Heating Systems

Coal-fired combined heat and power (CHP) plant designs in northern China have been widely adopted and prioritized by various urbanization policies. The efficiency benefits of coproduction need to be carefully weighed against the long-term incompatibility of a large coal CHP sector with decarbonization goals, as well as its immediate direct impact on renewable energy curtailment. Alternative heating technologies, predominantly based on electricity, should be explored and evaluated on a range of long-term emission reductions metrics. In the near term, similar to electricity-only plants, CHP plants have the potential for improved flexibility through both hardware and operational changes, as explored in Chapter 6 of this book.

3.4.1.3 Markets and Incentives: Pathways to Flexible Operation

The hardware and operational opportunities have to a large extent been overlooked because of the lack of incentives to deploy them. In China, electricity prices for generators do not vary over the time of day – the primary lever for incentivizing flexible balancing of renewable energy in most other countries. Instead, prices and quantities are largely fixed, with some limited market-based contracts on longer time horizons (monthly to annual), as discussed in Chapter 2. Price-based mechanisms could be complemented by mandatory measures, but China's mixed experience with renewable energy priority dispatch (in place since 2009) and minimum renewable energy share quotas (established in 2016) have demonstrated that mandatory measures alone are insufficient to reduce curtailment.

The heating sector, coupled to electricity through the large CHP fraction, has an even larger incentive problem, as heating prices in most cities do not adequately cover the cost of production, and there is limited metering, such that consumers do not pay according to how much they use. This leads to low appetite for improvements in flexible CHP and electrification. An efficient heating sector will require a constellation of changes, including better monitoring and control of heating supply, coordination among electricity and heating providers, incentives for flexible electricity supply, and rational heating prices.

Mandatory requirements on the grid company, such as renewable priority dispatch and minimum renewable energy share quotas, will be insufficient on their own to address these deficiencies. China is also piloting incentive-based measures, such as competitive peaking markets, that should be further studied. In the long term, an "economic dispatch" that naturally prioritizes zero-marginal cost renewable resources through a short-term competitive bidding market will likely be indispensable.

3.4.2 Appropriately Large and More Integrated Transmission Network

3.4.2.1 Managing Variability with Appropriate Interconnection

A large, well-functioning transmission network represents an important component of integrating renewable energy, smoothing its variability and allowing access to a larger number of flexible resources. China has undertaken substantial transmission line construction, becoming the world leader in UHV line deployment, and is planning and constructing many more [62]. Research by State Grid points to increased long-distance transmission as a necessary lever to reduce curtailment in northwest and northeast China [63]. Nevertheless, it is essential to establish clear criteria for transmission planning to ensure that the benefits outweigh the costs.

Transmission lines provide a wide range of potential benefits, from the typical production cost savings of accessing cheaper resources to reliability benefits and enhancing market competition [64]. The carbon and environmental impacts should be considered, as costs or benefits depending on the expected changes. Projects whose costs do not match these benefits should be rejected. When tabulating these, it is important to consider the distributional impacts of, for example, building lines that facilitate more coal generation in poorer, less dense areas that do not benefit from consuming the electricity. Some government documents worryingly use concepts such as larger "environmental capacity" and "ecological carrying capability" in poorer western regions as justification for these projects.

3.4.2.2 Regulating Long-Lived Assets for Future Scenarios

Pricing for use of the transmission line is another critical component of transmission regulation: in general, it should operate on a "beneficiary pays" principle and the more closely it matches actual network utilization, the better [65]. Current transmission pricing in China is rife with inefficiencies and poor practices. These include tariffs that do not reflect accepted principles of "rate-of-return" regulation, regional grids that overcharge for transmission, and rules with respect to receiving end prices that discourage market-based trading [66]. The current round of electricity reforms aims to mitigate some of these, but these changes will require a heavily strengthened independent regulator, which has been problematic throughout China's history of reform [67].

With the additional burden of planning for a decarbonizing world, how the transmission network will help or hinder this transition are important considerations – which would be unlikely to show up in a cost-benefit analysis with discounting. For example, building lines to connect a Chinese region with good wind resources is also frequently combined with additional mine-mouth coal-fired plants [68]. These plants will become more economical after the transmission line is built and, given their long lifetimes, may create additional barriers to decarbonizing.

3.4.2.3 Markets, Operations, and Regulations for Flexibility

Effectively regulating the transmission network is important not only because of its cost to consumers but also for its effect on competitive markets (see more discussions in Chapter 2) [69]. As incentives for flexible operation of coal and other generators are developed through markets, the transmission system must accommodate them. In particular, current practice distorts these by setting high expected utilization rates (thus encouraging more conventional units to fill up lines when it is not windy or sunny), fixing flow profiles a year or more in advance (thus making it impractical to vary according to renewable availability), and incentivizing the grid company to dispatch through expensive lines, not necessarily those that lead to the lowest system cost [70].

To effectively and flexibly integrate large quantities of low-carbon energy over large distances, China needs to move toward a system that separates regulated grid activities from market transactions (see relevant discussions in Chapter 2) [71, 72]. This means, first, that transmission lines need to be paid back according to how much they cost – including any incentives to reduce over-building – not by how much they are actually used. Second, when lines are congested, transmission tariffs should increase to encourage efficient utilization of scarce transmission, but these "congestion rents" should not add to the total revenue of the grid company. Third, line losses and other variable costs should be treated separately and recovered in a manner consistent with efficient system operation.

3.4.3 Storage Technology Development

3.4.3.1 Available Storage Technologies at Present

Electricity storage systems offer an option to absorb electricity from the grid when there is excessive supply, and feed electricity back to the grid at a later time when demand is high. It could play an important role in facilitating the integration of variable renewable resources by increasing the cost-effective penetration of renewable energy, reducing the investments in peaking units, and improving the utilization of installed capacity. An increase in storage capacity is also a common feature across future electricity scenarios that are designed to explore higher renewable penetration for China [73, 74]. For instance, the China 2050 High

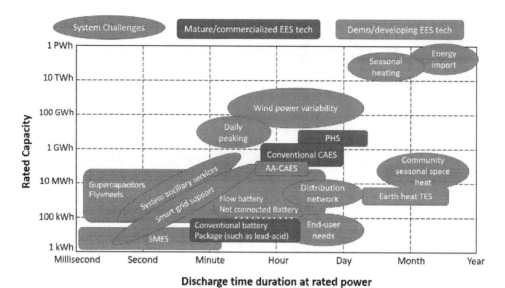

Figure 3.4 Electric energy storage technologies by discharge time, capacity, and technology availability.
(*Source*: Luo et al. 2015) [84]

Renewable Energy Penetration Scenario and Roadmap study found that achieving 85 percent renewable penetration by 2050 will require 140 GW of pumped hydro storage and 160 GW of chemical energy storage [75].

A wide range of electric energy storage technologies already exist, including batteries, pumped hydro, compressed air storage, and flywheels. These technologies have different characteristics in terms of discharge time, rated capacity, and commercial availability (Figure 3.4). For instance, pumped hydro energy storage is a mature technology that currently represents more than 99 percent of global total bulk storage capacity [76]. It has large energy capacity, a relatively low cost on a $/kWh basis ($5–$100/kWh), a long lifetime (40–60 years), and a discharge time duration from hours to days [77, 78]. By comparison, conventional battery technologies, such as lead-acid batteries, have low rated capacity, a high cost ($200–$400/kWh), a relatively short lifetime (5–15 years), and a short storage duration (minutes to hours) [79, 80]. Other popular battery systems being researched at present include flow batteries and liquid sodium cells.

3.4.3.2 Policies to Facilitate R&D and Deployment

The cost of grid-scale storage technologies is currently prohibitive as a means of balancing renewable energy, especially when compared with the two options discussed in Sections 3.4.1 and 3.4.2, i.e., flexible generation and integrated transmission. For instance, a study in the United States found that for two-hour storage, the economic value delivered by energy storage only exceeds current technology costs under strict emission limits [81]. It suggests that substantial cost reductions in battery technologies are necessary to justify large-scale deployment. PHS, by comparison, is by far the cheapest option to mitigate fluctuations in the power system. However, its deployment is constrained by the availability of hydropower resources. In China, since high solar and wind curtailment are currently happening primarily in the water-stressed northern regions, the role of PHS is limited in the absence of more flexible interregional transmission.

In the near term, electricity storage investments will require well-functioning wholesale markets and strengthened economic regulation to encourage private capital and cost-effective planning of utility-owned regulated assets. China's current pricing scheme makes even lower-cost PHS uneconomic [82]. These improvements in market practices will simultaneously help other methods of increasing system flexibility, whose cost-effective potential is large at present.

More importantly, continued investments in research and development are the key to accelerating cost reduction in grid-scale storage technologies, as well as to expanding the portfolio of available storage technology options in the future. For instance, besides batteries, prior studies also proposed a potential technology option of integrating combined heat and power (CHP) with heat pumps, which can be operated on regulating and reserve power markets to provide storage capacity [83]. Given the high cost of electricity storage technologies at present, China's public finance in storage would likely be more effectively directed at R&D to develop cheaper, more efficient storage technology in the future, as opposed to deploying current expensive storage technologies on a large scale.

3.4.4 Demand-Side Flexibility/Responsiveness

3.4.4.1 Value of Demand-Side Measures (DSM) for a High-Renewable System

Demand-side flexibility facilitates renewable integration in several different ways. First, for an electricity sector with high renewable penetration, incentives for electricity users to reduce their demand (such as through price signals) can reduce the total load as well as the net demand (i.e., demand minus wind and solar). These demand responses can in turn mitigate the need for reserve margin, especially during hours with low renewable availability, and hence improve the economics of the overall electricity system [85]. Traditionally, demand management measures were offered to large industrial and commercial customers with higher rates or limited supply during peak demand periods. Such options are rarely offered to smaller customers due to the need for expensive communications and metering equipment. However, this is changing with smart grid technologies that allow development of innovative rate structures and other mechanisms to more cost-effectively implement conservation and load shifting [86]. Demand-response programs such as direct load control (DLC) also allow utilities to directly control larger appliances, such as air conditioners and electric water heaters, to reduce peak demand.

Second, demand response provides more flexibility and stability in the electricity system. In the United States, for example, demand-response programs are increasingly providing load for utilities and system operators. Regions such as ERCOT derive 50 percent (the maximum level allowed by ERCOT market rules) of its contingency reserves from demand-response programs in the form of responsive reserves, i.e., disconnecting certain loads from certain electricity consumers when there appears to be a drop in frequency [87]. Since 2007, PJM Interconnection, a regional transmission organization in the eastern United States, has incorporated demand response resources in its forward capacity markets by procuring these resources to meet resources adequacy three years into the future [88].

3.4.4.2 Current Developments and Challenges of DSMs in China

Demand-response programs could play an important role in enabling renewable integration into China's relatively inflexible power grid. Utilities in China have implemented rate structures that vary during the day as generation costs change, i.e., time-of-use (TOU) pricing or tiered pricing in response to supply shortage or grid system constraints. In 2003, the National Development and Reform Commission (NDRC) began encouraging TOU rates for large industrial users and critical peak pricing where appropriate to promote electricity demand management [89]. Since then, China has implemented pilot programs to demonstrate the potential of demand response on improving power grid system efficiency. China started to encourage demand-response management nationally since the release of "Measures on the Orderly Use of Electricity" by NDRC in 2011 to better manage load shedding practices [90]. In the same year, China began implementing its first demand side management regulation, which required major grid companies to achieve annual energy savings and peak load reduction targets [91]. In 2014, Shanghai launched China's first large-scale demand-response city pilot. During the summer of 2014, 27 commercial and public building customers and 7 industrial customers responded to declared demand-response events, which delivered a 10 percent average reduction in peak demand [92]. A study estimated the market potential in 2030 to be 214 MW, 790 MW, and 2.5 GW in the "basic," "moderate," and "top-performing" scenarios respectively, equivalent to 0.3 percent, 1 percent, and 4 percent of the forecast peak demand in 2030 [93]. Therefore, China may be able to achieve higher reduction of peak demand by expanding such large-scale demand-response programs.

Price-induced demand response could also play a role in expanding renewable-based electric district heating in China. Renewables have a great potential in providing heating and cooling while reducing CO_2 emissions and air pollutants, as well as utilizing organic wastes. In 2015, renewables provided 28 percent of district heating in Europe, but only 1 percent in China, with great potential for scaling up in the future [94]. To expand renewable-based district heating, China will need to reform its current heating price system. In theory, China's current district energy prices structure could reflect actual cost of generation, transmission and operations, and maintenance. In reality, however, heat billing is based on a flat per-square-meter fee structure regardless of level of consumption [95]. Thus, consumers do not face price incentives to conserve heat. Policy reform should promote transparent pricing that reflects the real cost of electricity and heat production. Such price incentives could lead to reduced heating and cooling demand even in the short term, which may partly address the gas shortage challenge China is currently facing when switching from coal to natural gas for winter heating.

3.5 Conclusions

Increasing the scale of renewable integration is a key component of China's decarbonization strategy. While the immediate challenge is likely to reduce renewable curtailment and further improve its penetration rate, curbing climate change in the long term will require a fundamental transition in China's electricity system from one dominated by coal to one that consists primarily of renewables. The set of strategies that can help achieve marginal increases in renewable integration from the present-day level would be different from the set of strategies that can lay the foundation for a deeply decarbonized, renewable-dominated electricity system in the future. Therefore, one needs to focus not only on measures that can be achieved with current technologies and institutions but also on policies that must be put in place in the near term in order to plan for the longer-term transition.

We discussed four key elements of the foundations for a high-renewable system in China: flexible conventional generators, an appropriately large and more integrated transmission network, storage technology development, and demand-side flexibility/responsiveness. Some improvements can already be made using current capabilities, i.e., by deploying commercially available technologies at their present-day costs under current institutions. For instance, many measures being discussed in China's ongoing power system reform efforts are beneficial for renewable integration, especially those aimed at improving flexible generation of existing thermal units, improving grid connection and integration, and creating the

58   *Foundations for a Low-Carbon Energy System in China*

right price signals to enable demand-side responses (see more in Chapters 2 and 6). These measures can rely on existing technologies, and are largely compatible with China's current institutional setup, despite the need for some adjustments in market practices.

To open a wider set of opportunities for high renewable penetration by and beyond 2050, one needs to go beyond the mere focus on current technologies and measures that are easy to implement under current institutions. In comparison, R&D efforts that tackle fundamental engineering problems can enlarge the future technology portfolio from which one can choose to construct a decarbonized electricity system. For instance, China is leading the efforts in research and deployment of ultra-high-voltage transmission technology that could allow bulk renewable electricity transmission over a long distance [96]. Besides the need to invest in new storage technologies, developing new renewable energy technologies may dramatically reduce costs and increase efficiencies of future renewable technologies [97]. Furthermore, more sophisticated demand-side measures, such as smart appliances, could open the door for accommodating large variations in renewable electricity supply [98]. In sum, in addition to accelerating the deployment of existing renewable technologies, it is also of strategic importance for China to invest in new technologies that have the potential to become a critical part of the future technology portfolio required for deep decarbonization.

Notes

1 2.9 percent for wind and 3.3 percent for solar.
2 Most of Chile's renewable share of total primary energy sources (TPES) comes from biofuels and waste (21.2 percent), and hydropower (4.5 percent).

References

[1] G. He, A. P. Avrin, J. Nelson et al., "SWITCH-China: A systems approach to decarbonizing China's power system," *Environmental Science and Technology* **50** (2016), pp. 5467–5473.
[2] Energy Research Institute, National Development and Reform Commission, "China 2050 High Renewable Energy Penetration Scenario and Roadmap Study" (Beijing: People's Republic of China, 2015). Available at: www.efchina.org/Attachments/ Report/report-20150420/China-2050-High-Renewable-Energy-Penetration-Scenario-and-Roadmap-Study-Executive-Summary.pdf.
[3] UN Environment, Frankfurt School-UNEP Collaborating Centre UN and Bloomberg New Energy Finance, "Global Trends in Renewable Energy Investment" (Frankfurt am Main: Frankfurt School-UNEP Collaborating Centre for Climate & Sustainable Energy Finance, 2017). Available at: www.greengrowthknowledge.org/sites/default/ files/downloads/resource/Global%20Trends%20in%20Renewable%20Energy% 20Investment%202017_0.pdf.

[4] National Energy Administration, "Wind Power Integration and Operation 2018" (Beijing: People's Republic of China, 2019). Available at: www.gov.cn/xinwen/2019-01/29/content_5361945.htm.

[5] National Energy Administration, "PV Power Generation Statistics for 2018" (Beijing: People's Republic of China, 2019). Available at: www.gov.cn/xinwen/2019-03/20/content_5375353.htm.

[6] UN Environment, Frankfurt School-UNEP Collaborating Centre UN and Bloomberg New Energy Finance, "Global Trends in Renewable Energy Investment" (Beijing: People's Republic of China, 2020). Available at: www.fs-unep-centre.org/wp-content/uploads/2020/06/GTR_2020.pdf.

[7] National Energy Administration, "Wind Energy Development 13th Five-Year-Plan (2016–2020)" (Beijing: People's Republic of China, 2016). Available at: www.gov.cn/xinwen/2016-11/30/content_5140637.htm.

[8] National Energy Administration, "Solar Energy Development 13th Five-Year-Plan (2016–2020)" (Beijing: People's Republic of China, 2016). Available at: https://policy.asiapacificenergy.org/sites/default/files/IEA_PAMS_China_China13thSolarEnergyDevelopmentFiveYearPlan20162020.pdf.

[9] National Energy Administration, "Renewable Electricity Quota and Assessment Methods" (Beijing: People's Republic of China, 2018). Available at: http://zfxxgk.nea.gov.cn/auto87/201803/t20180323_3131.htm.

[10] Bloomberg News Editors, "China sets new renewables target of 35 percent by 2030." *Renewable Energy World* (September 26, 2018). Available at: .www.renewableenergyworld.com/baseload/china-sets-new-renewables-target-of-35-percent-by-2030/#gref.

[11] National Energy Administration, "Wind Industry Maintains Steady and Rapid Development Trend in 2013" (Beijing: People's Republic of China, 2014). Available at: http://energy.people.com.cn/n/2014/0306/c71890-24550768.html.

[12] National Energy Administration, "Wind Industry Surveillance Report 2014" (Beijing: People's Republic of China, 2015). Available at: www.chinapower.com.cn/informationtjzlqg/20160106/16581.html.

[13] National Energy Administration, "Wind Power Industry Development 2015" (Beijing: People's Republic of China, 2016). Available at: www.chinapower.com.cn/information&tjzl&qg/20160203/13900.html.

[14] National Energy Administration, "Wind Power Integration and Operation 2017" (Beijing: People's Republic of China, 2018). Available at: www.nea.gov.cn/2018-02/01/c_136942234.htm.

[15] National Energy Administration, "PV Power Generation Statistics for 2018."

[16] National Energy Administration, "Wind Power Integration and Operation 2018."

[17] National Energy Administration, "Wind Power Integration and Operation 2018."

[18] National Energy Administration, "PV Power Generation Statistics for 2018." (Beijing: People's Republic of China, 2019). Available at: www.gov.cn/xinwen/2018-01/24/content_5260072.htm#1.

[19] National Energy Administration, "PV Power Generation Statistics for 2018." Available at: www.gov.cn/xinwen/2019-03/20/content_5375353.htm.

[20] National Energy Administration, "Wind Power Integration and Operation 2018." Available at: www.gov.cn/xinwen/2019-01/29/content_5361945.htm.

[21] National Energy Administration, "Wind Industry Surveillance Report 2014." Available at: www.chinapower.com.cn/informationtjzlqg/20160106/16581.html.

[22] National Energy Administration, "Wind Power Industry Development 2015." Available at: www.chinapower.com.cn/information&tjzl&qg/20160203/13900.html.

60   *Foundations for a Low-Carbon Energy System in China*

[23] National Energy Administration, "Wind Power Integration and Operation 2017." Available at: www.nea.gov.cn/2018-02/01/c_136942234.htm.

[24] National Energy Administration, "Wind Power Integration and Operation 2016" (Beijing: People's Republic of China, 2017). Available at: www.nea.gov.cn/2017-01/26/c_136014615.htm.

[25] He et al., "SWITCH-China."

[26] Energy Research Institute of Academy of Macroeconomic Research, National Development and Reform Commission, "China 2050 High Renewable Energy Penetration Scenario and Roadmap Study." Available at: www.efchina.org/Attachments/Report/report-20150420/China-2050-High-Renewable-Energy-Penetration-Scenario-and-Roadmap-Study-Executive-Summary.pdf.

[27] M. R. Davidson, D. Zhang, W. Xiong et al., "Modelling the potential for wind energy integration on China's coal-heavy electricity grid," *Nature Energy* **1**(7) (2016), p. 16086. Available at: www.nature.com/articles/nenergy201686.

[28] National Development and Reform Commission, "The NDRC Announcement on Adjusting Feed-in-Tariffs for PV and Onshore Wind" (Beijing: People's Republic of China, 2016). Available at: www.gov.cn/xinwen/2016-12/28/content_5153820.htm.

[29] National Development and Reform Commission, Ministry of Finance and National Energy Administration," 2018 Announcement on PV Generation, 2018, Available at: www.ndrc.gov.cn/zcfb/zcfbtz/201806/t20180601_888637.html

[30] National Energy Administration, "Announcement on 2018 Wind Investment Surveillance Results," (March 5, 2018). Available at: http://zfxxgk.nea.gov.cn/auto87/201803/t20180307_3124.htm.

[31] National Development and Reform Commission and National Energy Administration, "Notice of the National Development and Reform Commission and National Energy Administration on Establishing and Improving the Guarantee Mechanism for Renewable Energy Power Consumption" (Beijing: People's Republic of China, 2019). Available at: www.gov.cn/xinwen/2019-05/16/content_5392082.htm.

[32] National Energy Administration, "Wind Energy Development 13th Five-Year-Plan (2016–2020)" (Beijing: People's Republic of China, 2016). Available at: https://policy.asiapacificenergy.org/sites/default/files/%E9%A3%8E%E7%94%B5%E5%8F%91%E5%B1%95%E2%80%9C%E5%8D%81%E4%B8%89%E4%BA%94%E2%80%9D%E8%A7%84%E5%88%92.pdf.

[33] State Council, "Announcement on Government Approved Investment Projects List" (December 20, 2016). Available at: www.gov.cn/zhengce/content/2016-12/20/content_5150587.htm.

[34] National Energy Administration, "National Energy Administration: Six Measures to Support Air Pollution Control Efforts in the Yangtze River Delta Region" (Beijing: People's Republic of China, 2014). Available at: www.nea.gov.cn/2014-12/12/c_133850786.htm.

[35] State Grid Corporation of China, Information on UHV. Available at: www.sgcc.com.cn/html/sgcc_main/col2017041259/column_2017041259_1.shtml.

[36] W. Peng, J. Yuan, Y. Zhao et al., "Air quality and climate benefits of long-distance electricity transmission in China," *Environmental Research Letters* **12**(6) (2017), p. 064012. Available at: https://iopscience.iop.org/article/10.1088/1748-9326/aa67ba.

[37] T&D World, "SPP Sets North American Record for Wind Power," (February 13, 2017). Available at: www.tdworld.com/grid-innovations/generation-and-renewables/art

icle/20969338/spp-sets-north-american-record-for-wind-power#:~:text=Southwest%
20Power%20Pool%20set%20a,given%20time%20with%20wind%20energy.

[38] L. Bird, J. Cochran, and X. Wang, "Wind and Solar Energy Curtailment: Experience and Practices in the United States," *NRELTP-6A20–60983* (Golden, CO: National Renewable Energy Laboratory, 2014). Available at: www.nrel.gov/docs/fy14osti/60983.pdf.

[39] International Energy Agency, "Energy Policies beyond IEA Countries: Chile 2018" (Paris: International Energy Agency, 2018). Available at: www.iea.org/reports/energy-policies-beyond-iea-countries-chile-2018-review.

[40] Bundesnetzagentur. 2015."Monitoring Report 2015" (Bonn: Bundesnetzagentur für Elektrizität, Gas, Telekommunikation, Post und Eisenbahnen, 2016). Available at: www.bundesnetzagentur.de/SharedDocs/Downloads/EN/BNetzA/PressSection/ReportsPublications/2015/Monitoring_Report_2015_Korr.pdf;jsessionid=EBE9DCFD35D44C5EF6F45492336CBDEF?__blob=publicationFile&v=4.

[41] B. Wehrmann, "The Energiewende's booming flagship braces for stormy times," *Clean Energy Wire* (June 14, 2017). Available at: www.cleanenergywire.org/dossiers/onshore-wind-power-germany

[42] Energy Research Institute of Academy of Macroeconomic Research/National Development and Reform Commission and China National Renewable Energy Centre, "China Renewable Energy Outlook 2017" (Beijing: China Energy Network, 2017). Available at: www.china5e.com/news/news-1009552-1.html.

[43] MIT Energy Initiative, "Managing Large-Scale Penetration of Intermittent Renewables" (Cambridge, MA: Massachusetts Institute of Technology Energy Initiative, 2011). Available at: http://energy.mit.edu/wp-content/uploads/2012/03/MITEI-RP-2011-001.pdf.

[44] N. Zhang, X. Lu, M. B. McElroy et al., "Reducing curtailment of wind electricity in China by employing electric boilers for heat and pumped hydro for energy storage," *Applied Energy* **184** (2016), pp. 987–994.

[45] Y. Kong, Z. Kong, Z. Liu et al., "Pumped storage power stations in China: The past, the present, and the future," *Renewable and Sustainable Energy Reviews* **71** (2017), pp. 720–731.

[46] National Energy Administration, "Hydropower Development 13th Five-Year-Plan (2016–2020)" (Beijing: People's Republic of China, 2016). Available at: https://policy.asiapacificenergy.org/sites/default/files/%E6%B0%B4%E7%94%B5%E5%8F%91%E5%B1%95%E2%80%9C%E5%8D%81%E4%B8%89%E4%BA%94%E2%80%9D%E8%A7%84%E5%88%92.pdf.

[47] MIT Energy Initiative, "Managing Large-Scale Penetration of Intermittent Renewables."

[48] S. Paltsev and D. Zhang, "Natural gas pricing reform in China: Getting closer to a market system?" *Energy Policy* **86** (2015), pp. 43–56.

[49] Paltsev and Zhang, "Natural gas pricing reform in China."

[50] J. Apt and P. Jaramillo, *Variable Renewable Energy and the Electricity Grid* (Washington, DC: RFF Press, 2014).

[51] M. R. Davidson, "Politics of power in China: Institutional bottlenecks to reducing wind curtailment through improved transmission," *International Association for Energy Economics IAEE Energy Forum* **4** (2013), pp. 41–43. Available at: https://mdavidson.org/2013-09-01-politics-power-china-wind-curtailment-transmission/.

[52] M. Milligan, B. Kirby, T. Acker et al., "Review and Status of Wind Integration and Transmission in the United States: Key Issues and Lessons Learned," *NRELTP-5D00–61911* (Oak Ridge, TN: U.S. Department of Energy, Office of Scientific and

Technical Information, 2015). Available at: www.osti.gov/biblio/1214995-review-status-wind-integration-transmission-united-states-key-issues-lessons-learned.

[53] Milligan et al., "Review and Status of Wind Integration and Transmission in the United States."

[54] International Energy Agency, "Status of Power System Transformation 2018" (Paris: International Energy Agency, 2018). Available at: https://webstore.iea.org/status-of-power-system-transformation-2018.

[55] International Energy Agency, "Status of Power System Transformation 2018."

[56] International Energy Agency, "Status of Power System Transformation 2018."

[57] International Energy Agency, "Status of Power System Transformation 2018."

[58] Paltsev and Zhang, "Natural gas pricing reform in China."

[59] Milligan et al., "Review and Status of Wind Integration and Transmission in the United States."

[60] International Energy Agency, "Status of Power System Transformation 2018."

[61] National Energy Administration, "Electricity Dispatch and Market Operations Supervision Report of Shandong and 6 Provinces" (Beijing: People's Republic of China, 2017). Available at: www.nea.gov.cn/2017-09/22/c_136629982.htm.

[62] Argonne National Laboratory, "Power Play: China's Ultra-High Voltage Technology and Global Standards" (Chicago: Paulson Institute, 2015).

[63] Y. Shu, Z. Zhang, J. Guo et al., "Study on key factors and solution of renewable energy accommodation," *Proceedings of the Chinese Society of Electrical Engineering* **37**(1) (2017), pp. 1–8.

[64] P. L. Joskow, "Incentive regulation in theory and practice: electricity distribution and transmission networks," in N. Rose, ed., *Economic Regulation and Its Reform: What Have We Learned?* (University of Chicago Press, 2014), pp. 291–344. Available at: www.nber.org/books-and-chapters/economic-regulation-and-its-reform-what-have-we-learned/incentive-regulation-theory-and-practice-electricity-distribution-and-transmission-networks

[65] M. Rivier, I. Pérez-Arriaga, and L. Olmos, "Electricity transmission," in I. J. Pérez-Arriaga, ed., *Regulation of the Power Sector* (London: Springer-Verlag, 2013), pp. 251–340.

[66] Z. Ming, P. Lilin, F. Qiannan et al., "Trans-regional electricity transmission in China: Status, issues and strategies," *Renewable and Sustainable Energy Reviews* **66** (2016), pp. 572–583.

[67] C. Tsai, "Regulating China's power sector: Creating an independent regulator without autonomy," *China Quarterly* **218** (2014), pp. 452–473.

[68] D. Yu, B. Zhang, J. Liang et al., "The influence of generation mix on the wind integrating capability of North China power grids: A modeling interpretation and potential solutions," *Energy Policy* **39**(11) (2011), pp. 7455–7463.

[69] Joskow, "Incentive regulation in theory and practice."

[70] Davidson, "Politics of power in China."

[71] Joskow, "Incentive regulation in theory and practice."

[72] Rivier et al., "Electricity transmission."

[73] He et al., "SWITCH-China."

[74] "China 2050 High Renewable Energy Penetration Scenario and Roadmap Study." Available at: www.efchina.org/Attachments/Report/report-20150420/China-2050-High-Renewable-Energy-Penetration-Scenario-and-Roadmap-Study-Executive-Summary.pdf.

[75] "China 2050 High Renewable Energy Penetration Scenario and Roadmap Study."

[76] Electric Power Research Institute (EPRI), "Electricity Energy Storage Technology Options" (Washington, DC: Electric Power Research Institute, 2011). Available at: www.epri.com/#/pages/product/1022261/.

[77] X. Luo, J. Wang, M. Dooner et al., "Overview of current development in electrical energy storage technologies and the application potential in power system operation," *Applied Energy* **137** (2015), pp. 511–536.

[78] M. Aneke and M. Wang, "Energy storage technologies and real life applications – A state of the art review," *Applied Energy* **179** (2016), pp. 350–377.

[79] Luo et al., "Overview of current development."

[80] Aneke and Wang, "Energy storage technologies."

[81] F. J. de Sisternes, J. D. Jenkins, and A. Botterud, "The value of energy storage in decarbonizing the electricity sector," *Applied Energy* **175** (2016), pp. 368–379.

[82] Zhang et al., "Reducing curtailment of wind electricity in China."

[83] H. Lund, S. Werner, R. Wiltshire et al., "4th Generation District Heating (4GDH): Integrating smart thermal grids into future sustainable energy systems," *Energy* **68** (2014), pp. 1–11.

[84] et al., "Overview of current development."

[85] U.S. Department of Energy, "Maintaining Reliability in the Modern Power System" (Washington, DC: U.S. Department of Energy, 2016). Available at: www.hsdl.org/?abstract&did=806857.

[86] F. Shariatzadeh, P. Mandal, and A. K. Srivastava, "Demand response for sustainable energy systems: A review, application and implementation strategy." *Renewable and Sustainable Energy Reviews* **45** (2015), pp. 343–350.

[87] Potomac Economics, "2015 State of the Market Report for the ERCOT Wholesale Electricity Markets" (Fairfax, VA: Potomac Economics, 2016). Available at: www.potomaceconomics.com/wp-content/uploads/2017/01/2015-ERCOT-State-of-the-Market-Report.pdf.

[88] Y. Liu, "Demand response and energy efficiency in the capacity resource procurement: Case studies of forward capacity markets in ISO New England, PJM and Great Britain." *Energy Policy* **100** (2017), pp. 271–282.

[89] National Development and Reform Commission, "Notice from the NDRC on Using Pricing Signals to Balance Supply Demand and Promote Rational Use of Electricity" (Beijing: People's Republic of China, 2003). Available at: www.nea.gov.cn/2011-08/16/c_131052527.htm.

[90] "Measures on the Orderly Use of Electricity" (Beijing: People's Republic of China, 2011). Available at: www.ndrc.gov.cn/fzggw/jgsj/yxj/sjdt/201104/t20110428_987489_ext.html.

[91] J. Guocheng, "The Development and Reform Commission and other departments issued the 'Measures for the Management of the Power Demand Side'." *China Today* (November 18, 2010). Available at: www.gov.cn/jrzg/2010-11/18/content_1748085.htm.

[92] M. Yew, M. Enoe, and A. Hove, "Stronger Markets, Cleaner Air: A High Reward Solution to Reduce Energy Use, Emissions and Costs" (Chicago: Paulson Institute, 2015).

[93] Y. Liu, N. Eyre, S. Darby et al., "Assessment of Demand Response Market Potential and Benefits in Shanghai" (Beijing: Natural Resources Defense Council, 2015). Available at: www.nrdc.org/sites/default/files/assessment-demandresponsepotentialbenefitsshanghai.pdf.

[94] Tsinghua University and International Energy Agency, "District Energy Systems in China: Options for Optimisation and Diversification" (Paris: International Energy Agency, 2017). Available at: www.iea.org/reports/district-energy-systems-in-china.

[95] "District Energy Systems in China: Options for Optimisation and Diversification." Available at: www.iea.org/reports/district-energy-systems-in-china.
[96] Argonne National Laboratory, "Power Play."
[97] MIT Energy Initiative, "The Future of Solar Energy." Available at: http://energy.mit .edu/wp-content/uploads/2015/05/MITEI-The-Future-of-Solar-Energy.pdf.
[98] P. D. Lund, J. Lindgren, J. Mikkola et al., "Review of energy system flexibility measures to enable high levels of variable renewable electricity," *Renewable and Sustainable Energy Reviews*, **45** (2015), pp. 785–807.

4

Enabling a Significant Nuclear Role in China's Decarbonization

Loosening Constraints, Mitigating Risks

MATTHEW BUNN

4.1 Introduction

Over the next several decades, China faces the immense challenge of expanding energy supply to fuel its growing economy while reducing and ultimately eliminating carbon emissions. It must also drastically reduce local environmental impacts, including the fine particulates that are choking China's cities.

What role could nuclear energy – which emits neither carbon nor other air pollutants – play in decarbonizing China's energy system? China's total final energy consumption in the middle of the twenty-first century is likely to be in the range of three to four terawatt-years per year and continue at that level thereafter [1].[1] Only part of that total will be electricity, though increasing electrification of sectors from industry to transportation will expand the fraction of the total that electricity represents.

Delivering that much energy without carbon emissions will be extraordinarily difficult. For nuclear energy or any other energy source to provide even one-tenth of the total low-carbon energy China will need would require growth to a scale that would deliver 300–400 gigawatt-years per year, which would be a dramatic expansion for either nuclear energy or renewables. Providing a larger share would require even larger-scale growth, and some technologies will certainly have to shoulder more than a tenth of the burden.

Decarbonizing China's energy system is likely to require every low-carbon technology available. Doing it without a major nuclear contribution would be substantially more difficult. But getting a major nuclear contribution will itself be a challenge. Hence, it makes sense to take action today to address enough of the problems that have limited nuclear energy's growth to make it a genuinely expandable option for China's energy future.

Reducing carbon emissions is only one of the reasons to shift away from China's heavy reliance on coal. Reducing air pollution (particularly fine

65

particulates) is politically salient within China and may be an even more important driver of China's energy decisions in the years to come. By some estimates, fine particulates in outdoor air cause over one million premature deaths per year in China and have a significant negative impact on GDP [2].[2] China's energy planners also value diversity in the energy mix, partly to strengthen energy security.

This chapter identifies the key constraints on nuclear energy's potential to grow to scales ranging from hundreds of gigawatts to a terawatt or more over the next several decades; the potential risks of such growth; and steps China could take to address these constraints and risks, so as to expand its nuclear energy opportunities. It offers suggestions for policies the Chinese government could implement in the near term (2018–2030) to maximize its nuclear energy options for the long term (2030–2100).

The most important constraints limiting nuclear energy growth at the scale of hundreds of gigawatts to terawatts are public acceptance – essential for siting the large number of facilities that would be needed – and economics. Other constraints are not trivial, but if the central two can be addressed, it is very likely the others can be as well. To address these critical constraints will require:

Avoiding catastrophes. Any Fukushima or Chernobyl-scale radiation release would likely doom prospects of gaining public acceptance for hundreds of nuclear reactors all over China. Hence, focusing seriously on, and making investments in, both safety and security should be seen as key investments in China's nuclear energy future.

Building public trust. Although China has an authoritarian political system, public opinion matters greatly in siting nuclear facilities. Two proposed fuel cycle facilities have already been canceled (or at least relocated) as a result of public protest, and the government is investing in public outreach efforts in towns where nuclear plants are proposed. A step-by-step process of building public trust, through genuine dialogue with affected publics and fulfilling promises made by nuclear organizations, will be essential to gaining the needed acceptance of nuclear energy.

Reducing cost and boosting revenue. As China shifts toward an energy system where market forces have more influence, the economics of nuclear energy compared with other options will loom large.[3] Steps to reduce the capital cost of reactors, maintain low-cost financing for them, and strengthen their revenues could have a major impact on the scale of future nuclear energy growth.

All three of these goals can be affected by both policy shifts and technological changes. Safety and security, for example, can be improved with rigorous regulation and steps to strengthen organizational cultures at existing facilities – and future reactor designs can offer expanded passive safety, relying less on pumps working or human operators taking the right actions to avoid an accident. This chapter, therefore, discusses both policy and technological approaches to address each issue it identifies.

For the near term, the most critical steps China can take to maximize its long-term nuclear energy options include:

- Expanded efforts to ensure both safety and security;
- Investing in public support for nuclear energy, particularly in step-by-step engagement with local communities;
- Carrying out research, development, and demonstration (RD&D) to develop new technologies that can be available within a few decades and that help address key constraints; and
- Avoiding near-term technological lock-in on costly, dangerous, and unneeded technologies, such as plutonium reprocessing and plutonium breeder reactors.

Given the importance of avoiding catastrophes, building public trust, and improving economics, those issues receive the most extensive treatment here. The chapter proceeds by focusing, one by one, on each of the most important constraints and risks that might limit nuclear energy's growth in China. The section on each concern discusses how challenging the particular issue is in the Chinese context, and how policy changes, advanced technologies, and, where relevant, changes in business models might help loosen the constraint or mitigate the risk. In addition to avoiding catastrophes, building public trust, and improving economics, the other issues addressed are waste management, proliferation resistance, government and industrial capacity (including human resources), regulatory delays, and integration into China's evolving energy infrastructure. Finally, the chapter concludes with suggestions on near-term steps to keep China's long-term nuclear energy options as open as practicable.

Nuclear energy's future in China matters not only for that country but also for the world. China is making larger investments in nuclear energy than any other country on Earth; as of late 2018, 29 of the 42 reactors brought online during 2013–2018 were in China [3].[4] Unless nuclear energy can grow enough to play a major role in decarbonizing China's energy supply, it will have little chance of playing a major role in global decarbonization.

4.2 China's Current Nuclear Energy Picture and the Scale of the Challenge

In 2017, China's nuclear plants had a capacity of 33.7 GWe [4–7]. Hence, growth to a scale that would provide even a tenth of the low-carbon energy China will need by mid-century would require scaling up by an order of magnitude – a truly

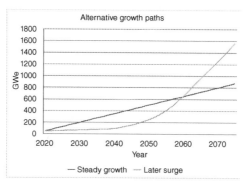

Figure 4.1 Either a slow, steady growth path or a slow growth path followed by a later surge could lead to hundreds of gigawatts of nuclear power capacity in China later in this century.
(*Source*: © 2021 Matthew Bunn)

transformational change. This would involve building hundreds of large reactors, or thousands of small modular reactors (SMRs).

A broad spectrum of possible paths to achieving such growth exists. At one end of the spectrum, in what might be called a "steady growth" scenario, China could build reactors at a steady pace of perhaps 5–10 GWe per year for decades. At the other end of the spectrum, in a scenario that might be called "later surge," China could deploy current-generation large light-water reactors at only a modest pace, and then accelerate deployments dramatically at some point in the 2030s–2060s, if and when advanced reactors with cost, safety, or other advantages became available (see Figure 4.1).

In either of these scenarios, nuclear energy might play a more important role in the second half of the twenty-first century than the first. While renewables may outcompete nuclear for low-cost low-carbon energy supply in the near term, achieving deep decarbonization with only intermittent sources and storage could be very costly; having some nonintermittent low-carbon backup would reduce overall system costs [8].[5] To preserve options for that future nuclear role, however, will require China to take a variety of steps in the nearer term, from avoiding catastrophes to investing in the next generation of technology.

China's current nuclear energy plans are ambitious, but not on the scale described for deep decarbonization. In 2012, following a review after the Fukushima Daichi nuclear accident, China shifted from a policy of "aggressive development" of nuclear energy to one of "safe and efficient development," reducing the nuclear energy target for 2020 from 70 GWe to 58 GWe [9]. That goal has remained unchanged since then, though it will not be met [10].

Indeed, nuclear energy growth has been slowing in China. In mid-2019, Chinese authorities approved starting construction on six new reactors – the first approvals

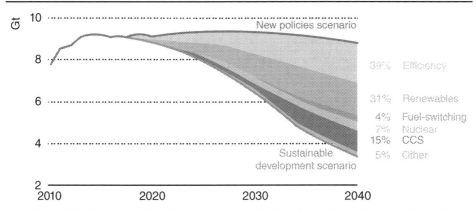

Figure 4.2 The International Energy Agency's Sustainable Development Scenario envisions only a modest role for nuclear energy in decarbonizing China's energy system.
(*Source*: International Energy Agency)

in over three years [11]. As of that time, the post-Fukushima hold on building reactors at inland sites had not been lifted. Recent reactor construction has suffered delays and cost overruns (while still remaining cheaper and faster than in Western countries), public opposition has been growing since the accident, there is little current need for additional electricity capacity, and China's nuclear industry, centered around a few massive state-owned firms, is suffering financially. As one strongly pro-nuclear Western observer put it, "all the negative factors that have afflicted nuclear programs elsewhere are also equally applicable there" [12].

Recent Chinese plans have not established official targets for longer-term nuclear growth. In 2015, the China Nuclear Energy Association (an industry trade group) projected that nuclear capacity would grow to 160 GWe in 2030 and 240 GWe in 2050 [13]. These figures now seem very unlikely to be reached.

Some experts believe that nuclear power in China is likely to level off after reaching a capacity of 100–150 GWe; should that occur, nuclear energy would play only a minor role in reducing China's carbon emissions. The International Energy Agency's "Sustainable Development" scenario, for example, projects only a small role for nuclear energy in decarbonizing the country's energy system over the next few decades [14] (see Figure 4.2). Hence, the questions that are the focus of this chapter – what the key constraints and risks are that limit likely nuclear energy growth, and how could they be addressed – are central to nuclear energy's future as a tool to reduce carbon emissions in China, and, by extension, worldwide.

For now, China's nuclear construction program is almost entirely focused on large light-water reactors. A two-unit demonstration pebble-bed plant, one small floating reactor, and one demonstration fast-neutron reactor are also under construction. China is investing in R&D for a number of advanced reactor concepts, and some US or other foreign firms with advanced nuclear proposals – such as the Terrapower concept financed in part by Bill Gates – were considering building their first demonstration units in China, where regulation is more flexible and government support is more available than in the United States [15, 16]. The Trump administration's decision to bar cooperation with China on advanced nuclear technologies, however, is forcing companies to reconsider those plans [17, 18].

4.3 Avoiding Catastrophe: Safety and Security

Avoiding major catastrophes – and convincing the public, relevant government authorities, and relevant investors that the plants will be safe and secure – is perhaps the most fundamental requirement for maintaining China's long-term options for large-scale nuclear energy growth. Increased safety concerns after the Fukushima accident led China to pause nuclear construction, impose new safety requirements, slow its nuclear growth plans, and halt – at least temporarily – plans for inland nuclear reactors. An accident or terrorist attack leading to a substantial radioactive release – particularly one that occurs in China – could make it impossible for nuclear energy to get the support needed to grow at the scale required to play a major part in decarbonizing China's energy system. Safety and security pose somewhat different issues, and this section discusses each in turn.

4.3.1 Safety

The Chinese government has long emphasized its commitment to a "safety first" policy on nuclear energy and has taken substantial actions to improve nuclear safety since Fukushima [19]. Nevertheless, there are clear reasons for concern, including the frequent major industrial accidents that occur elsewhere in China's economy; the quick pace and low cost of nuclear construction in China, which raises questions over whether corners are being cut; a regulator with a smaller, less experienced staff (and lower budget) than its US or European counterparts; the pace of nuclear growth, which has required bringing in construction firms without previous nuclear experience for less sensitive parts of projects, putting stresses on providing sufficient supplies of trained and experienced personnel; and an overall culture of deferring to authority that could pose challenges for maintaining an appropriate "questioning attitude" at nuclear facilities.

Reducing the risk of major accidental releases of radioactivity requires five major categories of action: (a) deploying systems with high levels of built-in safety, including substantial "defense in depth" along each plausible pathway toward a nuclear accident; (b) maintaining effective regulation and oversight; (c) maintaining strong "safety cultures" within the organizations building, operating, supporting, and regulating nuclear facilities; (d) ensuring that all personnel in safety-related positions have appropriate training and experience; and (e) advance planning for emergency response. China's approach in each of these areas has been evolving.

China's nuclear regulator, the National Nuclear Safety Administration (NNSA), under the Ministry of Ecology and Environment, has expanded rapidly in recent years in response to both the growth in the number of reactors in China and post-Fukushima safety concerns.[6] A new Nuclear Safety Law entered into force in early 2018.

After the Fukushima accident, China undertook a safety review of all its reactors then operating or under construction, paused in authorizing more construction until new safety approaches were agreed upon, and ultimately imposed more stringent safety requirements. By one account, the 2012 nuclear safety plan adopted by the State Council called for spending 80 billion CNY (US $12.5–$13 billion at then-current exchange rates, or over US $22 billion at PPP rates) on safety upgrades at the then-existing Chinese plants over the following five years [20]. An international review found that China's coastal plants typically have plant heights or seawalls 5–10 meters higher than the highest average historical tsunami in their areas [21]. But for plants close to sea level, China has required a variety of measures, including waterproofing of key equipment and construction of an expanded seawall at Qinshan.

China has been an active participant in international nuclear safety activities, regularly hosting both International Atomic Energy Agency (IAEA) and World Association of Nuclear Operators (WANO) reviews; Chinese reactors typically have one independent safety review per year [22]. Chinese officials have emphasized that China has never had a serious nuclear reactor accident and its plants' ratings on WANO safety indicators tend to be average or above average [23].

Nevertheless, both internally and internationally, the factors already mentioned have raised concerns about nuclear safety in China. The pace of nuclear growth – with operational nuclear reactors tripling between 2010 and 2016 – raises concerns over whether the supply of capable and experienced builders and operators, as well as the capability of regulators, will be able to keep up. The number of high-profile accidents in other Chinese industries has heightened questions about whether China can really maintain a very different culture of safety in the nuclear sector. NNSA has discovered welding flaws in safety-significant equipment that the agency attributed to factors such as poor supervision, quality assurance, and personnel skills. The agency also described insufficient equipment testing, inadequate analysis of inspection results, lack of process control, and inadequate approaches to learning from experience. All of this suggests that the safety culture issue may be a deep and difficult one [24].

72   *Foundations for a Low-Carbon Energy System in China*

The wide range of different reactor designs built and operating in China makes the overall nuclear enterprise more challenging to operate and regulate. These concerns are exacerbated by the corruption problem in China that President Xi Jinping has targeted, including high-profile cases in the nuclear industry; in 2010, for example, the president of China's largest nuclear company was jailed for life for taking some 6.6 million CNY (US \$2 million at PPP rates) in bribes [25, 26].

Finally, while China has taken steps to strengthen and expand NNSA – most recently with the new Nuclear Safety Law – NNSA still has less experience and funding than its counterpart agencies in the United States or Europe. The US Nuclear Regulatory Commission (NRC), for example, has a budget of just under a billion dollars a year, and oversees ninety-nine operating reactors with two more under construction, along with various other materials and facilities. China's NNSA in 2014 had a budget of 350 million CNY (about US \$100 million if converted at PPP rates) for overseeing, at that time, 20 operating reactors and 24 under construction, along with other materials and facilities. The NRC's staff was almost four times larger than the NNSA's and typically had substantially more experience [27].

These factors have led to a range of official and unofficial expressions of concern. In 2010, before Fukushima, China hosted its first IAEA Integrated Regulatory Review Service (IRRS) mission. The mission offered 39 recommendations for action and 40 suggestions – unusually large numbers – including on fundamental issues such as adequate independence and staffing of NNSA. A follow-up mission in 2016, however, found that in the intervening time, China had successfully addressed the vast majority of the concerns raised in 2010. The follow-up mission offered only a handful of new recommendations and suggestions – but one of those was that China should host another full IRRS mission by 2020 [28].

In 2011, after Fukushima, the State Council Research Office (SCRO), which advises China's powerful State Council, issued a report calling for a more cautious approach to nuclear energy, warning that moving too fast "could threaten the long-term healthy development of nuclear power." The SCRO report called for making NNSA an independent body reporting directly to the State Council (rather than being part of MEP), and quadrupling its staff by 2020; strengthening personnel training and efforts to build safety culture; improving quality control in manufacturing nuclear reactor components; and emphasizing safer "Generation III" nuclear reactors over the older-design "Generation II" reactors China (and other countries) have been operating to date [29].

China's reviews of nuclear safety after Fukushima found a range of issues that needed to be addressed, establishing short-, medium-, and long-term requirements for improvements. In September 2012, following these various reviews – and, strikingly, following a period of public comment – China's State Council approved a sweeping nuclear safety plan (which appears to have included at least some of the SCRO's ideas, such as a decision not to build any more Generation II reactors) [30]. By mid-2015, the Chinese government asserted that all the short-term and medium-term actions had been completed, and the longer-term actions were underway [31].

Prominent individual critics within China's nuclear establishment have also emerged – an unusual phenomenon given that public dissent from major government policies is rarely permitted in China. For example, He Zuoxiu, a physicist who participated in China's nuclear weapons program and has a strongly pro-government record, has described China's rapid nuclear construction as "insane," arguing that "China currently does not have enough experience to make sound judgments on whether there could be accidents." In 2015, He asserted that "there were internal discussions on upgrading [safety] standards in the past four years, but doing so would require a lot more investment, which would affect the competitiveness and profitability of nuclear power … Nuclear energy costs are cheap because we lower our standards" [32]. He has been especially opposed to inland reactors, asking: "Imagine if the Fukushima accident had happened on the course of the Yangtze River. Then how many people would have their food and water contaminated?" [33, 34].

Similarly, Wang Yinan, a researcher for the Development Research Center under China's State Council (and a protégé of He's), has fiercely opposed inland nuclear plant construction and become a popular antinuclear advocate in China [35, 36]. Of course, the overwhelming majority of the country's government and industry experts take a different view, arguing that China is achieving high levels of nuclear safety and nuclear growth should continue.

4.3.1.1 Strengthening Safety: Policies

Both strong policies and new technologies could help strengthen nuclear safety in China and keep open China's long-term options for large-scale nuclear energy growth. Several policy steps could help ensure nuclear safety.

Avoid rushing construction. China's government was wise to slow its nuclear construction plans after the Fukushima accident. A slower pace will allow more time to train builders and operators and let them gain experience, more time for regulators to check and recheck that each step in construction and operation is meeting requirements, less risk that corners will be cut to meet demanding schedules, and more opportunity to build public confidence.

Strengthen nuclear regulation. China's NNSA has expanded, gained experience, and updated some of its key regulations in recent years, but there is more to do to ensure that it has the resources, expertise, authority, culture, and independence needed to oversee nuclear safety in China. The country will need to continue expanding the budget and staff of NNSA and extend its cooperation with other countries' regulators [37].[7] In particular, while NNSA and the US NRC have extensive collaboration focused on their mutual challenge of regulating construction and operation of the AP1000 reactor design, this cooperation should increase to cover a much broader range of safety (and security) topics. It is also likely to be important to allow more transparency and genuinely independent public discussion. Opening the Nuclear Safety Plan for public comment was a useful step in the right direction.

Establish an effective industry-level nuclear safety organization. In the United States, the 1979 Three Mile Island accident provoked the nuclear industry to establish the Institute of Nuclear Power Operations (INPO), which provides in-depth peer reviews and ratings of safety performance [38]. INPO is widely credited with substantially improving the safety focus at US nuclear facilities. While INPO is the US branch of WANO, many see INPO as providing tougher oversight than is typical of WANO. China should establish a comparable body, taking advantage of the industry's common interest in avoiding disasters that would affect all the organizations in the industry.

Strengthen training, incentives, and other programs targeted on safety culture. Since the 1986 Chernobyl accident, it has been clear that safety culture – the degree to which everyone in nuclear organizations gives priority to safety and is always looking for ways to improve it – is critical to reducing the dangers of nuclear accidents. Building effective safety cultures is a difficult task, requiring focused, sustained leadership from the top of each major nuclear organization. Asian cultures often include respect for authority and reluctance to question instructions from on high, making a questioning attitude sometimes more difficult to achieve. China has launched a number of efforts to review and improve safety culture, but there is much yet to be done [39].

Counter nuclear industry corruption. China needs to target additional anti-corruption efforts – and more transparency in everything from major procurement contracts to oversight of on-the-ground construction and operation – to ensure that bribes and kickbacks do not lead officials to look the other way when corners are cut, or to cover up problems, as has occurred in many other industries in China, with sometimes disastrous results. In Russia, for example, Rosatom, the state nuclear corporation, invited Transparency International's Russian branch to take part in the design of a program to address corruption in nuclear procurement, despite the usually strong tensions between the government and anti-corruption nongovernment groups [40].[8]

4.3.1.2 Addressing Accident Risks: Technologies and Business Models

Most proposed advanced nuclear reactors are designed for greater levels of passive safety – that is, safety that does not require a human operator to push the right button, or a valve to work at the appropriate time – than are present in existing reactors. Some would potentially be able to survive a complete cutoff of all cooling for days or weeks without leading to a release of radioactivity. In the case of the fluoride high-temperature reactor (FHR), for example, which involves fuel encased in tiny particles embedded in graphite balls (which are able to withstand very high temperatures), floating in molten salt, one leading US nuclear safety expert remarked: "I cannot figure out how to engineer a release from this reactor."[9] It should be remembered, of course, that initial visions of the advantages of a reactor concept often do not pan out as the concept moves from paper to reality, but a range of approaches do appear to offer the potential for very significant increases in safety compared to current designs, which are already safer than previous designs.

In addition, some advanced systems would be located either underground or well offshore; in either case, there would be much less potential for large-scale radioactive releases to reach populated areas. Finally, in some cases (such as the underground plants idea, or reactors that could survive even a total loss of cooling) the safety concepts are simpler, easier for nonexperts to understand and find convincing, and have more potential for observable real-world demonstrations than the complex safety technologies for large LWRs.

4.3.2 Security

Terrorists or internal saboteurs could also be the cause of a Fukushima-scale disaster. Several terrorist groups have considered or planned attacks on nuclear reactors, and quite a number of sabotage events have already occurred, though none have come close to causing a radioactive release [41, 42].[10] Terrorists or thieves could also potentially steal weapons-usable nuclear material for a crude nuclear bomb from sites where such material is available. China has experienced increased terrorism in recent years, though most of the incidents have been relatively small-scale and low-tech [43].

Building more reactors would not necessarily provide more targets for terrorist theft, as long as the reactors were using low-enriched uranium (LEU) fuel, which is not usable in a nuclear bomb. More reactors, however, would mean more targets for potential attacks or sabotage. Spent fuel pools (and transports) are also potential targets; in a densely packed pool where hot, recently discharged fuel assemblies were stored in close proximity to each other, an attack that led to a loss of pool water could potentially cause a spent fuel fire, possibly resulting in a release worse than that of the Chernobyl disaster [44].

China's government takes nuclear security seriously and has identified it as an important area for US–Chinese cooperation [45]. China requires each nuclear operator to have defenses in place against a set of potential threats, with a variety of specific requirements within that overall objective. Reactors are protected by well-armed on-site guard forces, double fences with intrusion detection systems around the site, stringent access control systems, a variety of barriers, and more [46]. Each operator's security arrangements are regularly reviewed by regulators. China's government is considering a draft update of its nuclear security regulations, which, among other things, would require that operators put in place defenses based on a consistent national-level design basis threat (DBT), rather than relying on each operator to envision the threat it should defend against [47].

Nevertheless, there are reasons to be concerned. Since China has never acknowledged a significant attempted attack or theft of nuclear material at a nuclear facility, most people in China's nuclear industry do not see terrorism or sabotage as very serious threats, and hence put much lower priority on security as compared with safety. The regulatory effort devoted to security is therefore much smaller than that which is focused on safety. China does not regularly perform realistic tests of whether its nuclear security systems can really defend against intelligent adversaries looking for ways to defeat them – and China's experience of in-depth vulnerability assessment for its nuclear security systems is relatively limited. The country has initiated efforts to strengthen nuclear security culture at its facilities, but little information is available as to how successful those efforts have been. So far, with a few exceptions, US–Chinese cooperation on nuclear security has not involved US expert teams actually visiting major Chinese nuclear sites, so US government understanding of on-the-ground security practices is fairly limited, particularly in the military sector.

4.3.2.1 Strengthening Security: Policies

There are several policy steps China could take to limit the additional security risks from a dramatically larger nuclear fleet, starting with approving the updated nuclear security regulations. Strengthened security rules and practices should address the weaknesses previously noted, including, in particular, establishing regular, realistic "force-on-force" exercises to test the capabilities of security systems, focused programs to strengthen security culture and awareness of the threat, and comprehensive, multilayered defenses against insider threats [48, 49].

Most nuclear reactors do not use highly enriched uranium or separated plutonium that could be employed in a bomb – they are potential sabotage targets but are not locations for potential theft of weapons-usable nuclear material. Minimizing the number of locations and transports with weapons-usable nuclear material, and bulk processing of such material, would be an essential element of managing these risks as China's nuclear fleet grows. Reprocessing and recycling plutonium – involving bulk processing and transporting enough plutonium for hundreds or thousands of nuclear weapons every year – would be a major step in the wrong direction.[11]

4.3.2.2 Strengthening Security: Technologies and Business Models

Advanced nuclear systems could help make effective security easier to achieve. Systems with greater passive safety, making it harder for accidental events to cause a major radioactive release, also make it harder for attackers or saboteurs to cause such a disaster. As noted in Section 4.3.1.2, reactors located underground or offshore would offer less of a chance of an incident leading to radioactive releases that would reach populated areas. Underground reactors might also offer few points of potential attack, making them easier to defend; defending offshore reactors, by contrast, might be somewhat more difficult, though that would depend on the specifics of the arrangement. Reactors that could extend uranium resources without reprocessing would obviate arguments for proceeding with plutonium-recycling.

New technologies separate from civilian nuclear energy could also affect future nuclear terrorism risks, for better and for worse. As cyber technologies advance and merge with machine learning and other artificial intelligence approaches, they will create opportunities for more dangerous cyberattacks on nuclear facilities and more effective cyber defenses. Similarly, drones can offer new options for both defenders of nuclear facilities – including a better ability to monitor the areas beyond the fence line, to see attackers before they arrive – and for attackers. Social media now makes it possible for adversaries to identify people who are, for example, guards at a particular facility, and get information about their lives that would be helpful in attempting to recruit or entrap them.

4.4 Building Public Trust: Siting and Public Acceptance

Public and government acceptance of nuclear power plant sitings is perhaps the biggest single challenge to the kind of dramatic nuclear growth required for nuclear power to play a major part in China's decarbonization strategy. While China could expand nuclear energy use significantly by adding reactors at existing sites where public support has been established, there are limits to that strategy; for growth to the 0.3–2 TW scale, scores to hundreds of new sites are likely to be needed.

China's government remains sensitive to public opinion and protest, and public concerns about nuclear energy escalated sharply after the Fukushima accident [50]. In August 2016, consideration of one of the possible sites for a large spent nuclear fuel reprocessing facility was canceled after large-scale public protests [51]. Similarly, a 40-billion-CNY (approximately US $6.5 billion at then-current exchange rates) uranium processing facility, intended to meet half the 2020 demand for nuclear fuel in China, was canceled after mass protests in 2013 – though it appears that it will simply be relocated to other sites willing to host it [52].

In some cases, local government officials have been removed for their failure to control public opposition to other types of unwanted projects. Such demotions have "blown a chill wind through China's regional governments, leading to fears in the nuclear industry that it might have a tougher time attracting local support for nuclear projects" [53]. In early 2017, China's largest nuclear companies wrote to the State Council urging additional steps to build public support for nuclear energy and limit the scope of "not in my backyard" (NIMBY) opposition [54].

China's government has already tried a number of strategies to build local support for nuclear projects, including information campaigns aiming to increase the public's knowledge of nuclear issues and public engagement efforts focused on soliciting and responding to concerns. In 2014, the government published a handbook to guide such efforts [55].

Public concerns over the possibility of nuclear accidents – sharply heightened after Fukushima – are the biggest driver of the siting issue. Polling research indicates that citizens in many parts of China would be willing to pay substantial sums to avoid having nuclear power plants built near them, though citizens who received even a 10-minute introduction to nuclear energy were somewhat less resistant [56]. Another study, looking specifically at people who lived in towns where new plants were proposed, concluded that the most critical factors affecting local public acceptance were subjective belief in the importance of nuclear energy for China (described as "emotional identification") and trust in the government officials and scientists planning the project, while citizens' perceived level of knowledge about the technology had little impact on their acceptance [57]. In particular, the government's reluctance to approve nuclear power construction at inland sites – which are located along the major rivers that are critical to hundreds of millions of people in China – is based in significant part on concerns over the possibility of accidents that would contaminate those rivers, and concerns about the reactors' use of water in water-scarce regions [58, 59].

Over the coming decades, as climate change makes the need to reduce carbon emissions ever more apparent, there is a reasonable possibility that "emotional identification" with nuclear energy as an important technology for China's future will grow. But given the degree of opposition that has already begun to build, this should not be left to chance. Finding means to build public support for nuclear energy as a tool for providing energy without local air pollution or carbon emissions, while addressing public concerns about safety and other issues, is critical to the potential for large-scale nuclear growth in China.

4.4.1 Addressing the Siting and Public Acceptance Constraint: Policies

Clearly, the most critical single requirement for maintaining public confidence in nuclear energy in China, and hence in gaining approval for additional sites, is to avoid any major disaster at a nuclear facility – whether by accident or from terrorist action. As already discussed, this will require substantial efforts to strengthen both nuclear safety and security.

But building the level of public trust needed for widespread deployment of nuclear energy in China will take more than simply avoiding catastrophes. It is likely to require a level of transparency and engagement with the public that is so far rare in China's nuclear industry, or its rough-and-tumble energy and construction markets more broadly. Both international experience and research suggest that the public's trust in the organizations proposing nuclear facilities is critical and that information provided by the government and industry, often perceived as propaganda, is not enough. Instead, building trust requires a sincere willingness to engage with local publics, listen to and address their concerns, take step-by-step approaches with firmer decisions as more information is collected and analyzed, and ensure that nuclear organizations consistently follow through on all the promises they make [60, 61].

In particular, building and sustaining public trust is likely to require a greater tolerance of and support for genuinely independent voices than has generally been the case in China to date. Residents will want to be able to rely on independent experts who are not simply parroting the government line or working for the nuclear industry, and who have the expertise, resources, and access to information to analyze and comment on proposed actions. Open, transparent processes incorporating such independent experts can take more time, but they can also go a long way toward building trust. In the United States, the experience has generally been that rushing projects or trying to push them forward over public objections makes things worse rather than better; proponents of a new nuclear facility have to "go slow to go fast."

Specific policy actions that could help build public acceptance of nuclear energy in China include:

- Scaling up China's existing public engagement efforts at proposed nuclear sites.
- Expanding benefits offered to local communities being considered for, and then hosting, nuclear facilities. In Japan, for example, communities hosting nuclear

80   *Foundations for a Low-Carbon Energy System in China*

reactors or fuel cycle facilities receive substantial payments (known as kofu-kin), in addition to jobs and tax revenues.

- Establishing ongoing community engagement activities. In the United States, for example, many reactor companies sponsor regular "town hall" meetings where plant officials and workers – who typically also live in or near the host community – answer the public's questions and address concerns. Some plants organize more informal events such as picnics where local citizens can mix with plant staff and get answers to their questions. Some plants also organize citizen advisory boards, which meet regularly to discuss issues related to the plant in a focused and sustained way.
- Expanding local capacity to engage with and oversee the nuclear facilities. Most citizens do not know enough about nuclear technology to draw informed conclusions and must rely on trusted sources for information. It may be useful to provide support to train local representatives to engage with and monitor the nuclear facility in a more expert fashion, so that citizens have local sources of information not directly tied to the industry and government promoting the plant [62].[12]

4.4.2 Addressing the Siting and Public Acceptance Constraint: Technologies and Business Models

In general, such policy steps are likely to be more important in strengthening public acceptance of nuclear energy than are new technologies. But advanced technologies could also help in several ways.

Increasing demonstrable safety. Some advanced concepts have safety approaches that offer high levels of passive safety, potentially making it much more difficult for an accident or sabotage to lead to a major radioactive release. Moreover, in some cases, the concept may be simple enough to build public confidence that it really would be hard for anything to go seriously wrong. In particular, systems that could survive even a complete loss of cooling and failure to do anything at all to respond, along with reactors located underground, might help convince the public that there was little risk of a major radioactive release. Small systems with less radioactive material in their cores and greater inherent safety may require only small zones around them where planning for potential evacuation is needed, making it possible to site them near major populated areas.

Locating plants offshore. The idea of offshore nuclear power plants could make it possible to put plants near the huge coastal cities that are some of the world's largest sources of energy demand; onshore, the plausible land near such cities is typically already heavily used. With the reactors located far enough offshore to be largely or completely out of view – and with a strong safety case for them – it *might* be possible to greatly reduce public controversies over siting.

Reducing use of scarce water. One of the biggest concerns with the proposed inland sites in China is their potential use of, and threat to, scarce water resources, including major rivers. Already, existing technologies make it possible to locate nuclear power plants far from large bodies of water, if sources of piped water are available. But some advanced reactor concepts – particularly those that use coolants other than water – offer much greater potential for reduced water use, so they would not need to be sited near oceans, lakes, or rivers.

Overall, if China manages to avoid major incidents, builds public confidence and support, and invests in R&D on concepts that contribute to addressing some of the difficult siting challenges, it may well be possible to successfully site the large number of nuclear plants that would be needed for nuclear to play a significant role in decarbonizing China's energy system.

4.5 Improving Economics

Clearly, nuclear energy would grow faster if it were cheaper in comparison to other energy sources. In China, however, the economics of nuclear energy is not as much of a constraint on further deployment as it is in the United States or Europe, for four reasons: (a) nuclear plants are cheaper to build in China; (b) nuclear plants are cheaper to finance in China; (c) the competition from other energy sources is not as stiff, particularly as China does not currently expect to have large quantities of low-cost natural gas; and (d) China's government has been willing to set feed-in tariffs to provide stable revenue for nuclear plants, or provide other forms of support for what it regards as a strategic industry.

Cheaper to build: It appears that China can build nuclear reactors faster and at lower cost than has been the US or European experience in recent years, though lack of authoritative data and uncertainties in how best to compare prices across currencies create substantial ambiguities in this judgment [63].[13] The Organization for Economic Cooperation and Development (OECD), for example, reported government estimates in 2015 for the overnight capital cost (OCC) of a generic light-water reactor to come online in 2020 as either US $1,807 per kilowatt of installed capacity or US $2,615/kW for China. But in the United States, the study concluded that such a reactor, coming on line at the same time, would cost US $4,100/kW; cost estimates for European countries were higher still [64]. Similarly, a review of multiple sources over the period 2008–2015 estimated that overnight capital costs in China were US $1,500–$2,000/kW less than those in the United States or Europe; the review also concluded that total investment costs (including interest during construction) for the advanced European Pressurized Reactors (EPRs) being built at Tianshan were less than one-half those of the EPRs being built at Olkiluoto in Finland or Flamanville in France. The reason for the differences was that the delays and cost growth experienced in China were much less than those in Europe [65, 66]. The review noted that other reasons for reduced costs would include ongoing recent experience in reactor construction; lower costs for materials, equipment, and labor; and high levels of localization of manufacturing.[14]

Overall, in 2017, the China Nuclear Energy Association, an industry trade group, estimated that building 30 GWe of new nuclear energy in the 13th Five-Year Plan would cost 100 billion CNY per year, amounting to over 16,600 CNY/kW. That would be US $2,520/kWe if converted at currency exchange rates, or US $4,750/kWe if converted at PPP rates [67]. By comparison, by 2017, the estimated overnight capital cost of the two AP1000 reactors still under construction in the United States had risen to more than US $19 billion, amounting to over US $8,500/kW [68]. Recent US estimates of what such reactors might cost after several had been built and first-of-a-kind costs had been eliminated are just under US $6,000/kW [69, 70].

These are overnight costs, not including the costs of interest during construction. Those costs are lower in China as well, since (a) Chinese state-owned nuclear companies are able to access capital at low cost and (b) China typically builds reactors somewhat faster than has been the case in the United States and Europe. In mid-2018, for example, despite years of delays, China brought the first units of the AP1000 and EPR designs online, even though their counterparts in the United States and Europe had started construction years earlier [71].

Cheaper to finance. Nuclear plants in China are also cheaper to finance, as China's state-owned nuclear firms are able to finance nuclear plants at lower costs of money than are typically available to purely private firms. For an energy source where two-thirds to four-fifths of the total cost of electricity is the cost of building the plant, how much the owner has to pay for the money invested in construction can make all the difference between a profitable plant and a failing one. In other words, *the same reactor, costing the same amount to build, can be economic in one market and completely uneconomic in another, depending on the financing arrangements.*

Limited competition from natural gas. The competition is not as steep for nuclear energy because China does not yet enjoy the very low natural gas prices present in the United States. So far, natural gas production in China is modest, leaving the country heavily dependent on imported liquefied natural gas (LNG), which has been expensive. Plans for scaling up the use of natural gas electricity in China are also comparatively modest. Natural gas provides roughly half as much electricity as nuclear power does in China today, and in the IEA's "New Policies Scenario," gas would still be providing only 75 percent as much power as nuclear in 2040 [72].

Availability of feed-in tariffs or other support. As discussed in Chapter 2 of this volume, China is debating plans to introduce greater market competition in its electricity sector in the future, but for now, nuclear and renewable electricity sources typically enjoy fixed feed-in tariffs, allowing them to make a reliable profit.

In short, until recently the financial environment for nuclear investment in China was excellent, with strong state support, rapidly rising demand, low-cost second-generation reactors, low-cost government-backed financing, and certain, steady revenues from high and fixed feed-in tariffs. In the last few years, however, the environment has become much more uncertain, with excess capacity, state-owned companies exposed to more market forces, curtailment and future load-following reducing revenues, and cuts in tariffs. In 2017, for example, the Chinese government imposed reduced rates on some nuclear plants and indicated that future nuclear tariffs would be tied to the price of coal electricity [73]. In 2019, the Chinese government set the feed-in tariffs for the AP1000 and EPR plants that had recently been completed in the range of 0.42–0.44 CNY/kWh, well below what industry had hoped for, comparable to the tariffs for cheaper Generation II facilities. With these tariffs, the firms that built these plants will probably see little profit from them, potentially reducing investors' enthusiasm for nuclear projects [74]. Major Chinese nuclear firms are now also investing heavily in renewables, which currently appear to offer greater profit opportunities [75]. In the long term, as China moves toward deep decarbonization, there will presumably be strong state support for low-carbon energy sources, including nuclear energy. However, if China moves toward more market competition in the electricity sector, there is likely to be considerable competition among these sources, creating more uncertainty for investors. Ultimately, there may be tensions between deep decarbonization goals and government efforts to keep electricity prices low.

4.5.1 Addressing the Economic Constraint: Policies

Policy choices, new technologies, and different business models could all contribute to (or undermine) the economics of nuclear energy. On the policy side, the most important step would be to maintain the availability of low-cost financing. A second key step would be to continue at least a moderate pace of nuclear construction, to maintain a competitive nuclear construction industry and supply chain as well as a workforce with experience in nuclear construction and operations.

A third step would be to maintain strong and stable prices for nuclear energy, even if China moves toward more competitive electricity markets. This would make nuclear energy a more attractive and lower-risk target for private investment.

84 *Foundations for a Low-Carbon Energy System in China*

Finally, a fourth important move would be to maintain cooperative regulator–industry relationships. On the one hand, Chinese regulators need to be critical and independent enough to ensure safety. On the other hand, having a flexible approach that minimizes regulatory uncertainty and delays can also contribute to reducing nuclear energy costs, and to nuclear energy growth overall.

4.5.2 Addressing the Economic Constraint: Technologies and Business Models

A variety of approaches to modular design and construction, simplified systems, and enhanced passive safety could reduce construction costs and times, as well as the number of people needed to operate plants [76]. Smaller plant footprints and greater passive safety could also reduce the costs of security.

These potentials, however, remain to be realized. It is worth remembering that the Generation III plants, which were initially said to be cheaper to build than Generation II facilities, proved to be still more expensive. One survey of experts in the early 2010s found that, on average, US and European experts expected that the costs of both small modular reactors (SMRs) and Generation IV reactors would be slightly *more* expensive in 2030 than the costs of Generation III reactors were at the time of the survey [77]. All of the envisioned advantages of advanced reactors should be considered as possibilities that *may* come to pass, not as confirmed realities.

Modified business models might also improve nuclear energy economics. For example, if a reactor could provide electricity when the price was high and use its energy for other purposes (such as industrial process heat) when the price was low, the reactor could make more money. (By contrast, load-following as practiced at existing plants just means lowering output some of the time, meaning less electricity sold and less revenue.) In one approach, some high-temperature advanced reactors envision using the facility's energy to produce hydrogen or store heat when electricity prices are low and using hydrogen, natural gas, or stored heat to increase the plant's power output when prices are high and peaking power is needed [78]. Reactors that could go beyond the steady electricity baseload role of traditional nuclear power plants may become more important in a future world with grids incorporating large portions of intermittent renewables.

Some other concepts envision changing business models to reduce construction costs and deployment times. Engineers at the Massachusetts Institute of Technology (MIT), for example, have proposed both small and large reactors on offshore platforms similar to oil rigs [79]. These could be built in large numbers in factories (benefiting from economies of manufacturing scale) and towed to the sites where they would be used, greatly shortening construction times; they would eliminate the need to purchase land and drastically reduce the amount of nuclear-grade concrete that would have to be poured, also potentially reducing cost.

4.6 More Modest Constraints

4.6.1 Waste Management

Effective waste management is vital to any nuclear power program, both for protecting the environment and for maintaining public confidence. If nuclear wastes are managed appropriately, however, the cost of doing so is a small part of the overall cost of nuclear energy, and the impact on human health and the environment per kilowatt-hour is quite small compared with other energy sources. This is partly because of nuclear energy's ability to generate an enormous amount of energy from a small amount of fuel: for example, while a one-gigawatt coal plant needs an eighty-car train of fuel every day, a one-gigawatt nuclear plant needs one-half of one train car once a year.

In nuclear waste management, China may have the opportunity to succeed where the United States and others have so far failed. China has the following in its favor: large, sparsely populated areas for siting nuclear waste repositories; a unified and authoritarian government capable of making and sustaining decisions over time; nascent approaches to public engagement that seem to be showing positive effects; and the luxury of time to get waste management right, since dry cask storage of spent nuclear fuel provides a cheap and safe option for decades. Dry casks can offer time for the technology, politics, and economics of final spent fuel disposition to evolve [80]. It should be both politically and technically possible for China to provide large-scale spent fuel storage as nuclear power grows, and – eventually – one or more deep geologic repositories capable of containing all the spent fuel and other high-level radioactive wastes a growing nuclear program might generate.

4.6.2 Proliferation Resistance

Since China is already a nuclear weapon state, many in China (and elsewhere) believe that its nuclear energy choices have little impact on the spread of nuclear weapons. But there are at least three important elements of proliferation risk, even when systems are deployed in nuclear weapon states: the risk of nuclear theft if weapons-usable nuclear material is available in the fuel cycle; the risk of technology leakage; and the "example effect," increasing the probability that non–nuclear weapon states will pursue technologies such as enrichment and reprocessing that could increase their ability to build weapons if they chose to do so [81].

86 *Foundations for a Low-Carbon Energy System in China*

While the number of reactors China decides to build is not likely to have much effect on the spread of nuclear weapons, the specific technological choices it makes might have an effect. Hence, limiting proliferation risks should be an important consideration as China moves forward with its nuclear program. Enrichment and reprocessing – the two technologies that make it possible to produce bomb material – are the key intersections between civilian and military nuclear technologies, and decisions about them will have an outsized impact on proliferation risk. In particular, if China, as the country that will probably become the world's nuclear energy leader in the twenty-first century, chooses to rely on fuel cycles based on reprocessing and recycling plutonium, it will be more difficult to convince non–nuclear weapon states not to do the same.

In addition to these nuclear energy choices, it will be important for China to strengthen its enforcement of strategic trade controls, to limit proliferators' ability to acquire the nuclear and dual-use technologies they seek (many of which come from industries far afield from the nuclear industry) [82].

4.6.3 *Government and Industrial Capacity*

Dramatically increasing China's nuclear energy enterprise would require similarly substantial increases in governmental capacity to regulate and oversee nuclear plants and in industrial capacity to design, build, operate, and decommission them. This would require dramatically increasing the number of trained, experienced personnel in all of these areas.

Serious investments and training programs will be needed to avoid having these capacity issues constrain China's nuclear growth. But over time, it appears likely that if nuclear energy were to become a significant element of China's decarbonization strategy, the market would adjust, with the demand for nuclear experts (and resulting salaries) drawing more people into the field to fill the need. If institutional structures in government and industry can adjust as well, it should be possible to address the industry and government capacity constraints. Over the longer term, advanced reactor systems with increased passive safety and expanded modularity and automation in construction may require substantially fewer trained people per gigawatt of installed capacity.

4.6.4 *Regulatory Delays*

Regulatory delays and uncertainties – from approving construction of a new reactor to getting approval for a new design or a modified operating approach – have slowed nuclear growth in a number of countries and may well do so in the future. By affecting investor confidence in whether and when a reactor or new design will generate revenue, such delays can have reverberating effects.

China has already experienced unexpected regulatory delays – such as the extended pause in approvals for construction after Fukushima, and the ongoing (as of late 2019) hold on approval of inland sites. Overall, however, China's regulators have generally had a more cooperative relationship with industry than pertains, for example, in the United States. If China's government decides to make nuclear energy a major part of its decarbonization strategy, it is likely to be able to ensure that regulatory delays do not unduly constrain the necessary nuclear growth. Avoiding regulatory delays while maintaining the highest achievable standards of safety and security, however, will be a major challenge.

4.6.5 Integrating Nuclear Energy into China's Evolving Energy Infrastructure

As China moves toward deep decarbonization, intermittent renewables are likely to play a fundamental role in electricity supply. Nonintermittent low-carbon backup sources could be quite important to achieving 80–100 percent decarbonization at a reasonable cost [83]. Ideally, however, such backup sources would not simply provide steady power all the time, as nuclear plants typically do today, but would behave more like natural gas plants – offering steady power if desired, but also having the ability to shift output rapidly to follow requirements and offer peaking power when needed. Nuclear plants could generate more revenue and play a larger role in the overall energy system if they could go beyond providing baseload electricity. As noted in Section 4.5.2, some existing nuclear designs already do significant load-following, and some advanced designs envision being able to expand output for peaking power when prices are high, and use the reactor's heat for other purposes (ranging from storage to production of liquid fuels) when the grid has little need for the reactor's power. Even in a heavily electrified future, there will be many energy demands beyond baseload electricity.

4.7 Unlikely to Be a Major Constraint: Uranium Supply

Advocates of China's pursuit of plutonium reprocessing and fast-neutron "breeder" reactors have argued that such a "closed" fuel cycle is necessary because China has scarce uranium resources that will soon run out. These concerns have proven to be overblown. China has access to plenty of uranium to fuel even a greatly expanded nuclear enterprise for many decades to come, if not longer.

Domestically, by 2016 China had identified over 366,000 metric tons of uranium (tU); studies indicate that the total likely to be available in China is in the range of 2,000,000 tU, though much of this may only be available at fairly high costs [84]. That would be enough, even if no more were found and none purchased overseas, to fuel as much as half a terawatt of nuclear power for decades.

But estimates of the total uranium available will not remain fixed. China has been finding more uranium at a much faster pace than it has been using it; the previously reported estimate of China's identified resources, from only 2 years earlier, included only 265,500 tU, a 100,000-ton increase in just 2 years [85].

In part because much of China's uranium is costly to mine (though much less costly than reprocessing and breeder reactors are likely to be), China has also been buying uranium abroad – both on the open market and by purchasing foreign mines. In recent years, China has pursued a "three thirds" policy, getting a third of its uranium from each of these sources. To ensure that supply could not be cut off, China has built up a stockpile of roughly 10 years of fuel supply, ready for use when needed [86, 87].

Globally, uranium is abundant. As of 2016, the IAEA estimated total available resources of some 15 million tU, enough to fuel current consumption rates for more than 250 years [88]. Over time, these numbers have been going up, not down, as the world has generally found uranium faster than it has been used.

Some have projected that uranium prices would inexorably rise as the lowest-cost resources were mined out. This projection, however, ignores the parallel improvements in technology. On average, over the twentieth century the real price of mined minerals declined rather than increasing [89]. This trend is continuing, and there is little indication that uranium will be different. Indeed, the abundance of world uranium resources and the flexibility that abundance offered for fuel cycle choices was one of the key conclusions of MIT's 2009 study *The Future of the Nuclear Fuel Cycle* [90].

In short, lack of uranium is not likely to be a significant constraint on even large-scale growth of nuclear energy in China. The country can continue to ensure an adequate supply through both policy and technology choices.

4.8 China's Investments in Advanced Nuclear Systems

To address some of these risks and constraints, China is investing in research, development, and demonstration (RD&D) programs on advanced nuclear energy systems for the future. These include both near-term and long-term options.

There are good reasons to be optimistic about innovation in nuclear energy technologies. Many groups are developing new ideas; new materials, technologies, and construction approaches are opening fresh avenues of possibility; and advanced computer simulation accelerates the process of designing and assessing new concepts.

But there are also reasons to be pessimistic. No reactor concept other than an LWR has been successfully commercialized in over half a century. As noted in Section 4.5.2, the Generation III reactors were intended to be cheaper than Generation II systems but proved to be more expensive. The heat or electrons that reactors provide are commodities, the same as the heat or electrons from other technologies, so they cannot compete on the basis of unique features in the way a new smartphone can. The utilities that would buy a reactor are in the business of operating plants reliably for decades at costs slightly less than the price of the electricity, and they are deeply conservative, only wanting to buy systems that are reliable, tried, and true. As designs move from concepts to practical reactors, unexpected challenges appear, and they tend to become more expensive and problematic. In particular, everyone should be skeptical of claims of very low costs for advanced reactors, which have not proven out in the past; the recent MIT study of the future of nuclear energy concluded that "without design standardization and innovations in construction approaches, we do not believe the inherent technological features of any of the advanced reactors will produce the level of cost reductions needed to make nuclear electricity competitive with other generation options" [91].

Thus, in considering the *potential* benefits of advanced reactors, it is worth remembering the warning offered decades ago by Admiral Hyman Rickover, founder of the US nuclear navy, that an "academic reactor" would always have a huge number of advantages that a "practical reactor," one that was actually being built, would not have [92]. That, unfortunately, often remains the case today.

4.8.1 Chinese-Designed Sodium-Cooled Fast Reactors

China has started construction on a 600 MWe sodium-cooled fast-neutron "breeder" reactor called the China Demonstration Fast Reactor (CDFR), and envisions building larger commercial reactors based on this design in the future [93]. These systems would rely on reprocessing and recycling the plutonium they produce, creating large flows of plutonium. Traditionally, fast reactors have had even higher capital costs than LWRs, and at present, it appears unlikely that these designs will be commercially successful [94].

4.8.2 High-Temperature Pebble-Bed Reactors

China is completing construction of a two-unit demonstration "pebble bed" high-temperature gas-cooled reactor (HTGR) at the Shidaowan site in Shandong province [95]. These systems involve fuel in tiny particles coated in layers of carbon and silicon, which are embedded in tennis-ball-sized balls of graphite; the core, filled with these graphite balls, is cooled with helium. This offers high levels of passive safety, greater electricity production efficiency, and high-temperature heat usable for industrial applications. The reactors have proved to be more expensive than expected, however, and whether additional units will be built remains in doubt.

4.8.3 Molten Salt Reactors

For the longer term, China is funding R&D on molten salt reactor (MSR) concepts [96]. These include solid-fuel versions with pebbles essentially identical to those in the HTGR system, floating in molten salts rather than cooled by helium gas, and liquid-fueled versions in which the fuel would be dissolved in the salts. MSRs face a number of technical challenges, but could potentially offer very high levels of passive safety, high-temperature operation for efficiency and industrial process heat, and, in the liquid-fueled concepts, more efficient use of the uranium resource. Whether they will prove to be economically viable, however, remains to be seen.

4.8.4 Terrapower

Terrapower is a private US company, funded in part by Bill Gates, which is pursuing a sodium-cooled fast reactor that would breed fuel and burn it without reprocessing. In late 2017, Terrapower reached an agreement with Chinese firms to build a prototype facility in China, perhaps as soon as the mid-2020s. The Trump administration's decision to bar advanced nuclear reactor exports to China, however, has forced Terrapower to drop that plan [97, 98]. Nevertheless, should US–Chinese disputes be resolved, Terrapower and other US-origin advanced reactor technologies remain options for China's nuclear energy future. Terrapower, like other proposed "breed and burn" systems, would make it possible to extend uranium resources without reprocessing, and would also reduce volumes of nuclear waste. If successful, Terrapower might displace China's own fast-neutron reactor designs.

4.8.5 Lead-Cooled Fast Reactors

China is also pursuing early R&D on fast-neutron breeder reactors cooled with molten lead, rather than molten sodium, though these do not have priority similar to better-understood sodium-cooled systems [99]. Such reactors might have a number of advantages, including strengthened passive safety. Lead, unlike sodium, does not catch fire when exposed to moist air. Lead-cooled reactors are a longer-term possibility for China.

4.8.6 Accelerator-Driven Systems

China is continuing basic research on accelerator-driven systems, in which a reactor that is not quite able to sustain an ongoing chain reaction is driven by an accelerator supplying additional neutrons. Such systems might have advantages in safety and transmuting waste to shorter-lived species, but face daunting technical and economic challenges. These, too, appear to be a possibility only for the very long term [100].

4.8.7 Fusion Reactors

For the long term, fusion – generating nuclear energy by putting small atoms together, rather than splitting big atoms apart – represents a potentially important alternative to fission. Fusion systems would have very low safety, security, and proliferation risks, greatly reduced amounts of nuclear waste, and essentially unlimited fuel supplies. Like many other countries, China is making modest investments in fusion R&D. While there are companies attempting to find near-term solutions to fusion's technical and economic challenges, many experts believe those challenges will put commercial fusion energy systems at 2050 or beyond – if they ever are commercially successful [101, 102].

4.9 Conclusions

Like other energy sources, nuclear energy would have to grow dramatically to play a major part in decarbonizing China's energy system. As this chapter has described, doing so would require overcoming a variety of challenging constraints, and addressing important safety, security, and proliferation risks. Because of the immense challenges of decarbonization, and the role nuclear energy could play in meeting those challenges, it is worth doing what is practical to address the constraints on nuclear power growth, so that it could be a readily expandable option for the future.

China can take several steps in the next 10–20 years to maximize the nuclear energy options it would have available in 30–70 years. The most important of these steps are briefly described in the following sections.

4.9.1 Avoiding Catastrophes

Any large-scale nuclear accident or terrorist incident in China could effectively make significant nuclear growth politically impossible. Hence, the most fundamental steps China can take to keep its future nuclear options open are investments in safety and security to avoid such catastrophes.

As described in Section 4.3.1.1, China should strengthen its nuclear regulatory agencies and create an industry-level group, similar to INPO in the US, to establish best practices, conduct peer reviews, and track trends. It should also boost training, incentives, and other steps to strengthen both safety and security culture in its nuclear organizations. China should continue its decision not to start construction of additional Generation II reactors, emphasizing instead reactors with the greater passive safety features of Generation III and beyond. And it should avoid rushing reactor construction, giving builders, operators, and regulators time to do their work carefully, without cutting corners, and expanding their efforts at a moderate pace.

On the security side, China should ensure that all major nuclear facilities are effectively protected against the full spectrum of plausible adversary threats, and carry out regular, realistic tests of its nuclear security systems' performance. High degrees of passive safety – making it very difficult for either accidents or human action to cause large releases of radioactivity – should be a fundamental goal of China's advanced reactor development.

4.9.2 Building Public Trust

Public opposition to nuclear facilities is likely to be among the most substantial constraints to be addressed to achieve large-scale nuclear growth in China. China's nuclear organizations will have to invest in the slow, painstaking work of building trust with local communities, step by step – engaging with local residents, understanding and responding to their concerns, and building a reputation for following through on their promises. As noted in Section 4.4.1, this is likely to require more transparency and a bigger role for genuinely independent expert voices than has previously been the norm in China. The country should incorporate surveys and other data collection on the effectiveness of its public engagement efforts on nuclear energy, so that these support-building efforts can learn over time about what works and what does not.

4.9.3 Improving Economics

As it maps out its future energy and power generation approaches, decarbonization supports, and market reforms, China should ensure that it maintains a financial environment in which nuclear and other low-carbon sources can attract investment. This includes low-cost financing, strong construction management to minimize construction costs, and revenues that are at least reasonably predictable. Further cost reductions and revenue opportunities (such as using the energy from nuclear plants for more than just providing baseload electricity) should be a major focus of development of advanced nuclear energy systems.[15]

4.9.4 Avoiding Technological Lock-in on Dangerous and Unneeded Technologies

Just as China decided not to invest further in Generation II reactors, it should avoid major investments in technologies that are expensive, dangerous, and do little for the long-term future of nuclear energy. This includes plutonium reprocessing and breeder reactors that depend on reprocessing. Reprocessing is far more expensive than not doing so, and the capital cost – the main cost of nuclear energy – of breeder reactors has traditionally been significantly higher than the cost of light-water reactors [103, 104]. Processing spent fuel at high temperatures in volatile chemicals creates a variety of new safety risks. The large spent fuel pools, processing operations, liquid high-level waste storage, and plutonium storage and transport create potential targets for terrorist sabotage or nuclear material theft. A Chinese decision to rely on plutonium reprocessing and recycling would likely make it more difficult to stop the spread of reprocessing to additional non–nuclear weapon states, increasing proliferation risks.

There is no need for China to accept these costs and risks, since, as noted in Section 4.7, China has access to plenty of uranium to fuel its nuclear growth, and options for storage and disposal of spent fuel can provide safe nuclear waste management with lower costs and risks than reprocessing [105, 106].

4.9.5 Developing Options for the Future

Finally, to maximize its future nuclear energy options, China should continue to invest in and facilitate research, development, and demonstration (RD&D) on select advanced nuclear systems. This includes RD&D in China, cooperative RD&D with institutions in other countries, and monitoring of the promising results of foreign RD&D that China might adopt or adapt. The goal should not be to rush ahead, focusing only on those technologies ready for almost immediate demonstration and deployment, but to find technologies that could address key problems that have limited nuclear energy's growth in the past. China should seek to ensure that at least a small number of these advanced technologies are brought through the demonstration phase and ready for commercial deployment by mid-century [107].

China should focus its nuclear RD&D efforts on those advanced systems most likely to help overcome the key obstacles and risks described in this chapter,

94   *Foundations for a Low-Carbon Energy System in China*

including systems that could offer improved economics; increased passive, demonstrable, and understandable safety; broader siting options; strong security and proliferation resistance; and better ability to integrate with intermittent renewables and meet energy needs in addition to baseload electricity. To achieve such goals, China should build institutions for deciding on and implementing these RD&D efforts which are able to set priorities, allow different approaches to compete fairly, ensure goals are being met, and cut less promising projects, allowing resources to be reallocated to those that show the most promise for nuclear energy's future.

4.9.6 The Path Ahead

Achieving nuclear growth on the scale needed for nuclear energy to play a significant part in decarbonizing China's energy system will be a major challenge. There is no certainty today that the obstacles can be overcome. But with an approach that combines determination and care, China can maximize the nuclear energy choices it will have in the future, and have a chance to turn nuclear energy into a genuinely expandable element of the portfolio for mitigating climate change – for China, and for the world.

Notes

1 The 3.4 TW-yr of final energy the International Energy Agency envisions being consumed in 2040 in its "current policies" scenario [1] would represent roughly 50 percent growth compared to energy consumption of 2.55 TW-yr in 2016. In a "sustainable development" scenario, final energy consumption in 2040 would be about a third lower, in the range of 2.8 TW-yr/year. Many other projections are broadly similar.

2 For a discussion of the role coal energy plays in contributing to these particulate concentrations, and of pollution as a motive for China's efforts to reduce coal use, see Chapter 6 of this volume.

3 For a discussion of China's evolving approach to electricity regulation and markets, see Chapter 2 of this volume.

4 Statistics from the International Atomic Energy Agency's "Power Reactor Information System" database (see [3]).

5 Note that other non-intermittent low-carbon sources not examined in the MIT study, such as fossil energy with highly effective carbon capture, could also serve this role.

6 The Ministry of Environmental Protection was reorganized to become the Ministry of Ecology and Environment in 2018. The director of NNSA is now a Deputy Minister. The Minister, Li Ganjie, is a former head of the nuclear regulatory agency.

7 For a broader set of recommendations for regulatory reform (though now somewhat dated, as some of the recommendations have since been implemented, at least in part), see [37].

8 The 2013 Rosatom annual report [40] includes a preface from Elena Paniflova, director of the Center for Anti-Corruption Research of Transparency International-Russia, briefly describing their work with Rosatom. This is not to say, of course, that the corruption issue in the nuclear sector in Russia is resolved; it remains an ongoing problem.

9 Remarks at a workshop on low-carbon energy technologies, MIT, May 2015.

10 In 2014, for example, an insider at the Doel-4 reactor – as yet unidentified as of 2019 – opened a locked valve and allowed all of the coolant for the turbine to drain away, causing the turbine to overheat and destroy itself. This type of attack could not have led to a radioactive release, and

Enabling a Significant Nuclear Role in China's Decarbonization 95

hence appears not to have been intended for terrorism. See discussion in [41]. For a list of relevant incidents, see [42].

11 For a brief discussion of the importance of bulk processing as a nuclear security vulnerability, see [41, pp. 59–60].

12 In the United States, for example, the Department of Energy established citizens' panels near its major nuclear facilities to provide advice, discuss issues at the site, and represent the point of view of local citizens – some of whom are supporters of the facility, while others are critics. Some members of these boards have been experts – in some cases because they once worked in the nuclear industry – or have developed expertise over time through their service on the panels. For a discussion of both the advantages of these boards and the major challenges that still exist in genuinely engaging the public, see [62].

13 For projects where most of the costs relate to internationally traded goods and services, currency exchange rates are the best way to compare costs between different currencies, while for projects with mostly domestic content, "purchasing power parity" (PPP) exchange rates are more useful. In China's case, the two are quite different: the average market exchange rate for the three years leading up to 2018 was in the range of 6.6 CNY/\$, while the PPP exchange rate for those years was in the range of 3.5 CNY/\$ [63]. For nuclear projects, which combine international and domestic content, a realistic comparison is probably between these two exchange rates. Both are reported in this chapter.

14 Localization often reduces costs in China, where manufacturing is typically managed more efficiently, with lower labor costs, than it is in other locations where such nuclear equipment would be manufactured.

15 Similarly, the recent MIT report on the future of nuclear energy recommends that: "Future research, development, and demonstration (RD&D) funding should prioritize reactor designs that are optimized to substantially lower capital costs, including construction costs. Innovations in fast reactors that are advertised on the basis of fuel cycle metrics are unlikely to advance commercial deployment" [8, p. 83].

References

[1] International Energy Agency, "World Energy Outlook 2017" (Paris: International Energy Agency, 2017), pp. 700–701.

[2] Hu J., Huang L., Chen M. et al., "Premature mortality attributable to particulate matter in China: Source contributions and responses to reductions," *Environmental Science and Technology* **51**(17) (2017), pp. 9950–9959.

[3] International Atomic Energy Agency, "Power Reactor Information System" (Vienna: International Atomic Energy Agency, n.d.). Available at: www.iaea.org/pris/.

[4] M. Hibbs, *The Future of Nuclear Power in China* (Washington, DC: Carnegie Endowment for International Peace, 2018).

[5] World Nuclear Association, "Nuclear Power in China" (London: World Nuclear Association, October 2017).

[6] M. V. Ramana and A. King, "A new normal? The changing future of nuclear energy in China," in Peter van Ness and Mel Gurtov, eds., *Lessons from Fukushima* (Canberra: Australia National University Press, 2017), pp. 103–132. Available at: https://press.anu.edu.au/publications/learning-fukushima.

[7] M. Schneider and A. Frogatt, with J. Hazemann, T. Katsuta, M. V. Ramana, J. C. Rodriguez, A. Rüdinger, and A. Stienne, "World Nuclear Industry Status Report 2017" (Paris: Mycle Schneider Consulting, September 2017), pp. 198–202.

[8] J. Buongiorno, M. Corradini, and J. Parsons, co-chairs, "The Future of Nuclear Energy in a Carbon-Constrained World" (Cambridge, MA: MIT Energy Initiative,

2018). Available at: http://energy.mit.edu/wp-content/uploads/2018/09/The-Future-of-Nuclear-Energy-in-a-Carbon-Constrained-World.pdf.

[9] M. Bunn, H. Zhang, and L. Kang, "The Cost of Reprocessing in China" (Cambridge, MA: Belfer Center for Science and International Affairs, January 2016), pp. 12–13.

[10] "Goals set for nuclear energy development in next five years," *China Daily* (January 18, 2017). Available at: www.chinadaily.com.cn/business/2017-01/18/content_27988526.htm

[11] S. Tabeta, "China approves first new nuclear reactors in 3-plus years," *Nikkei Asian Review* (August 2, 2019). Available at: https://asia.nikkei.com/Business/Energy/China-approves-first-new-nuclear-reactors-in-3-plus-years.

[12] S. Kidd, "Assessing China's slowdown," *Nuclear Intelligence Weekly* (November 30, 2018), p. 7. Available at: www.energyintel.com/pages/about_uiw.aspx.

[13] World Nuclear Association, "Nuclear Power in China."

[14] "World Energy Outlook 2017."

[15] S. Stapczynski, "Nuclear experts head to China to test experimental reactors," *Bloomberg Technology* (September 21, 2017). Available at: www.bloomberg.com/news/articles/2017-09-21/nuclear-scientists-head-to-china-to-test-experimental-reactors.

[16] C. F. Yu and G. Peach, "China: CNNC commits to TWR development," *Nuclear Intelligence Weekly* (October 6, 2017). Available at: www.energyintel.com/pages/about_uiw.aspx.

[17] US Department of Energy, National Nuclear Security Administration, "U.S. Policy Framework on Civil Nuclear Cooperation with China" (Washington, DC: National Nuclear Safety Administration, October 2018).

[18] C. F. Yu, "China: U.S. export ban paves way for competition," *Nuclear Intelligence Weekly* (October 19, 2018). Available at: www.energyintel.com/pages/about_uiw.aspx.

[19] National Nuclear Safety Administration, "The People's Republic of China: Seventh National Report Under the Convention on Nuclear Safety (2013–2015)" (Beijing: Ministry of Environmental Protection, 2016).

[20] World Nuclear Association, "Nuclear Power in China."

[21] P. Y. Lipcsy, K. E. Kushida, and T. Incerti, "The Fukushima Disaster and Japan's Nuclear Plant Vulnerability in Comparative Perspective," *Environmental Science & Technology*, **47** (2013), pp. 6082–6088.

[22] World Nuclear Association, "Nuclear Power in China."

[23] Y. Dejian, "Nuclear Safety Regulatory Framework and Challenges in China," presentation to the 40th Annual Meeting of the Spanish Nuclear Society, October 2014.

[24] Hibbs, *The Future of Nuclear Power in China*, p. 87.

[25] "Former China nuclear head jailed for life over bribes," *BBC News* (November 19, 2010).

[26] H. Zhang, "China's Nuclear Security: Progress, Challenges, and Next Steps" (Cambridge, MA: Project on Managing the Atom, Harvard University, 2016), pp. 5–7. Available at: http://belfercenter.hks.harvard.edu/files/Chinas%20Nuclear%20Security-Web.pdf.

[27] Lipcsy et al., "The Fukushima disaster and Japan's nuclear plant vulnerability."

[28] International Atomic Energy Agency, "Integrated Regulatory Review Service (IRRS) Follow-Up Mission to China," IAEA-NS-IRRS-2016/06. (Vienna: International Atomic Energy Agency, 2016). Available at: www.iaea.org/sites/default/files/documents/review-missions/final_report_china_follow-up.pdf.

[29] "Maintain nuclear perspective, China told," *World Nuclear News* (January 11, 2011). Available at: www.world-nuclear-news.org/NP_Maintain_nuclear_perspec tive_China_told_1101112.html.

[30] Lipcsy et al., "The Fukushima disaster and Japan's nuclear plant vulnerability."

[31] C. Guohan, "Safety Enhancement of the NPPs in China After the Fukushima Accident," presentation to the 3rd Regulatory Conference of the European Nuclear Safety Regulators Group, June 29–30, 2015.

[32] E. Graham-Harrison, "China warned over 'insane' plans for new nuclear power plants," *The Guardian* (May 25, 2015).

[33] C. Buckley, "China's nuclear vision collides with villagers' fears," *New York Times* (November 21, 2015). Available at: www.nytimes.com/2015/11/22/world/asia/ chinas-nuclear-vision-collides-with-villagers-fears.html?_r=0

[34] Z. Yue, "China's nuclear expansion threatened by public unease," *China Dialogue* (September 23, 2014). Available at: www.chinadialogue.net/article/show/single/en/ 7336-China-s-nuclear-expansion-threatened-by-public-unease.

[35] Buckley, "China's nuclear vision collides with villagers' fears."

[36] Yue, "China's nuclear expansion threatened by public unease."

[37] L. Jinging, Y. Fuqiang, J. Portner, et al., "Recommendation for the Reform of China's Nuclear Safety Regulatory System" (Beijing: Natural Resources Defense Council, December 2013).

[38] J. V. Rees, *Hostages of Each Other: The Transformation of Nuclear Safety Since Three Mile Island* (Chicago: University of Chicago Press, 1996).

[39] L. Zhang, "Nuclear Safety Culture Construction in China," presentation, IAEA Workshop on the Use of a Harmonized Safety Culture Framework, Vienna, October 23–25, 2017.

[40] Rosatom, "Public Annual Report-2013: Performance Results of the State Atomic Energy Corporation 'Rosatom'." (Moscow: Rosatom, 2014). Available at: www .rosatom.ru/upload/iblock/f6e/f6eb142a59cc7b93cb8a254ee7dd11a4.pdf.

[41] M. Bunn, M. B. Malin, N. Roth et al., "Preventing Nuclear Terrorism: Continuous Improvement or Dangerous Decline?" (Cambridge, MA: Project on Managing the Atom, Belfer Center for Science and International Affairs, Harvard Kennedy School, 2016), p. 29. Available at: http://belfercenter.ksg.harvard.edu/files/PreventingNuclear Terrorism-Web.pdf.

[42] T. Hegghammer and A. Daehli, "Insiders and outsiders: A survey of terrorist threats to nuclear facilities," in M. Bunn and S. Sagan, eds., *Insider Threats* (Ithaca: Cornell University Press, 2017), pp. 10–41.

[43] R. Gramer, "The Islamic State just pledged to attack China next: Here's why," *Foreign Policy* (March 1, 2017). Available at: https://foreignpolicy.com/2017/03/ 01/the-islamic-state-pledged-to-attack-china-next-heres-why/

[44] F. von Hippel and M. Schoeppner, "Reducing the danger from fires in spent fuel pools," *Science & Global Security*, **24**(3) (2016), pp. 141–173.

[45] H. Zhang and T. Zhang, "Securing China's Nuclear Future" (Cambridge, MA: Project on Managing the Atom, Harvard University, 2014). Available at: https:// www.belfercenter.org/sites/default/files/files/publication/ securingchinasnuclearfutureenglish.pdf.

[46] Y. Zhou, "The security implications of China's nuclear energy expansion," *Nonproliferation Review* **17**(2) (July 2010), pp. 347–363.

[47] L. Wang, "On China's Nuclear Security Regulations," presentation, Harvard-Tsinghua workshop on "Opportunities for Cooperation on Regulating Nuclear Safety and Security," Beijing, June 2, 2017.

[48] Zhang, "China's Nuclear Security."

[49] Zhang and Zhang, "Securing China's Nuclear Future."

[50] Ramana and King, "A new normal?," pp. 117–120.

[51] C. Buckley, "Thousands in eastern Chinese city protest nuclear waste project," *New York Times* (August 8, 2016).

[52] H. Zhang, "China's Enrichment Capacity: Rapid Expansion to Meet Commercial Needs" (Cambridge, MA: Project on Managing the Atom, Harvard Kennedy School, August 2015), pp. 17–18.

[53] "China: Reprocessing plan faces new domestic challenges," *Nuclear Intelligence Weekly* (August 25, 2017). Available at: www.energyintel.com/pages/about_uiw .aspx.

[54] Yu, "China: Reprocessing plan faces new domestic challenges."

[55] Y. Guo and T. Ren, "When it is unfamiliar to me: Local acceptance of planned nuclear power plants in China in the post-Fukushima era," *Energy Policy* **100** (2017), pp. 113–125.

[56] C. Sun and X. Zhu, "Evaluating the public perceptions of nuclear power in China: Evidence from a contingent valuation survey," *Energy Policy* **69** (2014), pp. 397–405.

[57] Guo and Ren, "When it is unfamiliar to me."

[58] Buckley, "China's nuclear vision collides with villagers' fears."

[59] Yue, "China's nuclear expansion threatened by public unease."

[60] J. Vera, "Winning public trust: The siting of a nuclear waste facility in Eurajoki, Finland," *Innovations: Technology, Governance, Globalization* **1**(4) (Fall 2006), pp. 67–82.

[61] M. Bunn, J. P. Holdren, A. Macfarlane et al., "Interim Storage of Spent Nuclear Fuel: A Safe, Flexible, and Cost-Effective Approach to Spent Fuel Management" (Cambridge, MA: Project on Managing the Atom, Harvard University, and Project on Sociotechnics of Nuclear Energy, University of Tokyo, June 2001), pp. 33–56.

[62] J. Weeks, "Advice – and Consent? The Department of Energy's Site-Specific Advisory Boards" (Cambridge, MA: Project on Managing the Atom, Belfer Center for Science and International Affairs, Harvard Kennedy School, August 2000). Available at: www.belfercenter.org/index.php/publication/advice-and-con sent-department-energys-site-specific-advisory-boards.

[63] Organization for Economic Cooperation and Development, "Purchasing Power Parities (PPP)." Available at: https://data.oecd.org/conversion/purchasing-power-par ities-ppp.htm (Accessed March 24, 2021).

[64] Organization for Economic Cooperation and Development, International Energy Agency and Nuclear Energy Agency, "Projected Costs of Generating Electricity" (Paris: Organization for Economic Cooperation and Development/International Energy Agency/Nuclear Energy Agency, 2015), p. 41.

[65] N. Barkatullah and A. Ahmad, "Current status and emerging trends in financing nuclear power projects," *Energy Strategy Reviews* **18** (2017), pp. 127–140.

[66] World Nuclear Association, "The Economics of Nuclear Power" (London: World Nuclear Association, version updated August 2017). Available at: www.world-nuclear .org/information-library/economic-aspects/economics-of-nuclear-power.aspx.

[67] China Nuclear Energy Association, "China Nuclear Energy Guide 2017" (Beijing: China Nuclear Energy Association, 2017). Available at: www.niauk.org/wp-content/ uploads/2018/04/CNEA-China-Nuclear-Energy-Guide.pdf.

[68] "Direct Testimony and Exhibits of Tom Newsome, PE, CFA, Philip Hayet, and Lane Kollen," *In the Matter of: Georgia Power Company's Seventeenth Semi-Annual*

Enabling a Significant Nuclear Role in China's Decarbonization   99

Vogtle Construction Monitoring Report, Docket No. 29849 (Augusta, GA: Georgia Public Service Commission, December 1, 2017).

[69] US Energy Information Administration, "Capital Cost Estimates for Utility Scale Electricity Generating Plants" (Washington, DC: Energy Information Administration, November 2016). Available at: www.eia.gov/analysis/studies/powerplants/capitalcost/pdf/capcost_assumption.pdf.

[70] Lazard, "Lazard's Levelized Cost of Energy Analysis – Version 11.0" (New York: Lazard, November 2017). Available at: www.lazard.com/media/450337/lazard-levelized-cost-of-energy-version-110.pdf.

[71] International Atomic Energy Agency, "Power Reactor Information System."

[72] International Energy Agency, "World Energy Outlook 2017," pp. 702–703.

[73] "China: NEA codifies nuclear load-following," *Nuclear Intelligence Weekly* (March 10, 2017). Available at: www.energyintel.com/pages/about_uiw.aspx.

[74] "China: Lower-than-expected tariffs for first AP1000s and EPRs," *Nuclear Intelligence Weekly* (April 5, 2019). Available at: www.energyintel.com/pages/about_uiw.aspx.

[75] "China: Nuclear players shift to renewables," *Nuclear Intelligence Weekly* (April 6, 2018). Available at: www.energyintel.com/pages/about_uiw.aspx.

[76] Buongiorno et al., "The Future of Nuclear Energy in a Carbon-Constrained World," pp. 31–58.

[77] L. D. Anadon, V. Bosetti, M. Bunn et al., "Expert judgments about RD&D and the future of nuclear energy," *Environmental Science & Technology* **46**(21) (November 2012), pp. 11497–11504.

[78] C. Forsberg, L. W. Hu, P. Peterson et al., "Fluoride-Salt-Cooled High-Temperature Reactor (FHR) for Power and Process Heat: Final Project Report," MIT-ANP-TR-157 (Cambridge, MA: Massachusetts Institute of Technology, December 2014).

[79] J. Buongiorno, J. Jurewicz, M. Golay et al., "The offshore floating nuclear plant (OFNP) concept," *Nuclear Technology* **194**(1) (April 2016), pp. 1–14.

[80] Bunn et al., "Interim Storage of Spent Nuclear Fuel," pp. 33–56.

[81] M. Bunn, "Proliferation-Resistance (and Terror-Resistance) of Nuclear Energy: How to Think About the Problem," presentation, Engineering and Public Policy Seminar, Carnegie-Mellon University, December 12, 2014. Available at: www.belfercenter.org/sites/default/files/legacy/files/prolif-resist-talk-2014.pdf.

[82] M. Bunn, M. B. Malin, W. C. Potter, and L. S. Spector, eds., *Preventing Black Market Trade in Nuclear Technology* (Cambridge: Cambridge University Press, 2018).

[83] et al., "The Future of Nuclear Energy in a Carbon-Constrained World," pp. 5–29.

[84] Nuclear Energy Agency, Organization for Economic Cooperation and Development, and International Atomic Energy Agency, "Uranium 2016: Resources, Production, and Demand" (Paris: Nuclear Energy Agency/Organization for Economic Cooperation and Development, 2016), pp. 201–204. Available at: www.oecd-nea.org/ndd/pubs/2016/7301-uranium XE "uranium" -2016.pdf.

[85] H. Zhang and Y. Bai, "China's Access to Uranium Resources" (Cambridge, MA: Project on Managing the Atom, Belfer Center for Science and International Affairs, Harvard Kennedy School, May 2015). Available at: https://www.belfercenter.org/sites/default/files/legacy/files/chinasaccesstouraniumresources.pdf.

[86] Nuclear Energy Agency, Organization for Economic Cooperation and Development, and International Atomic Energy Agency, "Uranium 2016," p. 3.

[87] Hibbs, *The Future of Nuclear Power in China.*

[88] Bunn et al., eds., *Preventing Black Market Trade in Nuclear Technology.*

[89] E. Schneider and W. Sailor, "Long-term uranium supply estimates," *Nuclear Technology* **162**(3) (June 2008), pp. 379–387.

[90] M. Kazimi and E. J. Moniz, co-chairs, "The Future of the Nuclear Fuel Cycle: An Interdisciplinary MIT Study" (Cambridge, MA: MIT, 2011). Available at: http://web.mit.edu/mitei/research/studies/documentsnuclear-fuel-cycle/The_Nuclear_Fuel_Cycle-all.pdf.

[91]   et al., "The Future of Nuclear Energy in a Carbon-Constrained World," p. xii.

[92] Admiral H. Rickover, memorandum, June 5, 1953. Available at: http://ecolo.org/documents/documents_in_english/Rickover.pdf.

[93] Bunn et al., "The Cost of Reprocessing in China," pp. 32–34.

[94] T. B. Cochran, H. A. Feiveson, W. Patterson et al., "Fast Breeder Reactor Programs: History and Status" (Princeton, NJ: International Panel on Fissile Materials, February 2010). Available at: http://fissilematerials.org/library/rr08.pdf.

[95] Hibbs, *The Future of Nuclear Power in China*, p. 72.

[96] Hibbs, *The Future of Nuclear Power in China*, pp. 51–53.

[97] Yu and Peach, "China: CNNC commits to TWR development."

[98] J. Greene, "Trump's tech battle with China roils Bill Gates nuclear venture," *Wall Street Journal* (January 1, 2019). Available at: www.wsj.com/articles/trumps-tech-battle-with-china-roils-bill-gates-nuclear-venture-11546360589.

[99] Hibbs, *The Future of Nuclear Power in China*, p. 53.

[100] Hibbs, *The Future of Nuclear Power in China*, p. 53.

[101] E. Cartlidge, "Fusion energy pushed back beyond 2050," *BBC News* (July 11, 2017). Available at: www.bbc.com/news/science-environment-40558758.

[102] Hibbs, *The Future of Nuclear Power in China*, pp. 57–58.

[103]   et al., "The Cost of Reprocessing in China," pp. 12–13.

[104] Rickover, memorandum, June 5, 1953.

[105] M. Bunn, "Assessing the Benefits, Costs, and Risks of Near-Term Reprocessing and Alternatives," testimony before the Subcommittee on Energy and Water, Committee on Appropriations, US Senate, 14 September 2006.

[106] F. von Hippel, "Managing Spent Fuel in the United States: The Illogic of Reprocessing" (Princeton, NJ: International Panel on Fissile Materials, January 2007).

[107] M. J. Ford and D. P. Schrag, "A tortoise approach for US nuclear research and development," *Nature Energy* (July 30, 2018), pp. 810–812. Available at: www.nature.com/articles/s41560-018-0221-1.pdf.

5

Transitioning to Electric Vehicles

HENRY LEE

5.1 Introduction

Over the past two decades, China's transportation sector has grown dramatically, rivaling the country's unprecedented growth rates in the energy sector. This rapid expansion has brought measurable economic and social benefits, but it has also brought costs in the form of growing dependence on foreign oil, increasing traffic congestion, and stifling air pollution. While these problems are the focus of government initiatives, transitioning China from a carbon-intensive economic structure to a decarbonized energy mix will grow in importance as the country enters the next decade.

Currently, pollution from the transportation sector – both conventional and unconventional – is dwarfed by emissions from the power and industrial sectors. This gap may continue for the next few years but as growth in CO_2 emissions from other sectors declines, the reduction of emissions from passenger vehicles and trucks will become an essential part of China's long-term decarbonization strategy. To truly decarbonize, China must reduce its greenhouse gas emissions to nearly zero. This means eliminating fossil fuels from every sector, including transitioning passenger vehicles to electricity – either directly through the deployment of battery electric vehicles (BEVs) or indirectly through hydrogen and fuel cells.

The size of this transition is daunting. At the end of 2019, China had 225 million fossil-fueled passenger vehicles and 27 million trucks on the road [1, 2].[1] On a per capita basis, vehicle ownership was about one-half of that in the United States. Assuming continued economic growth, by 2040 China's per capita vehicle ownership should increase at least 50 percent to around 350–400 million trucks and cars. If China is to electrify 80 percent of them, it will have to electrify 280–320 million vehicles. Such a transition will place significant incremental demand on the electric grid. It will also require building a new infrastructure to transport, distribute, and market power to a sector that heretofore has not consumed electricity.

The scale of this transition will be enormous, requiring China to install millions of individual electricity charging units. It will also require that utility regulations be reformed, which in turn will affect electricity prices and investment decisions.

Transportation trends that are beginning to emerge will accelerate. Chinese consumers will continue to expand their reliance on rail for intercity transportation. By default, cars will become an intracity mode of transportation, encouraging the use of smaller electric vehicles for shorter trips. Without incremental power and the ability to transport it to millions of charging units, consumers will be reluctant to purchase electric cars. Without a supportive regulatory system, investors – mostly state companies – will lose money and hesitate to invest in needed infrastructure. All of these elements must be pursued together, and this synchronization will not happen overnight. Hence, if China is to electrify its transport system in the 2030–2060 time frame, it must begin now.

This chapter will assess both the opportunities and challenges to decarbonize the transport sector. As will be shown, passenger vehicles and trucks account for a majority of the carbon emissions from this sector; hence, they are our focus.

What has transpired in China's transportation sector over the past two decades is indeed impressive. In 2019, auto sales exceeded 21 million vehicles, or 4 million more than were sold in the United States [3]. Today, China is the world's largest car market, and this sector will continue to grow.

Between 1992 and 2013, China spent three times more on transportation infrastructure (as measured by percent of GDP) than Western Europe or North America [4].[2] Today, the highway network in the eastern part of the country is close to complete, and the focus of the 13th Five-Year Plan is to expand that network to the central and western parts of the country [5].

The scale of China's development is nothing short of astounding. In 1988, China had only 110 kilometers of expressways. Today, it has over 123,000 kilometers. It has the world's longest railroad network. Its high-speed rail systems serve almost every city in China with a population of over 500,000 people. In fact, the passenger railroad system has been so successful that intercity highway trips by passenger vehicles began to decline in 2013, as motorists shifted to using railroads [6]. Interestingly, the opposite phenomenon is occurring with freight, as railroads are being replaced by trucks, which are perceived as more flexible and convenient.

While the growth in China's transportation system has been impressive, it has not occurred without high social costs. For example, in Beijing, approximately 31 percent of its PM $_{2.5}$ and 58 percent of its NOx are generated by the transportation sector [7]. While the data on CO_2 emissions from the transportation system is poor, recent estimates suggest that emissions have grown from 581.4 million tons of carbon dioxide in 2010 to 843 million in 2016 [8].

The transportation sector accounts for 9 percent of China's CO_2 emissions, and this percentage will increase as emissions from stationary sources stabilize and the number of vehicles on the roads increases [9].[3] Yet CO_2 emissions have not been the principal driver of Chinese efforts to reduce the environmental and social costs of transportation. Rather, concerns over conventional air pollution, traffic congestion, and energy security have pushed successive governments to design and implement new policies and programs – some of which have the added benefit of reducing CO_2 emissions, and some of which do not.

5.2 Energy Security

China's oil imports grew from 3.8 million barrels in 2009 to 8.4 million barrels in 2017 [10]; it is currently the largest oil importer in the world. Approximately 48 percent of its oil is consumed in the transportation sector and that percentage is growing [11]. China has three options to manage its energy security problem – it can diversify its sources of foreign oil; it can build overland oil pipelines and thus reduce the volume of oil moving through strategic pinch points, (such as the Straits of Malacca, which is only 1.7 miles across); or it can invest in energy efficiency. To an extent, China has done all three, but these actions have slowed the rate of growth in imported oil, without reducing it. By 2040, China's import levels are forecast to exceed 13 million barrels per day [12].

5.3 Traffic Congestion

Traffic congestion in the major cities has made commuting a nightmare. Trips that should take 20 minutes often take 2 hours as gridlock chokes major arteries. To combat this problem, Chinese cities have invested billions of yuan in mass transit and have instituted regulatory restrictions on driving. In larger cities, consumers aspiring to buy a new vehicle compete to obtain a registration permit, the number of which is severely limited. But as urban populations increase, these actions have had a limited effect on relieving traffic congestion.

5.4 Air Pollution

By 2014, ambient levels of conventional pollution in China's major eastern cities had become a political embarrassment, forcing both the central and provincial governments to take action. While many of the recent abatement initiatives have focused on reducing coal combustion from industrial sources and electric generating units, China has promulgated emissions standards for new cars that are even more stringent than those in the United States. The government requires all vehicles to be inspected once a year, and more frequently for older vehicles. If the latter do not pass inspection, they must be scrapped within a certain number of days, and a scrappage certificate is required before the owner can purchase a new vehicle. Finally, China's State Council has set a goal to improve new automobile fuel efficiency for passenger cars to the equivalent of 47.7 MPG by 2020 (the US standard is 55 MPG by 2025, which translates to an on-the-road estimate of 37.3 MPG) [13].

5.5 Trade and Manufacturing

In addition to improving local air quality, reducing traffic congestion, and enhancing energy security, there is a fourth imperative – economic upgrading. China is determined not to fall into what it perceives as the "middle income trap," stuck in low-value manufacturing and dependent on foreign innovation.[4] The automobile industry has been a key player in China's efforts to become a global economic force. However, the structure of the industry limits its ability to fulfill this vision. China has over 120 vehicle manufacturing companies. Many of them are owned by provincial governments and are an important source of revenue for provincial treasuries. To protect these revenue flows, local governments restrict the sales of vehicles across provincial borders, while the central government historically limited foreign ownership to joint ventures. These rules, along with restrictive technology transfer policies and high import tariffs, have protected the Chinese industry, but as a result, Chinese vehicle manufacturers have not been competitive in the global marketplace.

5.6 Deploying Electric Vehicles

Starting in 2009, China embraced the development and deployment of electric vehicles (EVs) as a means to meet three of its four policy goals. First, the government believed that EVs would allow China to leapfrog the technological barriers that restricted the country's ability to be a major player in the world market, hoping to replicate the Japanese and Korean experience with efficient small and midsized sedans in the 1970s. Second, deployment of EVs would reduce gasoline and diesel consumption and lower dependence on foreign oil; and third, it would reduce local air pollution, such as particulates and NOx emissions. While deployment of EVs will not reduce congestion, an electric car caught in traffic uses less energy than a conventional gasoline-fueled car, and thus may be better suited for Chinese city driving.

5.7 What about CO_2?

China has committed to stabilizing its CO_2 emissions by 2030 and to dramatically increasing the percentage of energy from nonfossil energy sources. Its carbon stabilization strategies, have, to date, been heavily focused on electricity generation, but if China is to move beyond stabilization and significantly lower its carbon emissions, it will have to transition its transportation systems away from reliance on petroleum fuels. To an extent, the electrification of the railroad system is a step in this direction. While there are alternatives to jet fuel (such as biofuels), it will be more difficult and expensive to transition airlines and large ships away from fossil fuels. However, these modes accounted for only 15 percent of China's CO_2 emissions from the transportation sector in 2014 [14].[5] Therefore, ground transportation will be the primary focus of any effort to decarbonize this sector.

5.8 Magnitude of Transition

Under a business-as-usual scenario, China will have more than 350 million vehicles (passenger vehicles and trucks) on the road by 2030 and possibly 500 million by 2040. If the power to fuel these vehicles was sourced from conventional fossil fuel or nuclear facilities, China would need approximately 120 generating plants of 1 GW each. If the power was sourced from wind or solar generation, that number would be twice as high due to their intermittent availability. We are assuming that the average EV only drives 25 miles per day and consumes about 1 kWh for every 3 miles it drives. The actual number is sensitive to when the vehicle is charged – during the night or in daytime. But in almost every scenario, investment needs for new generation and an expanded grid will be large.

The fundamental point is that substantial deployment of electric vehicles will require more electricity, which in turn will require investment in new transmission and distribution infrastructure. The total cost could be between US $500 billion and $1 trillion. While this number is high, over a 30- to 40-year transition period, it is well within China's capacity.

5.9 Is Electrification of China's Vehicle Fleet the Optimal Path for China?

Would it be less expensive to reduce CO_2 emissions from the power and industrial sector, thus allowing China to ignore the transportation sector? There is some validity to this argument because an aggressive program to reduce emissions from stationary sources is likely to be less expensive and perhaps less disruptive than attempting to transition the vehicle transportation sector to electricity. However, at some point, the marginal cost of reducing emissions from stationary sources will be greater than the marginal cost of electrifying a portion of the Chinese transport sector. Where these cost curves cross will differ from one part of China to another. If China's goal is to realize deep decarbonization in the 2060 time frame, it will need to transition its transport sector off of fossil fuels.

There are other options, such as biofuels and hydrogen, but to date the technology and the resource base, as well as political momentum, favors electrification.

If China is serious about electrification, and all its actions and statements indicate that it is, the country must answer three questions:

(1) Will electrification actually reduce carbon emissions?
(2) What are the key challenges and barriers to deployment in electric vehicles that must be addressed?
(3) What policies will enhance this transition?

Let's look at each of these in turn.

5.10 Will Electrification of the Vehicle Fleet Result in CO_2 Emission Reductions?

Several studies have attempted to answer this question, and while their assumptions and results differ, their basic answer is that in the short term and mid-term, CO_2 emissions will increase in most regions of China as a result of rapid deployment of electric vehicles, but will decrease in the longer term, as nonfossil fuel generation backs out coal. In 2013, Hong Huo and several of his colleagues studied the impact of EVs on both conventional air emissions and greenhouse gases in China [15]. They looked at three regions – Beijing-Tianjin, the Yangtze River Delta, and the Pearl River Delta. They found that greater penetration of electric vehicles would reduce local emissions of conventional pollutants, but the additional demand on the electric grid would require the availability of additional generation capacity. In those areas where a majority of the power plants burned coal, electrifying the transportation sector would increase CO_2 emissions, but for those regions that relied on renewables – primarily hydro – for a large percentage of their power, CO_2 emissions would decrease. The authors assumed that electric vehicles in China would be smaller and use less electricity per mile driven than similar vehicles in the United States.[6] They concluded that in the Yangtze and Pearl River Delta regions, electric vehicles would reduce greenhouse gases by 20–40 percent as compared with internal combustion vehicles. This conclusion was based on the percentage of nonfossil fuel generation that they assumed would be incorporated into the grid by 2025 and beyond. Electric vehicles would increase greenhouse gas (GHG) emissions 3–10 percent in 2012 in the Beijing-Tianjin area due to its greater reliance on electricity from coal-fired power plants.

It is useful to look at the assumptions behind these numbers. First, the authors assume that China will be adding substantial amounts of renewable energy and reducing the amount of its coal-fired capacity that is actually used. While the amount of power from renewable sources will increase, the uncertainty is whether coal use will decrease in the next two decades. As pointed out in Chapter 6, the data on planned new coal plants suggests otherwise.

To deal with the conventional pollution problem in its eastern cities, China is not eliminating coal, but rather moving its capacity westward. The 13th Five-Year Plan states that the government "will restrict coal resource development in the east of the country and optimize it in the west" [16]. From a CO_2 emissions perspective, it doesn't matter where the coal is burned, while it does matter for NOx, sulfur, and small particulate emissions. Emitting pollutants in regions where there are fewer people translates into fewer exposures and lower mortality and morbidity rates.

Second, much of China's coal power plant fleet was built during the last 15 years and has at least another 25 years of useful life. Is it reasonable to expect that China will retireu a significant percentage of these plants prematurely? The latest five-year plan calls for a nationwide effort to upgrade its existing coal-fired fleet to achieve lower emissions of conventional pollution and improved efficiency. The latter will reduce facility-specific GHG emissions 5–10 percent, but it will also ensure that these facilities will be producing power – and emitting significant amounts of CO_2 – for many years into the future.

Third, even if China had no interest in electrifying its transportation sector, electricity demand is almost certainly going to increase over the next several decades. China is committed to electrifying a significant percentage of its industrial base and to transitioning the economy to a greater reliance on service industries, which will translate into greater electricity consumption in the commercial sectors. Both of these actions will increase the demand for power, regardless of what changes occur in the transportation sector.

A portion of this increase will be offset by efficiency gains in the operation of the grid, as outlined in Chapter 2, and part will be offset by increases in energy productivity. These two factors will not be sufficient to keep electricity demand neutral or negative.

The forecasts that EVs will reduce GHGs are built on very optimistic scenarios – in which China scraps its coal-generated plants 20 years before the end of their useful lives, and reforms its electricity grid and seamlessly integrates massive amounts of nonfossil fuel energy at rates unprecedented anywhere in the world. All of this would have to happen at a time when China is worried about increasing its financial exposure – particularly provincial debt – and maintaining its current rate of urbanization. China has amazed the pundits before and may do so again, but it would be fair to say that the probability of this scenario coming to pass is not high.

If the power sector is not going to rapidly transition to high dependence on nonfossil fuel generation, then a surge toward electric cars will almost certainly increase GHGs, particularly in the northern parts of the country that do not have access to large amounts of hydroelectricity.

If moving rapidly to electric vehicles in the next 10–20 years is likely to increase GHG emissions, should China step back from its present efforts to develop and deploy electric vehicles? The answer is almost certainly no. Twenty years of slightly higher GHG emissions to achieve much lower emissions for the remainder of the century is a trade-off worth making. China's ultimate goal should be to reach a state of low or negligible carbon emissions. The present portfolio of transportation and electricity technologies will not be sufficient to reach this goal. The country must develop new battery and charging technologies. It must develop new business strategies and new regulatory and governance reforms. Finally, it must expand and enhance its energy technology innovation and research process. However, to wait for a low-carbon grid to be in place or for new, more efficient battery technologies to emerge before starting to electrify the transport sector would extend the transition to a lower carbon scenario by decades. All of these actions need to be pursued simultaneously.

5.11 Realizing Deeper Deployment of EVs

The ultimate goal is to develop and deploy electric vehicles that are more attractive options than traditional fossil-fueled vehicles. This means producing vehicles that fit the needs of the Chinese consumer and are as attractive in terms of performance and price as cars and trucks with internal combustion engines (ICEs). Simultaneously, China will need to design and establish a charging infrastructure that is accessible, affordable, and convenient. To put the challenge in perspective, a deep decarbonization effort would mean electrifying the vast majority of China's passenger vehicle fleet by 2060. Under such a scenario, manufacturing and selling gasoline- or diesel-fueled vehicles would probably not be a profitable business, and the remainder of the fleet would transition to electricity soon thereafter. There were about 1.5 million electric vehicles on the road in China in 2017, and officials predict that this figure will exceed 80 million by 2030 (or about 15–18 percent of the projected passenger vehicle fleet). If this trend continues, China will have upwards of 350 million EVs on the road by 2060. For this to happen, China would have to develop and install the capacity to build, sell, maintain, and charge these vehicles.

5.12 EVs: The Vehicle of Choice?

Electric vehicles have several inherent advantages over internal combustion-engine vehicles (ICEs). They perform better with quicker acceleration, are less noisy, and have fewer maintenance problems because they have fewer moving parts. In the United States, consumers tend to balance multiple attributes in purchasing a new vehicle. They typically want a vehicle superior to their current one. American consumers also purchase cars that can support their longest trip with the most baggage. Hence, range has been a barrier to EV sales in the United States and Europe. To address "range anxiety," European and US manufacturers are designing vehicles with ever-larger battery capacity.

Chinese consumers may have a different perspective. First, many Chinese still do not own a car, and thus a high proportion of annual sales are to first-time buyers, who are not comparing their purchases to their present car, but rather are weighing their actual transportation needs. Second, urban residents, who use a car to commute, or simply to travel around the city, often find themselves caught in traffic gridlock for significant portions of their trips. Electric cars are more efficient than petroleum-fueled vehicles when traffic congestion is the norm.

In China, range anxiety is offset, in part, by the availability of the best intercity railroad system in the world. If a person travels from Beijing to their family home 500 miles away, they have an option – comfortable and rapid train service – that is not available to the US traveler. The consequences are twofold. First, range anxiety is less of a barrier to EV sales. Second, Chinese vehicle manufacturers have the option of selling smaller and less expensive EVs with reduced battery capacity. Purchasing a smaller urban electric car will almost certainly be a more attractive proposition in China than in Europe or the United States. Further, the charging infrastructure for cars that drive 30 miles per day will be smaller and less expensive than one in which motorists want the option (admittedly, one they will rarely use) to drive 200 miles per day.

Up until 2016, smaller Chinese EVs were found almost exclusively in rural areas, and for safety reasons, they were not allowed to use the highway system. But these vehicles are being superseded by slightly larger and safer models that can be driven on all roads. For example, BYD, one of China's larger car manufacturers, has announced that it will emphasize less expensive "low-end EVs" and will significantly improve their performance. Other Chinese manufacturers plan to aggressively market a portfolio of EVs that will include both low-end and larger models, including hybrids. In total, there will be many different EV models available in Chinese showrooms by 2025. Obviously, some of these will fail to attract buyers and will disappear, but their advent suggests that Chinese consumers will not have a problem finding an EV model that meets their needs.

What about fleet vehicles, such as buses, taxis, and commercial vans? China has already made significant strides in deploying electric fleet vehicles. Over the past five years, much of the subsidy monies earmarked for electric vehicles have supported the purchase of taxis, buses, and government service vehicles.

110   *Foundations for a Low-Carbon Energy System in China*

Admittedly, this trend is more pronounced in some cities and localities than others. Areas with state-owned EV manufacturers have been more aggressive than areas without such companies. Further, the generous subsidy programs for EVs have targeted specific regions, and not the entire country.

5.13 Freight Transport

Freight transportation presents a larger and different problem. While passenger trains have taken business away from the roads and airlines, the opposite has occurred with freight. For the period 1995–2012 there has been a 16-fold increase in truck usage as measured by ton miles [17]. As China moves to a more consumption-oriented economy, demand for trucks – particularly midsized and smaller models – will increase. China, for environmental reasons, is now locating its coal-fired power plants away from eastern cities and siting them closer to coal mines. Power is moved by high voltage transmission lines as opposed to moving coal by rail. As China invests in more renewables and long-distance transmission, revenues from hauling coal will decrease at an even faster rate.

If truck transportation grows and freight railroads shrink, carbon emissions from this sector will increase, since the latter mode is significantly more energy-efficient than the former.

5.13.1 Can China Convert Trucks to Electricity?

Trucks differ in terms of size and the distances that they cover. Short-haul trucks that deliver goods from the regional warehouses to local stores, or packages to homes, are smaller and often drive less than 150 miles per day. The batteries used to power these trucks can be 75 kWh or less, and can be recharged in a central garage at night. Electrification is a viable option for smaller trucks, which dominate intracity deliveries.

Intercity freight transportation is handled by long-haul trucks that usually carry more than 36,000 kilograms over distances greater than 250 miles per day. The size of the battery needed to power a vehicle of this size would be very large. Further, there are attractive alternatives to diesel-fueled trucks. LNG has become an increasingly popular option in OECD countries and may be an attractive option – both economically and logistically – to electrifying China's long-haul truck fleet. The cars and trucks that will be on the road in 2060 will not look like those in the showrooms of 2020 or even 2030. Battery technologies will continue to evolve, as will infrastructure equipment. Hydrogen may emerge as a viable fuel and LNG will continue to be a competitive fuel. While electrifying heavy trucks

5.14 What Are the Economic Challenges to Passenger EV Penetration?

Electric vehicle technologies have been commercially available for almost two decades. In the early years, installed battery costs hovered close to US $800 per kilowatt. Today their costs have been cut in half, and investors – both electronic and vehicle manufacturers – are allocating significant funds to developing ever more efficient and less costly batteries. At installed battery costs equal to or below the US $200-per-kWh threshold, electric vehicles will be cheaper than conventional gasoline-fueled cars [18]. While one cannot accurately foretell the future, it is likely that this threshold could be breached by the mid-2020s, if not sooner.

The major barriers to consumer acceptance have been threefold: (1) price, (2) skepticism about new technologies, and (3) the lack of an easy and accessible option to charge the vehicle. To overcome the first two barriers, the Chinese government, at both the central and local levels, offered generous subsidies, up to US $7,000 per vehicle. Such subsidies were financially viable for the government when sales were in the 400,000 vehicles per annum range, but in any scenario in which penetration rates are much higher, large subsidies become unaffordable. Further subsidies serve as a deterrence to technology innovation, since they induce consumers to purchase an asset that is not yet economically competitive, as opposed to keeping the pressure on manufacturers to develop ever-better technologies. That is, they can lock in – at least temporarily – less efficient and more expensive technologies and actually slow down the rate of innovation. Subsidies do create benefits, but studies show that these benefits primarily take the form of learning – for the manufacturers, the government, and the consumer – as opposed to reducing environmental externalities. Hence, some level of subsidy is beneficial, but governments should resist pressures to extend and expand them.

Recognizing these limitations, China announced its intention to phase out EV subsidies, beginning with a 20 percent reduction in 2022 [19]. Instead, it plans to use regulatory tools to incentivize consumers to purchase electric vehicles. For example, a person purchasing a new car in many larger Chinese cities must obtain a registration or permit from the government. These permits are rationed to purchasers of conventional vehicles, but are readily available to purchasers of EVs. In some cities, cars can only drive into the center of the city on certain days, based on their number plates. Again, EVs are exempted from this restriction. Garages in locations with limited space provide preferential parking for EVs. All of these steps are designed to stimulate EV sales.

In the last few years, Chinese consumers have been buying small EVs as a second car to circumvent these driving restrictions. In many instances, consumers drive these cars more than their larger diesel or gasoline models, because they are a better fit for urban traffic. Further, Chinese motorists are not as locked into larger gasoline cars as their US counterparts, and the Chinese government encounters less political resistance when it uses its regulatory authority to influence driving preferences.

5.15 Charging Infrastructure

From both the technological and regulatory perspective, a scenario in which electric cars replace traditional gasoline-fueled vehicles seems plausible. What is uncertain is how fast this transition will occur. History tells us that system transitions are usually slower than their advocates predict. If China's goal is deep decarbonization, speed is not as important as the eventual magnitude of the transition. The transition is not likely to be slowed by delays in the development of efficient and cheaper battery technology or consumer resistance to unfamiliar technologies. Rather, it is the absence of an effective charging infrastructure – a system which, as of the end of 2017, remained costly, undeveloped and, in many cases, unavailable – that is most likely to be the major factor in any delay in making the transition.

Advocates often focus on a particular asset, such as more renewable generation or more electric vehicles, without understanding that those assets are part of a greater system. When a household purchases electricity, they are also paying for the wires that transported the electrons, the voltage that moves the power, and frequency regulation that ensures high quality electricity, essential for many of today's home electronics.

The same paradigm is true for transportation systems. Over the past 50 years, countries have built a transportation system that relies heavily on single-vehicle ownership. To support these vehicles, governments have built thousands of miles of highways and roads. The oil industry has developed a fueling infrastructure with the capacity to refuel a vehicle in less than 5 minutes. The cost of this system – the retail station plus storage and transportation minus the cost of the commodity (gasoline or diesel) and taxes – is relatively small. In most countries, it is less than 17 percent of the total cost of the refined fuel [20].

A system designed to support electric cars for passenger transportation will look quite different. The industry is still in its nascent stages, and there is substantial uncertainty around its eventual structure. However, several fundamental characteristics are unlikely to change.

Technologies exist that can charge electric vehicles at a slow rate – measured in hours – for costs that are less than those paid to fuel a gasoline or diesel vehicle. This statement is especially true for China, which has higher gasoline prices than in the United States, but lower electricity prices.

Faster charging technologies are now available for commercial stations that can charge a vehicle to drive 100 miles in under 20 minutes, but the total cost in most jurisdictions is much higher than slow charging.

5.16 Home Charging

Chinese households are unlikely to purchase single-family homes with their own garages or driveways. Most of the urban population lives in high-rise apartments and parks on the streets, in public or private lots, or public garages. Unlike many US homeowners, the average Chinese motorist cannot plug his car into his private garage outlet or rewire her house to allow her to install faster charging equipment. Although there have been incidences of impressive ingenuity – for example, extension lines have been dropped from the fifth floor of multi-story apartment buildings to EVs parked on the street below – it is not credible to design a charging system around such practices.

Whatever charging system is developed in China must be aligned with the existing housing system, in most cases high-rise apartment buildings. The country has two options – the first is a system of widespread public charging units and the second is the development of a system of commercial fast-charging stations. Neither of these will be easy; both will require a significant amount of upfront capital, and as mentioned earlier in this chapter, the latter will be expensive in the initial deployment stages.

In the United States, home charging equipment (capacity approximately 6.6 kW) costs around US $1,500 per unit. To this figure, one needs to add the cost of trenching (if the charging equipment is located in an outside lot or along a street) and rewiring, particularly if the equipment is located in an existing building. These costs can vary, depending on the type of building, its location, and the existing level of wiring. A low-cost system will require from US $3,000 to $5,000 per unit.[7] These capital costs will have to be recovered from payments by the users or be subsidized by the government. To these capital expenses, one must add the cost of the power, which varies depending on the time of day. Power used at 6:00 pm is costlier than power consumed in the middle of the night. (Costs are rarely accurately reflected in tariffs.) It is true that smart metering technology can optimize the demand, and thus reduce the cost, over a 10-hour period, but this technology is not cheap and will have to be paid for.

114   *Foundations for a Low-Carbon Energy System in China*

By the end of 2017, the Chinese government had overseen the installation of 214,000 public charging units [21]. Most of these are slow charging (7 kW) and would take about 4–6 hours to recharge a small car with a 30-kWh battery [22]. Theoretically, one could repower 3 cars over a 12-hour period, but this means that one-third of the people would have to move their car (or the charger) in the middle of the night. In our analysis, we assume that this will not happen and that the car parked at a charger remains in that space until the morning. For two-thirds of the time, the vehicle will not be receiving power. Further, many of these units will not be used during the day, since a significant subset of the users will be away from home.

Assuming a cost of power of US $0.10 per kWh and a capital recovery cost for the investment and installation of charging equipment of another US $0.10 per kWh, the total cost would be in the vicinity of US $0.20 per kWh. This figure could be lowered by installing more charging units per apartment or office building, since economies of scale at single locations will reduce the total cost of installation. China now requires that new buildings include the wiring and equipment to accommodate electric vehicles, and these costs are incorporated into the building's construction cost. Assume that the total cost is reduced below US $0.20 per kWh and the average motorist drives 32 miles per day and pays about US $32 per month or US $384 per year. This figure will be lower for Chinese motorists than the equivalent cost of fueling a gasoline or diesel car by about a factor of two.

The challenge is not simply developing better battery charging technologies but also developing a business model by which the users cover most of the fixed and variable costs of both charging and power. If there are 300 million electric vehicles on the road in 2040 and the power they need to cover their daily driving costs US $1 per day, the overall annual cost of charging all the BEVs in the country would be US $110 billion, excluding any additional costs for generation capacity, transmission lines, or improvements to the distribution system.

5.16.1 Fast-Charging Stations

What about fast-charging stations? The answer depends on how one defines this term. Units in fast-charging stations have a capacity in the vicinity of 50 kW or higher, which would charge a 30-kWh battery in about 30 minutes. Tesla is installing 120-kW chargers at some of their new stations, and a consortium of several major European automobile manufacturers has announced that they are developing a 350-kW charger [23]. The cost of the infrastructure to serve fast-charging stations will be much higher than the cost for the smaller systems. Most stations will have multiple charging units, similar to contemporary gasoline filling stations. So, if a station has five 350-kW units, it would be drawing 1.75 MW of power at peak use. The electrical infrastructure to support such a facility would require investments in wires, transformers, and distribution equipment with the ability to handle a 1.75-MW load (or 350 homes). The costs will be substantial and will vary from location to location.

To cover these fixed costs, the station will either have to place a large surcharge on every kilowatt-hour of power sold or be located on a site that could generate a high flow of customers. In the United States and Europe, such utilization rates are possible at highway rest stops and perhaps at major shopping centers. A 350-kW charger – which is not presently available commercially – could provide 100 miles of power in 6 minutes. Under this scenario, EVs would top off their batteries to a level needed to reach their destination, as opposed to completely recharging them. This would allow the station owner to increase his utilization rates – the percent of time a unit is in use and earning revenue – which is critical to a station's profitability.

Will such stations have a large market in China? Perhaps not, since range anxiety among Chinese consumers is less acute than among US motorists, given China's excellent intercity transportation alternatives. Chinese manufacturers may also be less inclined to market expensive cars with 100-kWh battery packs and may emphasize a domestic market characterized by less expensive cars with smaller battery packs. All of these trends point to greater reliance on home charging.

Due to its higher fixed cost, in 2020 power from fast-charging stations cost three times as much as that available at the local garage or at home, so motorists may deliberately forgo using fast-charging stations to access the cheaper power source at home or at their job. The cost of fast charging decreases rapidly when utilization is over 20 percent during a 24-hour period, 12 months per year [24]. This threshold, however, will not be easy to meet in a country that may use EVs as an "urban" car for short trips.

5.17 Will the Growth in Renewables Affect the Economics of Electric Cars?

On the one hand, if generation from renewables grows rapidly, the increase in CO_2 emissions from rapid deployment of electric cars will be less. At rates of fossil-fueled power generation below 50 percent, EVs will reduce CO_2 emissions, as compared with using diesel- or gasoline-fueled vehicles. However, reducing the use of coal in the electricity sector below the 50 percent threshold will not be easy nor realized soon.

As discussed in Chapter 3, more renewables will increase the need to invest in modernizing China's electric grid, building more transmission capacity, and eventually integrating storage into the system. The result is almost certainly costlier power, since fixed costs per unit of electricity will rise. Increased power costs will reduce demand and, at the margin, push Chinese consumers to demand more energy-efficient EVs (which will require more efficient batteries) and will induce some to hold onto their gasoline- or diesel-fueled cars.

The intermittency of wind and solar power will impact regions of China differently. The southern provinces have access to large supplies of hydroelectricity (which can flatten the fluctuations in power supply) while the northern provinces do not. Therefore, the cost of integrating renewables, and thus the price, will be higher in the north. However, concerns about the health effects of local air pollution and the desire to improve energy security are higher in northern China, and these factors will drive the commitment to electric vehicles – regardless of any short-term cost impacts.

In summary, the commercial success of electric vehicles will depend, in part, on China's capacity to reform its electricity system. These reforms include not only technological advances in the form of storage, smart metering, and nonfossil generation but also regulatory reforms, changes in grid operations, dispatch protocols, and tariff protocols. Improved planning, including improvements in intergovernment coordination and cooperation, will also be essential. A system of electric cars requires a modern and technologically sophisticated electricity system.

5.18 Are There Reasonable Scenarios in Which Electrifying the Transportation Sector Fails?

We have painted a cautiously optimistic picture of the potential for electric vehicles. While the rate of deployment might be slower than the government predicts, the China of 2060 is likely to have a transportation sector that is heavily electrified. Cost-competitive electric vehicles should become readily available by the end of this decade. This does not mean that every Chinese consumer will go out and purchase one, since an effective and widely available charging infrastructure may take more time to emerge. There are strong forces pushing China in the direction of electric vehicles, but there is significant uncertainty around the speed of that transition.

What could change this picture? The problems that are pushing China toward electric vehicles – conventional air pollution, energy security, global markets, and climate change – will not disappear. China will continue to commit resources and political capital to addressing these four problems. So, the question now becomes – are there alternative remedies to these problems that would be less costly and more effective than EVs?

The first option that comes to mind is autonomous vehicles. But these are as likely to be electric as the nonautonomous vehicles. Charging systems would be somewhat easier to design, but the land required for storing and parking such vehicles would, in many cities, be expensive. Further, autonomous vehicles are as apt to increase congestion as decrease it. Their future will have to be the subject of another chapter in another book. But much uncertainty remains, and it is not clear that they are superior to the nonautonomous alternatives.

What about hydrogen vehicles? The present cost of purchasing and operating a hydrogen vehicle is 50 percent greater than the cost of owning and operating a similar EV. Technology could evolve in a way that lowers costs. Still, there would be three additional hurdles to overcome.

First, public concerns over safety would need to be assuaged. Second, the hydrogen fuel would have to be produced, and the two most likely options will be to use the existing fleet of power plants – many of which remain coal-fired – or to produce the hydrogen through coal gasification, which would emit greater amounts of CO_2. Third, in the same way that electric vehicles require the establishment of a charging infrastructure, hydrogen will need its own fueling infrastructure, which would require a substantial investment.

Another option touted by some is biofuels. But the amount of land needed to fuel 300 million Chinese electric vehicles makes this idea more of a boutique alternative that might be used for certain transportation modes where electrification is not a practical option – such as airplanes and heavy trucks.

The final option would be to develop and manufacture superefficient vehicles that would attain efficiencies of around 70–80 MPG. This option would use the existing gasoline infrastructure and thus might be less expensive than the electric or hydrogen option. Yet, as stated in this book's Introduction, to effectively address the climate threat, countries have to eliminate almost all greenhouse gas emissions. This means striving to reach a level as close to zero emissions as possible. Superefficient gasoline-fueled cars will not achieve that level; thus, they become, at best, an interim or bridge strategy that will be replaced by EVs or hydrogen-electric vehicles.

5.19 Conclusions

In the short term, China's decarbonization efforts, like those in many other countries, will emphasize stationary sources – both power generation and large manufacturing. At some point, though, countries will have to turn their attention to the transportation sector. In China, this process has been accelerated by the pervasive problem of conventional air pollution (especially in its large eastern cities), its growing concerns around energy security, and traffic congestion in those same cities. Investments in electric cars has grown and the government has made a strong commitment to support their deployment by increasing research and development, designing strong regulatory nudges, and subsidizing the installation of charging units in buildings, parking areas, and streets.

As we have pointed out, there will be bumps in the road, not all R&D efforts will result in deployable technologies, and not all regulatory programs will be successful. Further, in the short term, the greater success in deploying electric vehicles, the greater the possible increases in carbon dioxide emissions as the existing coal-fired plants are operated for more hours and new coal plants come online. However, in the long run these increases in emissions will be offset by renewable energy investments and by the potential growth of electric vehicles due to the development of the charging, regulatory, and marketing infrastructures that will support them. This infrastructure and these institutions will emerge only if China is willing and able to continue its strong commitment to EVs.

Two of the challenges to EV deployment are likely to prove more difficult to overcome. The first is the development of a Chinese solution to the lack of an effective electric charging infrastructure. Home charging is the least expensive option, but Chinese homes are large apartment buildings and office buildings with limited garage or parking space. Fast charging will be significantly more costly because of land prices in urban areas, installation and equipment expenses, and the necessary upgrades to electric distribution systems. Unless utilization rates in fast-charging stations are high or the government agrees to subsidize their development and/or the power they sell, investors will lose money.

China does enjoy a major advantage of having a terrific intercity rail network and well-run mass transit systems. However, many are running at close to capacity, and space (or capital) to expand them is limited. Smaller electric cars may be a viable response to growing mobility constraints. We are beginning to see more small electric vehicles on the city roads. However, developing a charging infrastructure that is both accessible and available will become an ever-greater challenge as the percentage of EVs in use increases.

The second challenge is the need to provide this infrastructure with more electricity. Technologies are improving, particularly those related to smart grids and more efficient charging equipment, but if the Chinese grid is going to meet the incremental demands from industrial users, the growing commercial sector, and a rapid electrification of the transportation sector, it will need to embrace significant reforms in how power is dispatched, priced, and distributed – issues discussed at length in other chapters. Theoretically, the government could subsidize these uses, but in a world with millions of electric vehicles as well as an electrified industrial sector, the subsidization option is likely to be much too expensive to be sustainable. In the short term, the government could require the grid companies to eat the difference between costs and retail prices, but such actions will only result in underinvestment. In the end, China will have to remove the inefficiencies in its pricing, dispatch, and investments in its electricity systems; only then will it be able to achieve its ambitious targets to transition a major portion of its passenger vehicle fleet to electricity.

Notes

1 The *South China Post* in its April 19, 2017 edition estimates the figure to be 300 million. Most sources put this figure closer to 220 million passenger vehicles.
2 China sold 7.2 million vehicles in 2006.
3 Transportation accounted for about 28 percent of US CO_2 emissions.
4 Interview with Wang Qing, Division Chief of the Market Economy Division of the State Council Development Research Center.
5 Note: data excludes international marine bunkers and international aviation bunkers.
6 The average electricity consumption in the United States is around 0.37 kWh per mile, while the BAIC Motor Works uses the EVISO as a point of comparison. The EVISO uses approximately 0.25 kWh per mile.
7 It is possible to charge an EV by plugging into the existing outlet, but it would require more than 10 hours to charge the vehicle.

References

[1] https://statista.com/statistics/278423/amount of passenger cars-in China/.
[2] https://statista.com/statistics/278424/amount-of-trucks-in-china/.
[3] "China – Flash Report, Sales Volume, 2019." Available at: www.marklines.com/en/statistics/flash_sales/salesfig_china_2019.
[4] McKinsey Global Institute, "Bridging Global Infrastructure Gaps" (McKinsey & Company, 2016). Available at: www.un.org./pga/71/wp-content/uploads/sites/40/2017/06/Bridging-Global-Infrastructure-Gaps-Full-report-June-2016.pdf.
[5] National Development and Reform Commission, "13th Five-Year Plan for Economic and Social Development of the People's Republic of China (2016–2020)" (Beijing: People's Republic of China, 2016), pp. 79–84.
[6] National Bureau of Statistics of China, *China Statistical Yearbook 2016* (Beijing: China Statistics Press, 2016).
[7] S. Su, "The Transport Emissions & Social Cost Assessment" (Beijing: WRI China, 2017). Available at: www.wri.org.cn/en/The-Transport-Emissions-and-Social-Cost-Assessment.
[8] H. Ritchie and M. Roser, "China: CO_2 Country Profile." Available at: http://Ourworldindata.org/co2/country/china?country=chn.
[9] Ritchie and Roser, "China: CO_2 Country Profile."
[10] United States Energy Information Agency. "Today in Energy," (February 5, 2018). Available at: www.eia.gov/todayinenergy/detail.php?id=34812.
[11] International Energy Agency, "China (P.R. of China and Hong Kong, China) Balance 2018." Available at: www.iea.org/sankey/#?c=China%20(P.R.%20of%20China%20and%20Hong%20Kong,%20China)&s=Balance.
[12] International Energy Agency, "World Energy Outlook 2017" (Paris: International Energy Agency, 2017).

[13] International Council on Clean Transportation, "Chart Library: Passenger Vehicle Fuel Economy" (International Council on Clean Transportation, 2018). Available at: www.theicct.org/chart-library-passenger-vehicle-fuel-economy.

[14] International Energy Agency. 2017. "CO_2 emissions by product and flow." IEA CO_2 Emissions from Fuel Combustion Statistics (database). (Paris: International Energy Agency, 2017). Available at: www.oecd-ilibrary.org/energy/data/iea-co2-emissions-from-fuel-combustion-statistics_co2-data-en.

[15] H. Huo, H. Cai, Q. Zhang et al., "Life cycle assessment of greenhouse gas and air emissions of electric vehicles: A comparison between China and the US," *Atmospheric Environment*, **108** (2015), pp. 108–116.

[16] National Development and Reform Commission, "13th Five-Year Plan for Economic and Social Development of the People's Republic of China (2016–2020)" (Beijing: People's Republic of China, 2016), pp. 84–85.

[17] W. Li, H. Li, H. Zhang et al., "The analysis of CO_2 emissions and reduction potential in China's transport sector." *Mathematical Problems in Engineering*, (January 2016), pp. 1–12. Available at: https://doi.org/10.1155/2016/1043717.

[18] H. Lee and A. Clark, "Charging the Future: Challenges and Opportunities for Electric Vehicle Adoption" (Cambridge, MA: Belfer Center for Science and International Affairs, September 2018). HKS Working Paper No. RWP18–026, pp. 13–14.

[19] E. Barrett, "China is rolling back the subsidies that fueled its electric-vehicle boom," *Fortune.com* (January 5, 2021). Available at: https://fortune.com/2021/01/05/china-electric-vehicle-subsidies-sales-tesla/#:~:text=Subsidies%20on%20electric%2Dvehicle %20purchases,roughly%2050%25%20of%20global%20sales.&text=To%20get% 20the%20market%20back,phase%2Dout%20deadline%20of%202022.

[20] U.S. Energy Information Administration, "Gasoline Explained: Factors Affecting Gasoline Prices" (Washington, DC: U.S. Energy Information Administration, n.d.). Available at: http://www.eia.gov/energyexplained/index.php?page=gasoline%20XE %20"gasoline"%20_factors_affecting_prices.

[21] F. Li, "China has the most public EV charging stations worldwide," *China Daily.com* (January 11, 2018). Available at: www.chinadaily.com.cn/a/201801/11/ WS5a5759d9a3102c394518e9e1.html.

[22] National Energy Administration and China Electric Vehicle Charging Infrastructure Promotion Alliance, "China Electric Vehicle Charging Infrastructure Development Annual Report," 2016–2017. Available at: www.nea.gov.cn/136376732_ 14978397401671n.pdf.

[23] Lee and Clark, "Charging the Future," pp. 21–22.

[24]   "Charging the Future," p. 39.

6

From Barrier to Bridge

The Role of Coal in China's Decarbonization

MICHAEL R. DAVIDSON

6.1 Introduction

Coal accounts for more than 80 percent of China's energy-related and process-related CO_2 emissions and is a major contributor to air and other environmental pollution [1].[1] Rapid economic growth, particularly since 2000, has relied predominantly on coal-fired electricity and coal use in industry, but the economic, environmental, and health costs are large and increasingly salient politically. In response, government policies aim to restrict coal's growth, including retiring or banning coal plants and certain heavy industry in key regions, as well as mitigating some of its impacts through improved environmental controls. In order for China to meet its commitments under the Paris climate agreement and dramatically reduce carbon emissions by mid-century, coal use will need to peak within the next decade and then decline at an unprecedented rate.

Despite these restrictive policies and the falling costs of alternatives, the transition away from coal is neither automatic nor just around the corner. Numerous barriers – technological, political, and historical – help to maintain coal's dominance. For China to prepare for deep decarbonization pathways by mid-century, it must convert coal from a barrier to a bridge, productively repurposing its assets for flexibility as it opens the way for clean, low-carbon generation and industrial processes.

First, in a decarbonizing electricity sector, coal plants will need to take on significantly different operational roles as they move from providing relatively flat "baseload" power to more variable power, balancing growing intermittent renewable energies. China's current hybrid plan-market electricity system does not appropriately value these services, making the economic case for flexibility retrofits and more variable operation difficult.

Second, coal power is also closely integrated with heating supply in northern cities, where combined heat and power plants coproduce both commodities. This

121

centralized district heating infrastructure could either be abandoned in favor of end-use electrified options or repurposed to generate heat centrally from electricity or gas – both at high cost.

Furthermore, over half of China's coal is used outside the electricity and heating sectors, as fuel and feedstock for industry and by households. In many of these sectors, China has lower rates of electrification and is less efficient than leading international industry. Closing the "efficiency gap" is the main priority of many government efforts, but current incentives to expand new, more efficient technologies have the potential to lock in large overcapacity in coal-intensive processes that should be replaced by electrification in a decarbonizing China.

The socioeconomic impacts of this transition are immense. The Chinese economy is heavily invested in coal infrastructure that would be at risk of becoming stranded costs. Virtually every province is facing coal generation overcapacity, putting pressure on generating companies to defend their production, even at relatively low levels of renewable energy generation. Direct coal users – e.g., heavy industry – and upstream sectors – e.g., mining – are major employers important to local and provincial governments. For these, large layoffs would be extremely disruptive, similar to what China faced in the 1990s when restructuring the state-owned sector. A successful transition must include bridges to help governments, firms, and workers mitigate the socioeconomic consequences.

This chapter lays out the details of these challenges, beginning with an historical perspective on the rise of the coal industry and its politics. China's electricity grid and challenges of shifting coal's role from "baseload" to more variable operation as more substitutes come on the grid are described. Technical challenges to increasing flexibility of coal plants are also outlined. The large uses of coal in industry, where substitutes are diverse and more context-specific, are examined. The chapter concludes with a range of opportunities in facilitating this transition in a politically acceptable manner.

6.2 Rise of China's Coal Industry

Coal resources are historically the backbone of China's economic growth, and from the very beginning of the economic reforms of the 1980s, coal shortages threatened to derail market creation efforts. As a result, new institutions were developed to expand mine creation and ensure delivery in electricity generation, cement, iron and steel, and other sectors. It also became an essential part of urbanization as coal-based district heating served China's rapidly growing northern metropolises. Over the decades, employment and investment potential in direct and indirect (downstream) coal sectors have become a defining feature of local politics in many areas of China as well as embedded in formal institutions. These factors

Figure 6.1 Employment in coal mining and washing sectors by province, 2015 (data for Tibet unavailable).
(*Source*: National Bureau of Statistics of China) [7]

remain obstacles to change, .despite overwhelming economic, environmental, and social imperatives to transition away from coal.

6.2.1 Key Pillars of Industrialization and Urbanization

China's proven coal reserves stand at roughly 140 billion tons (roughly 40 years at current consumption rates), fourth largest in the world [2]. Despite this potential, China has periodically faced coal shortages. At the time of market reforms in the 1980s, coal was mined and distributed under a planned system that coordinated prices and rail transportation with the Ministry of Railways and was organized through the annual Coal Conference, at which contracts were signed [3]. Prices were kept particularly low to meet quotas for key downstream sectors such as electricity and steel [4]. Under initial liberalization policies, some central mines were transferred to local ownership, and mines were encouraged to sell some coal outside of the plan, for which they could charge higher prices [5].

Small mines opened up across the country, outpacing central mine production expansion and helping to address shortages by the mid-1990s. These new firms, many of which were "township and village enterprises" or privately owned mines, became key economic drivers on their own, as well as a growing source of jobs. Employment in coal mining and washing reached a peak of around 5.2 million in 2010, recently falling off to around 4 million [6]. This expansion occurred at different rates across the country (see Figure 6.1). Shanxi, for example, has eight times the national average per capita employment in coal mining and washing.

While markets increasingly determined coal prices for electricity generation, electricity tariffs for generators were still heavily regulated by the government. This has led to numerous challenges for electricity generation companies, swinging between excessive profitability and large losses. When coal prices rise, generation companies cannot pass through increased costs and may even refuse to produce, which can result in local electricity shortages [8]. Larger firms have responded by greater consolidation between upstream and downstream activities. Many generation companies own some mines, and the China Energy Investment Corporation (formerly Shenhua Energy) built its own rail lines in the 1990s to bypass difficulties with regulated transportation contracts [9].

Over half of China's coal is used outside the electricity and heating sectors, as a heat source or feedstock to industry, or for heating and cooking by households. Coal provides 54 percent of the country's direct industrial energy demand, comparable with India, but much larger than Japan (30 percent) and the United States (8 percent) [10]. The largest of these sectors include iron and steel, cement, and chemical manufacturing, which have been key inputs to China's economic growth, some for export and others to support domestic industrial development and urbanization.

China's massive urbanization – a major consequence of economic reforms – is also a huge driver of coal consumption. The number of Chinese cities with urban populations greater than 1 million people has increased from 31 in 1990 to 156 in 2016 [11]. Urban infrastructure drives demand for many of the products that rely on coal-intensive processes. The construction sector accounted for 23 percent of metal products (including steel) and 61 percent of nonmetal products (including cement) in 2015 [12].

Centralized district heating (DH) is dominant for city dwellers in the north – as opposed to building or household-level heat – most of which is provided by coal, though some limited areas are converting to natural gas. DH capacity – including dedicated coal boilers and combined heat and power (CHP) plants that also generate electricity – reached 493 GW-thermal in 2016 [13].

6.2.2 Early Energy Conservation Efforts

The energy intensity of China's economy (energy per unit GDP) fell over the course of the reform period with the introduction of more efficient technologies and some degree of production shifting to lower energy-intensive sectors. Energy conservation has long been a central government priority; hence, while these technological shifts are in part driven by market forces, they are also the result of command-and-control efforts. Even prior to the more recent introduction of explicit coal consumption caps and reduction targets, economy-wide energy conservation policies largely focused on coal use.

Following China's accession to the WTO in 2002, energy use expanded faster than economic growth, resulting in the reversal of the declining energy intensity (see Figure 6.2). As a result, in the next Five-Year Plan (11th, 2006–2010), China established energy intensity reduction targets and scaled up its program of early retirements of small and inefficient coal power plants, cement kilns, iron and steel

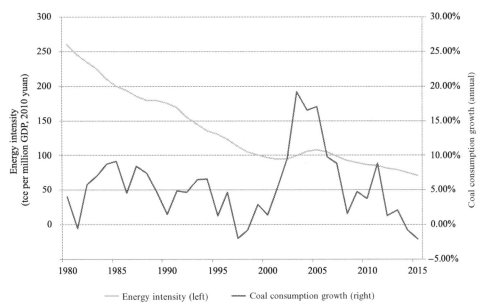

Figure 6.2 Energy intensity and coal consumption growth rates, 1980–2015.
(*Source*: National Bureau of Statistics of China) [14]

smelters, and other industrial facilities, known as "build large, press small" (上大压小 *shandayaxiao*). In electricity, this resulted in over 100 GW of coal power plant retirements, which were replaced and expanded by newer, larger plants (see Figure 6.3). China's coal power fleet is now more efficient on average than that of the United States, as discussed in Section 6.4.

An important, latent premise of these programs was that they did not alter coal's crucial role in the economy, but rather sought to increase the productive efficiency of this resource. These programs were not specifically targeted at substituting – or finding substitutes – away from coal. Coal use – and its accompanying politics – thus continued.

With old capacity being replaced many times over by new capacity, now with technical lifetimes exceeding 2050, these programs also potentially lock in electricity and other sectors (e.g., iron and steel) to coal-intensive processes long after more stringent climate policies should come into effect. Under the scenario where new coal infrastructure is banned in the 2020s, these may increase cumulative carbon emissions [15].

6.2.3 New Drivers for Substitutes

China's long period of sustained energy-intensive growth wavered slightly in 2015, as electricity growth was nearly stagnant and coal use fell [16]. At the same time, to stimulate economic recovery and reduce burdens from government

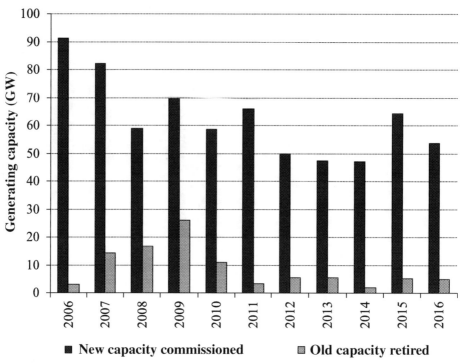

Figure 6.3 Coal capacity retirements and additions, 2006–2016.
(*Source*: Author's calculations based on NEA, CEC, and NBS data)

regulation, many investment-permitting responsibilities were devolved to local authorities [17]. These resulted in predictably large investments by eager localities and contributed to a severe overcapacity situation across virtually every coal-consuming sector, resulting in low prices, low utilization rates, and low or negative profits. Now, sectors including coal mining, electricity, iron and steel, and cement are establishing capacity reduction plans (去产能 | *qu channeng*) – this time without massive co-located reinvestment programs [18]. Some policies target outdated and inefficient plants for retirement, but others, such as the forced closure of mines discussed in Section 6.3, apply uniformly.

The non-climate environmental and health impacts of China's energy use have also increased in magnitude as well as political salience over this period, now representing the second largest driver for contracting the coal sector. For example, one estimate of the cost of air pollution placed damages at 5 percent of GDP, compared to 7–10 percent GDP growth rates in the 2000s [19]. Isolating coal's contribution is complicated, but the electricity and heating sector alone could contribute as much as one-quarter of particulate matter (PM) during high pollution episodes in northern cities [20].

Some of the measures under the Air Pollution Action Plan announced in 2013 are similar to earlier conservation efforts, though on a larger scale: forced shutdowns of coal plants and industrial facilities in eastern regions are followed by a massive build up in the west of "mine-mouth" coal plants connected by long-distance transmission lines as well as relocated heavy industry [21, 22]. However, other measures are qualitatively different: electricity or natural gas-based heating are encouraged over coal-based infrastructure in select cities; non-coal-based cooking options in rural areas are promoted; and the profile of renewable and nuclear energy as substitutes for coal electricity has been raised [23]. Many provinces in China have also instituted explicit coal consumption caps, and nationally, there is an indicative coal consumption cap as well as a binding target in the 13th Five-Year Plan (2016–2020) to reduce coal's share in the energy mix to 58 percent by 2020 [24, 25].

With large capacity reduction targets in coal and crude steel (500 million tons and 100–150 million tons respectively by 2020), lost jobs requiring new placements (according to government estimates, 1.3 million and 500,000 respectively) are immense [26]. The lack of social safety nets has been identified by the International Monetary Fund as a major barrier to economic restructuring reforms [27]. China's social welfare ministry has proposed several strategies to address dislocation, including internal transfers within companies, finding new employment in related areas, and providing basic social welfare support [28]. Workers in large SOEs may find it relatively easy to transfer internally, because these groups have already diversified into an array of different industries [29],[2] while smaller local mines have greater difficulties. Exacerbating the job placement problems, smaller mines can have 25 times the labor intensity of open-pit automated mines [30]. There is thus constant tension between fulfilling central priorities of reducing capacity and satisfying local political needs, such as employment.

6.3 Politics of Coal and the Grid

The abundance of coal and the speed with which it could be exploited to generate power and for industrial processes not only fueled China's economic growth, but it also shaped the institutions of growth that now represent barriers to decarbonizing the grid. Compared with other large emitting sectors, electricity generation has perhaps the greatest range of substitutes for coal that are also of comparable cost. Additionally, in other sectors – such as heating and industrial processes – the most viable substitute often relies on some electrification, thus shifting the burden from direct coal use to the electric grid. Finally, more generally, decarbonization pathways rely on substantial electrification across the economy, including

128 *Foundations for a Low-Carbon Energy System in China*

traditional non-coal sectors, such as transportation. For these reasons, electricity demand is likely to increase in a decarbonizing China. Thus, this section focuses on the politics of the electric grid related to coal.

6.3.1 Planning Coal Electricity amid Broader Liberalization

Early on, observers recognized reliable electricity supply as a key precondition for industrial growth. Despite persistent electricity shortages in the early 1980s, new investment lagged due to rigid central planning and lack of finance. In 1985, the government relaxed central planning of generation investments by giving some permitting authority to local governments and allowing special (higher) tariffs to encourage new builds [31]. The grid and the majority of generating assets remained with the state-run ministry. Local government-owned enterprises and private firms were now able to build and operate their own generators, helping to alleviate shortages by the mid-1990s [32].

While investment was partially liberalized, prices and annual generation were not subject to significant competition and efficiency incentives. New projects could obtain tariffs that essentially guaranteed recovery of costs plus a generous profit for an extended period. This system, essentially rate-of-return regulation common to many countries with vertically integrated utilities, led to inflated costs and overinvestment [33]. Furthermore, the profits were returned to the owners of these plants, in many cases, provincial governments that controlled permitting. Following formal unbundling in 2002, this approach was replaced by a "benchmark tariff" system that applied uniformly to all new coal generators in a province and whose levels were set by the pricing department in the National Development and Reform Commission, mostly with an aim to control inflation [34].

Selecting generation and consumption quantities – the shared role of local governments and the electricity ministry – also led to distortive allocation. When facing shortages, all generation was used and industrial consumption was rationed on universal rules of thumb such as "on 3 days, off 4 days" rather than willingness to pay (i.e., marginal profit) [35]. When shortages were no longer an issue, generators would seek an allocation from government-run annual planning processes and then be dispatched on a daily basis by the grid company, and neither step had efficiency at its core. For example, an overriding priority of ensuring equity tended to equalize utilization ratios across multiple generators in a process that came to be known as "equal shares dispatch" [36]. In addition, there were claims that the grid company gave preference to its own generators, with a famous case of Er'tan hydropower plant in Sichuan, a high-profile World Bank-funded project that was reported to be underutilized compared to the Sichuan grid's own generators [37].

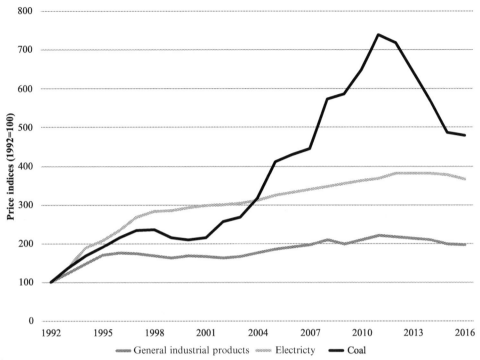

Figure 6.4 Producer price indices for electricity, coal, and general industrial products, 1992–2016.
(*Source*: National Bureau of Statistics of China) [39]

With guarantees of prices and equitable sharing (with some variation) of the generation plan regardless of cost, investment in coal-fired power boomed. This is unsurprising: compared to the case of a typical power market where only generators with competitive marginal costs are allowed to generate, equal shares planning will lead to excessive market entry.[3] Furthermore, with permitting thresholds given to local governments, smaller and lower-efficiency generators tended to be built more quickly [38].

Throughout this period, most coal was bought at the government-directed annual coal conference at essentially fixed prices. As the coal market started liberalization, market forces drove an increase in coal prices over the late 1990s and 2000s, while benchmark electricity tariffs grew much more slowly. An official policy intending to "couple" electricity tariffs with coal prices was put in place, but has not been implemented consistently (see Figure 6.4). Investment continued over this period because of the equal shares guarantee and despite the incomplete cost pass-through.

The current round of power sector reforms inaugurated in 2015 includes the goals of rationalizing power system planning and operation, letting market forces play a bigger role, and degrading the power of the grid monopolies. These have the potential to break down some of the institutions that have propelled and maintained coal's dominance in the electricity sector. However, central government commitments to reducing its own role, as well as that of other government entities, contrast with further encroachment by the state – for example, by its forced closure of all coal mines for 90 days in 2016 to drive up depressed coal prices, and by handing over most new electricity market designs and operations to local governments without changing their underlying incentives [40].[4] In Sections 6.3.2 and 6.3.3, the institutional incentives of two key actors – local governments and grid companies – are examined.

6.3.2 Local Government Incentives

Power plant construction results in large investments (typically from central banks) and a surge in construction activity, both of which reflect well on local economic indicators that are crucial to local officials' career advancement. Abundant power capacity can also help attract energy-intensive industry to the area. Thus, when more approval authority is given to local governments, more plants tend to get built. This was the case in the 1980s as well as following the 2014 release of authority for all sizes of coal plants to localities.

The "equal shares" dispatch rule, which is being degraded by current market reforms, has also helped local governments in this task by guaranteeing the viability of new investments. State-owned generation firms, for their part, are also incentivized to continue investing in a crowded market because internal personnel assessments strongly favor indicators such as total capacity and generation more than profit.[5]

On the other hand, local governments are typically more concerned with lowering electricity prices for industry than in protecting the health of generating companies. First, generating companies have been increasingly consolidated by central government state-owned enterprises (SOEs), which now control over 75 percent of generating capacity, leaving only a handful of provinces with large shares by locally owned groups, e.g., Zhejiang and Guangdong [41]. Second, this concentration of state ownership in this sector is much greater than is the case for the overall economy. Relative to generation, large electricity consumers thus have greater ownership by local governments and private firms.

Self-generation plants connected to the grid built on the sites of industrial facilities are another example of distorted incentives. These plants can be particularly economical for large users as a way to generate electricity at a lower cost than purchasing it at the central government benchmark. Thus, they have proliferated in certain industry-heavy provinces. They do not participate in

From Barrier to Bridge: The Role of Coal in China's Decarbonization   131

dispatch in the same way as normal generators, reducing their flexibility and leading to barriers to integrate renewable energy, which are discussed further in Section 6.4 [42].

Local governments generally welcome other generation sources, of which wind and solar are the major types. However, in general, enthusiasm for renewables is lower than for coal for both employment and fiscal reasons. While renewable energy also generates construction and manufacturing employment, coal mining and coal-fired power lead to large numbers of long-term employees producing the fuel and operating the plant. Leveraging new investments in large renewable energy equipment manufacturing facilities could significantly enhance local governments' interest in renewable energy [43].

Tax breaks for renewable energy generators, which are administered by the central government, reduce local tax revenue since a share of centrally collected taxes are redistributed to localities [44]. Thus, once built, local governments may prefer to support coal as compared to alternatives through annual generation planning and electricity market designs [45].[6] Some central policies, such as the elimination of local taxes on coal resources, counteract this trend, but overall, many local governments derive greater benefits from coal than wind and solar.

6.3.3 Grid Company Incentives

China is served primarily by two large state-owned grid companies – State Grid and Southern Grid – which have provincial and local subsidiaries where most electricity settlement takes place. Under the current tariff system, grid company revenues are simply the difference between the government-set retail and generation prices [46]. Grid companies thus make more money the more they sell and they have an incentive to favor sources with lower average tariffs. This stands in contrast to typical economic regulation of natural monopolies, such as transmission and distribution networks, which focus on recovering costs plus acceptable profits. In some cases, they include performance incentives, but should not depend on market transactions [47].

China's electricity dispatch is also distinct from typical electricity market setups, which prioritize low marginal cost generators (in which wind and solar have a natural advantage because they do not require fuel), thereby ensuring sufficient revenues for long-term investment [48]. According to the difference-based tariff, grid companies would have an incentive to favor low *average cost* generators, not necessarily low *marginal cost plants*. Under this setup, wind, solar, and nuclear would be at a disadvantage with respect to hydropower as well as cheaper coal. Grid companies are required by law to accept all renewable energy that they can, though curtailment (forced spillage) is high, reaching up to 40 percent in some regions, and enforcement is weak: for example, there is no instance of any grid company paying compensation for curtailment.

Coal generators have another advantage with respect to grid company revenues: they can be built near load centers, thereby reducing transmission line costs as well as losses. By contrast, building lines to connect to more distant renewable resource regions within a province incurs additional costs and losses that would not be directly recovered, even if overall system costs were lower.

Current energy sector policies to combat air pollution in key eastern regions prioritize shutting down coal plants near load centers and building up coal capacity near mines in western and northern provinces, which grid companies also favor [49]. Owners of interprovincial lines are paid per unit of electricity shipped, with the price set by the central government, and thus the higher the utilization the greater the revenues for the grid company. The same line designed to transmit only renewable energy would likely have lower utilization because of intermittency and the inflexibility of schedule coordination between regions (months to years). Instead, grid companies designate many of the "air pollution corridors" as coal-renewable hybrids, because they transmit at a relatively flat, predictable, and high level, with a small fraction of renewable energy balanced by much larger, newly installed capacities of coal [50].[7]

From workflow and evaluation perspectives, grid companies may also prefer coal over its alternatives. Coal generation can be planned months in advance; this simplifies scheduling practices, which include the important task of meeting government generation plans. Wind, solar, and hydropower introduce greater uncertainties that must be managed on shorter timescales and require greater efforts to maintain grid reliability. Current reforms call for short-term "spot" markets based on marginal costs, but fully realizing these would dramatically change prevailing grid company incentives, representing a large uncertainty that the grid companies may prefer to delay. Historically, grid companies did not fare well in earlier attempts at spot market pilots, which led to their suspension [51].

6.4 Rewiring the Coal Generation Fleet

China has over 1,000 GW of coal-fired power capacity, much of which needs to be productively repurposed in a bridge future. Coal-fired power plants have operational restrictions that limit output, changes in output, and startups and shutdowns. For the system of 10 years ago, designed for relatively flat load profiles and no intermittent renewable energy, these inflexibilities were less important. As a bridge, coal must play a balancing role, which significantly depends on both technologies and compensation mechanisms. Ongoing market reforms, as well as mandatory retrofit programs, are moving in this direction, but some technology development programs still underemphasize this role for coal. A highly uncertain, but potentially game-changing, technological advancement would be cost-effective carbon capture, utilization, and sequestration at commercial scale, but the technology for this is still in its infancy.

6.4.1 Engineering Challenges of Flexible Operation

Starting in the 1990s, China began to import advanced coal power plant technology, built on supercritical boilers that operate at high temperatures and pressures and require new materials. Soon after, central research and development programs began, with the aim of "indigenizing" these technologies. Three Chinese equipment manufacturers were directed to make strategic ventures and licensing agreements with international firms, and within a decade, China had installed its first domestically manufactured supercritical plant [52].

Crucially, this and subsequent ultra-supercritical technology programs were organized primarily around peak performance efficiency targets, specifying temperatures and pressures to be reached if the plant were operating as intended at a high, flat level (i.e., "baseload") [53]. In addition to peak efficiency and domestic manufacturing capability, coal technology plans scaled up in the 12th Five-Year Plan (2011–2015) also consider pollution control technologies [54].

CHP plants coproducing district heating in large cities have also historically been planned for peak and stable operating conditions during the winter season. The prevailing dispatch principle is to "use heat to determine electricity" (以热定电 | yiredingdian), because of the important heating obligation. CHP plants have also been exempted from most of the restrictions on new coal plant permitting, which has led some plants to find small heating demands nearby to justify expansion. This inefficient expansion of coal eventually led to tighter restrictions on new CHP plants by mandating minimum heating loads [55].

However, the output of coal plants in a decarbonizing system will fluctuate more frequently, operating below peak outputs and for fewer hours per year. This creates a cascade of effects, all of which must be addressed in a world with coal as a bridge. First, when prices do not vary, the high capital costs of coal plants mean that those with low utilization ratios are at risk of not recovering costs. While average costs fall with increasing penetrations of renewable energy, price volatility in spot markets (discussed in Section 6.4.2) may increase, and thus overall profits need not decline.

Second, coal plants are frequently run in a conservative and inflexible manner. Minimum stable outputs – technically, a threshold below which production costs escalate, but which is, in practice, the result of political as well as economic

134 *Foundations for a Low-Carbon Energy System in China*

considerations – contribute significantly to renewable energy curtailment [56]. A comparison of designs used in Europe shows that some Chinese plants are, in fact, technically capable of reaching low outputs – below around 50 percent, possibly even 20–40 percent – thus providing more space for renewable energy [57]. Coal plants in China are also only infrequently turned off and on ("cycled"), which is justified in a mixture of technical and economic terms.[8] Once on, they stay on for lengthy periods, despite voluminous technical literature showing that it is feasible to cycle in less than 24 hours [58, 59].[9]

Third, coal plant efficiencies fall at low outputs, losing some of the gains of newer technologies: below roughly 80 percent, a supercritical plant will revert to the less efficient subcritical mode. Thus, generating 500 MW from a 1,000 MW ultra-supercritical plant may require *more* coal than generating the same amount from a 600 MW subcritical plant [60]. Fewer than 20 percent of plants were operating above this 80-percent threshold in 2013, a statistic that has likely deteriorated since then due to falling capacity factors [61]. Low loadings also make it difficult for some pollutant control technologies to meet air quality standards [62, 63].

Natural gas is often raised as a potential bridge to a low-carbon grid because of its lower carbon intensity and greater flexibility in operation, including in China [64]. Natural gas price-setting has likely suppressed some supply as well as consumption in the electricity sector, and reforms for this are currently underway [65]. However, natural gas likely cannot supplant the important bridge role for coal in China. First, while China's natural gas consumption is growing, only around 15 percent goes to electricity generation [66]. Furthermore, China depends heavily on both pipeline imports and expensive liquefied natural gas (LNG), which accounted for 39 percent of consumption in 2017, a figure that has risen rapidly in the years since [67]. Finally, the large push to switch from coal to gas in recent years as been geared at addressing air pollution, e.g., replacing many "baseload" applications such as district heating in large cities and rural heating and cooking – not flexible "peaking" generation [68].

6.4.2 Economics of Flexible Operation

At fixed average tariffs, coal plants have no incentive to proactively become more flexible. This is because they earn the same revenue regardless of whether they generate when there is plentiful renewable energy or when supply is scarce. Grid companies, with a limited political mandate to put pressure on coal plants, as well as limited information on individual plant capabilities, also see little benefit in testing the flexibilities during dispatch. By comparison, curtailing renewable energy is easy to implement and has no direct economic costs, since curtailment is uncompensated.

Flexibility is addressed naturally in a cost-based vertically integrated utility or in a standard electricity "spot" market, where operations are optimized according to least marginal cost. When renewable energy is abundant and/or demand is low, fewer fuel-burning generators are required, which lowers the marginal price at that time and encourages inefficient units to ramp down or shut off. When renewable energy is scarce and/or demand is high, more fuel-burning generators are required, raising the marginal price and encouraging more units to start and ramp up to meet demand. Crucially, these market signals do not carry over if dispatch is based on average costs – the preferred contract pricing method for current market efforts in China – which may or may not align with marginal costs.

In lieu of time-varying energy prices, China's grids compensate generators for a uniquely Chinese concept of "peak regulation" ancillary services (调峰辅助服务 I *tiaofeng fuzhu fuwu*), which is quite distinct from more traditional ancillary services in power systems (reserves, frequency regulation, etc.). Peak regulation compensates generators if they are asked to go below their minimum outputs or to shut down on short notice, in effect paying for "negative energy." New market-based peak regulation mechanisms are now being implemented across the country; these improve renewable integration, but at high cost and inefficiency. For example, regulators administratively set minimum outputs and price caps to control the size of the market. Nevertheless, compensation is well beyond what are likely direct costs of providing "peak regulation."[10]

CHP, with high minimum outputs in winter, is increasingly being brought into these new dispatch rules, e.g., through participation in the peaking markets. One challenge is that district heating prices, especially for residential consumers, are in general not cost-reflective [69]. Thus, CHP generators face greater difficulties maintaining profitability for a given level of electricity generation when the heat they produce is sold at a loss.

6.4.3 Retrofits and Markets: An Uncertain Future

There are three stages at which coal plant technologies can be enhanced for flexibility: research and development, project design, and postconstruction retrofits. While China has already settled on designs for its ultra-supercritical fleet up to 1,000 MW, it does have ongoing R&D programs into the next generation of coal plants, known as "advanced" ultra-supercritical or simply "700°C," referring to the desired peak temperature. More ambitious than previous efforts, this program is attempting to achieve advances in materials that are not yet in commercial operation anywhere in the world [70]. Despite the dramatic changes in the power sector recently, there are no explicit considerations for economic performance, such as more flexible operation for integrating renewable energy.[11]

China's equipment manufacturers are also limited in their choice of technologies to those from specific international partners and with certain design criteria selected one to two decades previously by central government research and development program officials [71]. While Chinese companies have domestic manufacturing capability, they still rely on imported design software, high temperature materials, and specialized steel [72]. Technology agreements based on certain designs stymie tailoring projects to specific circumstances: for example, an agreement may include software for calculations of a 1,000 MW unit, but not for an 800 MW unit, which would require various changes [73].

Retrofitting existing plants to improve flexibility and efficiency is also possible and happening in various systems around the world [74–76]. China has begun various technical retrofit pilot programs, and targets flexibility retrofits of 220 GW of generating capacity in the 13th Five-Year Plan period (2016–2020) [77]. Early results – for example, reducing minimum outputs from 50 percent down to 30 percent – show large technical potential [78].

The basic regulatory and market regimes to promote greater flexibility are still underdetermined for retrofits (i.e., how do plants recover the cost of these upgrades and the lost revenues from the potential reduced generation, when operating more flexibly?). In the same 13th Five-Year Plan, 340 GW of energy-efficiency retrofits and 420 GW of "ultra-low-emissions" retrofits are targeted, and presumably some of this capacity overlaps with the flexibility retrofits [79]. Will these retrofitted plants be willing to reduce output after making large investments to improve overall efficiency? Perhaps more importantly, if these plant designs can only maintain "ultra-low-emissions" when operating at stable peak outputs, ramping down for flexibility will degrade their air pollution mitigation benefits.

6.4.4 Carbon Capture, Utilization, and Sequestration (CCUS)

Many future global low-carbon scenarios show a strong role for technologies that capture CO_2 from combustion or other industrial processes and store it underground as a means of avoiding its climate impacts. China-focused modeling studies highlight the important contribution of CCUS to both the power sector and industrial emissions reductions after 2030 [80]. These scenarios are largely speculative, since CCUS projects to date are limited and costly. Eighteen projects of greater than 0.4 million tons of CO_2 (0.4 $MtCO_2$) captured per annum are currently operational globally, most of which are in enhanced oil recovery (EOR) that does not involve dedicated geological storage [81].

China has one operational demonstration project and several more in the planning stages. Most of these use captured CO_2 for EOR, which can be cost-effective because of increased oil production, but these have limited scale and are site-dependent. A detailed analysis with source-sink matching indicates that there is greater potential (roughly 360 $MtCO_2$/yr) for such low-cost capture and storage in China [82]. However, the largest potential (up to 2,500 $MtCO_2$/yr) would have a complete capture-to-storage cost of up to $70/$tCO_2$. These analyses contain a significant amount of uncertainty in terms of capture costs – which depend on the capture process, specifically whether it is a concentrated CO_2 stream, such as with industrial flue gases, or more dilute, such as in post-combustion capture. In addition, there is still uncertainty regarding the specific geological mechanisms for reliable permanent storage [83].

CCUS/CCS creates a parasitic load on power generation, because of the energy requirements for capture, compression, transportation, and storage. Hence, in the absence of other changes to the power system, it would increase coal use and enhance energy security concerns. Some interesting technologies are being explored to make partial-capture CCS "flexible" by storing extra CO_2 in a tank that can be sequestered at a later time, effectively acting like a battery and shifting the time when the parasitic capture load occurs. Modeling results on the coal-heavy MISO grid in the United States show that this can decrease costs and CO_2 emissions under a stringent CO_2 cap relative to inflexible CCS [84].

6.5 Direct Coal Use: The Other Half of the Challenge

Roughly 54 percent of the nearly 4 billion tons of coal that China consumes annually goes to sectors and uses outside of the power and district heating sectors. These direct uses of coal are a large fraction of energy-related (i.e., combustion-related) and the bulk of process-related CO_2 emissions, in total accounting for 42 percent of China's CO_2 emissions [85].[12] The industrial sector is also the largest consumer of electricity, and thus responsible for a large amount of indirect emissions.

6.5.1 Overview of Direct Coal Use

The demand for coal-intensive products and services exhibits largely the same drivers as coal use as a whole – energy-intensive economic activities and urbanization. In contrast to electricity generation, however, the industrial products and other services that rely on direct use of coal are far more heterogeneous and geographically constrained. These include steel, cement, and chemical production as well as household heating and cooking (see Figure 6.5). In general, this means that less coal-intensive substitute processes are sector-, context- and, possibly, product-specific, complicating the planning of low-carbon technology transitions.

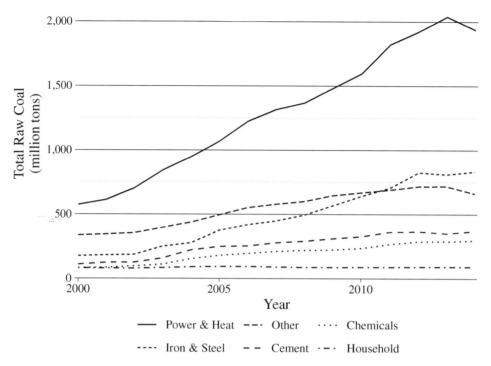

Figure 6.5 Total coal use by sector, 2000–2014. Calculated from direct use of raw coal as well as embedded raw coal in intermediate coal products (e.g., coke). (*Source*: National Bureau of Statistics of China) [86]

Some common elements are discussed here before diving into the steel sector in Section 6.5.2.

China's industrial production is more energy-intensive than that of its leading international competitors, and the foremost reason is the high reliance on coal as opposed to cleaner energy sources. However, as with coal power as elaborated in Section 6.2, there is a wide variation even among Chinese firms using similar processes, often because of local incentives to rapidly expand production at small scales that are less efficient. Mitigating the environmental impact of these processes usually takes the form of adopting the more efficient current technologies at larger production scales, with a secondary emphasis on substituting other fuels and feedstocks for coal.

Reducing overcapacity – and the resulting impacts on the market – is another major central policy objective, which can align with improving efficiency in the sector. The "build large, press small" program has included retiring significant numbers of small cement kilns, iron and steel smelters, and other "backward" production facilities. However, while overcapacity is now rampant in the sector, new production continues to come online, outpacing retirements in the cement sector, for example, by five to one [87].

Efficiency upgrade options vary widely across industry and product. In cement, for example, technology options largely center around the combustion process, such as taking advantage of the high temperatures to efficiently incinerate household waste as well as introducing better coal combustion technologies [88]. In steel, opportunities largely involve increasing reuse of scrap steel and recovering and reusing heat such as is released during cooling processes [89].

However, a true decarbonization pathway for energy-intensive industries will require combinations of replacing primary fossil feedstocks with biomass, electrification, and possibly carbon capture and sequestration (CCS) [90]. These different technology pathways point to the need to avoid overinvesting capital in efficiency improvements for old plants and technologies, which could quickly become irrelevant and create their own stranded costs. The massive amounts of new capacity coming online now, which is at the efficient frontier for coal-intensive processes, will be difficult to retire early and thus are likely barriers to technological upgrading in the medium term. In contrast to coal power, these old retrofitted technologies do not have readily available additional markets for their services (such as balancing renewable energy).

According to official statistics, direct household use of coal, primarily for heating in northern regions, amounted to 93 million tons in 2015 [91]. However, the small-scale nature of this consumption makes statistical accounting difficult, and this difficulty is enhanced by chronic issues of small mines operating without approval. Some claim this figure is as high as 200 million tons [92]. Relative to urban populations, rural areas use significantly more coal: over 85 percent of residential coal, but only 45 percent of residential electricity, is consumed in rural areas [93]. Major efforts are underway to provide cleaner heating options for rural areas around major cities, which include electrification as well as increased natural gas availability [94]. Because of the urgent air pollution issues as well as maintaining longer-term decarbonization options, these trends must continue.

6.5.2 Iron and Steel Sector

Iron and steel represent the largest coal users in China outside of the electricity and heating sector. China's steel production now accounts for 50 percent of the world's production, with 87 percent of that amount consumed domestically [95]. It is also significantly more energy-intensive than other major steel-producing countries – e.g., roughly 55 percent higher than the United States [96]. This is primarily the result of the coal-intensive process that China adopts, as well as efficiency gaps within the sector.

Steel can be produced through two main channels – Blast Furnace-Basic Oxygen Furnace (BF-BOF) and Electric Arc Furnace (EAF) – as well as the outdated and inefficient Open Hearth Furnace (OHF). The two processes are not directly interchangeable, as they take different inputs. In the BF-BOF process, iron ore and coke (coal that has been processed to drive off impurities) are first converted to a purer form of liquid iron (or "hot metal") at high temperatures in a blast furnace, which could be heated by burning coal or other fuels. In a basic oxygen furnace, the hot metal is then turned into steel by blowing oxygen over it [97]. Up to 30 percent of the BOF input can also be from recycled, or "scrap" steel [98].

The EAF process directly uses electricity to form steel from already processed iron – either scrap steel or purer iron streams such as direct reduced iron (DRI) produced through an alternative natural gas–based process [99]. By using processed iron – not iron ore – and substituting electricity for coal as the primary energy input, EAF requires two to three times less energy than BF-BOF [100]. Crucially, these higher efficiencies are obtained when EAFs use scrap steel, which may be limited due to availability of post-consumer scrap and/or is costlier than the inputs necessary for BF-BOF.

China uses BF-BOF for over 90 percent of its steel production, and this ratio has been steadily rising over the last 30 years (see Figure 6.6). Furthermore, the efficiencies of its steel mills vary dramatically: of the 86 medium-to-large-scale enterprises in 2012, the BF ironmaking process of the worst performers was 40 percent more energy-intensive than the best performers [101]. Closing the efficiency gap in the BF-BOF process, which typically involves recovering and reusing heat at various stages from the production of coke to the steel-making process, is the primary policy focus in the sector [102]. One of the primary levers to achieving this goal in the 13th Five-Year Plan is to increase the sector's scale and concentration, with the 10 largest enterprises to account for 60 percent of production by 2020, and overall capacity to be reduced to 1,000 million tons [103].

In a decarbonizing pathway, electrification is essential. EAF processes, and their declining share, receive little official emphasis in industry plans. An accompanying government document explains that EAF is constrained in China due to low scrap production and high electricity costs [104]. However, scrap limitations in the medium term are uncertain, with some government and industry sources pointing to a potential surplus in 15 years [105]. In addition, low coal prices and the lack of carbon pricing have likely suppressed EAF production: when coal prices nearly doubled at the end of 2016, the demand for scrap steel increased as mills shifted inputs away from primary iron ore, leading to a price increase of roughly 20 percent [106].

From Barrier to Bridge: The Role of Coal in China's Decarbonization 141

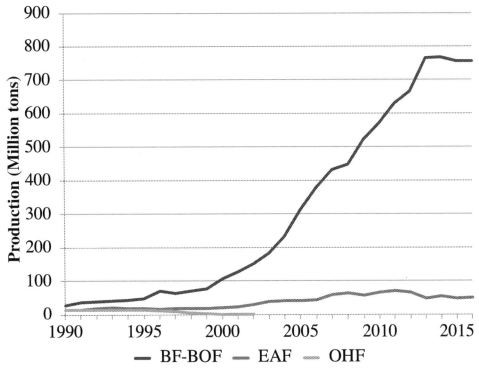

Figure 6.6 Steel production by process in China, 1990–2016.
(*Source*: World Steel Association)

The economic viability and carbon reduction benefits of EAFs will depend on the electricity sector and its price signals, as well as any other compensating ancillary services. The indirect emissions from electricity consumption depend on the overall generation mix. In addition, EAFs cycle roughly once per hour, with power loads concentrated in about 45 minutes, so their utilization could be changed on an hourly basis to respond to changes in the availability of renewable energy [107]. If all of the targeted 1,000 million tons of steel capacity in 2020 were EAFs (assuming an average of 480 kWh per ton), the potential load available for demand response could exceed 70 GW [108].[13] (See Chapter 3 for more discussion on demand response.)

6.6 Conclusions: Opportunities for the Coal "Bridge"

China's most difficult task in decarbonizing is to alter the institutions and technologies that support continued coal use. These are deeply embedded in China's economic growth strategy and have become a common fixture of local and central-level politics. Reaching very low levels of greenhouse gas emissions will

142 *Foundations for a Low-Carbon Energy System in China*

require substantial electrification of industry, transportation, and heating, while simultaneously replacing much of the coal capacity with low-carbon alternatives. To achieve this outcome, coal-based infrastructure needs to be productively repurposed as a "bridge" to an efficient, electrified, and flexible energy economy. We offer suggestions in three areas – technologies, economic, and political institutions, and socioeconomic consequences – for facilitating this transition.

6.6.1 Technology Recommendations

(1) Pursue expansive coal plant flexibility retrofits holistically with low-emission and energy efficiency retrofits.

Compared with European designs, China's current coal-fired power plants may not be as inherently flexible, due to technology choices made during rapid electricity growth years. However, existing coal capacity generally has the capability of achieving more flexible operation – in particular, low minimum outputs – with hardware and/or software changes. The current pilot retrofits have shown great promise in this area.

Retrofits for flexibility must be coordinated, however, with low-emission and energy efficiency retrofits to be successful. If low-emission and efficiency retrofits are focused on improving performance at peak loading conditions, they may ignore or even exacerbate inflexibilities in low-load and variable-load operation. If chosen end-of-pipe environmental controls are not functional at low-load operation, then additional measures must be taken to ensure that air pollution, efficiency, and climate goals are met.

(2) Design all new coal plants for flexibility.

Despite the questionable need for additional capacity in many regions of China, new coal plants will continue to go online for years to come. For example, China's 13th Five-Year Plan (2016–2020) allows for an increase of 200 GW of coal capacity during this period. Possible inefficiencies of these investments can be mitigated if plants are designed to operate flexibly with intermittent resources from day one. Improved technical parameters and experience can allay plant operators' fears about issues with low and variable outputs. Greater transparency on these capabilities can also inform grid operators, who will continue to play a dominant role in determining system flexibility until a large spot market develops, and even likely beyond that time.

Some of these changes involve software and simple hardware changes identified in the existing retrofit programs. Greater improvements may be better achieved earlier in the design process. These may require additional technical collaborations and possibly technology licensing with international equipment manufacturers, but the investments in these should be compared with much higher expected costs of retrofitting at a later date.

(3) Incorporate advanced district heating and residential heating technologies, such as heat storage and heat pumps, which improve flexibility and efficiency in new and existing heating grids.

With expanding electricity and urban heating systems, there was little impetus historically to consider flexibility options in CHP units and heat boilers. China did not pursue thermal heat storage, which was deployed in systems in northern Europe. Given the increasing conflict with low-carbon electricity sources during dispatch in winter, more flexible options need to be considered for providing heat to China's northern cities.

Many options exist for improving efficiency and incorporating diverse low-carbon sources, such as building-level controls for peak-shaving, more active regulation of CHP using heat storage, heat pumps (running on renewable electricity), and storage on daily (current capabilities) up to seasonal (research focus) timescales [110]. Modeling studies reveal that such technologies, if deployed in China, could result in large reductions in curtailment of renewable capacity [111].

(4) Increase electrification of direct coal users in industry, and close the "efficiency gap" where it does not lock in old, coal-intensive technologies.

With over half of coal consumption occurring outside the electricity and heating sectors, China will need to surpass international levels of electrification in industry on any decarbonization pathway. Current energy-intensive iron and steel processes should be replaced with more flexible electric arc furnaces, which can still take up to 30 percent of liquid iron made from raw ore as China builds up a large steel scrap market. Electrification processes that are flexible in responding to electricity supply conditions (e.g., through energy price signals and ancillary services markets) should be especially researched and prioritized in deployment policies. Some international examples already exist [112].

China's energy-intensive industries are still less efficient than many leading international firms, which has prompted a large body of research and central policies to "close the efficiency gap." Some efforts involve retrofits, but a substantial amount of new production capacity is being brought online to replace and expand older facilities. These new plants, still predominantly using coal-intensive and not electricity-intensive processes, could become substantial barriers to the low-carbon transition of the industry [113].

(5) Reduce direct and embedded use of coal in buildings through more efficient end-use technologies and longer lifetimes.

Of all energy consumed in the country, roughly 12 percent is embedded in construction materials for the building sector [114]. This is driven largely by

144   *Foundations for a Low-Carbon Energy System in China*

demand for steel and cement – approximately 23 percent and 61 percent of which, respectively, go to construction [115]. Furthermore, growth in building floor area has large uncertainty going forward, in part driven by speculation in the real estate market, where some analyses point to 21 percent of urban residences lying vacant [116].

Demolition of older buildings is also proceeding at a rapid pace, which can generate long-term benefits in terms of energy efficiency – e.g., electricity and heating. The energy intensity of residences (per unit area) has been relatively flat in urban areas since 2000, offsetting increases in comfort with stricter energy codes, and commercial buildings have seen slight declines since 2012 [117]. Ensuring best available efficiency technologies and long lifetimes of the newly built dwellings is critical to reducing coal use.

(6) Expand carbon capture, utilization, and sequestration (CCUS) research and demonstration projects, as a potential option to accelerate the transition.

Currently, incentives in China align with demonstrating CCUS/CCS as a future technological option and not necessarily deploying it at scale, due to concerns over energy security, cost, and technology development/licensing with international partners [118]. However, CCUS/CCS research and development is not growing elsewhere in the world, and has, in fact, been in decline in recent years in the OECD [119]. Given its presence as a "backstop" technology in most $1.5°C/2°C$ climate change scenarios, substantially more investment is needed globally at all technological stages of the process and in scientific monitoring of storage for leakage.

China is potentially well positioned to lead this effort, through comprehensive research and development programs on the entire CCUS/CCS chain. First, China has an unusually vertically integrated energy sector, giving companies such as China Energy Investment Corporation the ability to conduct research and pilots covering all stages of the process. Second, because coal-intensive industry creates purer streams of CO_2 – and hence, lower-cost capture – China's reductions are potentially less costly than those of other countries that would be primarily capturing from dilute power generation exhaust streams. Finally, China may need this backstop technology earlier than most, due to its limited ability to cost-effectively scale up natural gas in the medium term. This could give China the lead in early pioneering of efficient capture and related technologies, with potential export opportunities down the road.

6.6.2 Economic and Political Institution-Building Recommendations

(1) Prepare new revenue streams for conventional electricity generation from spot markets and other compensated electricity services.

From Barrier to Bridge: The Role of Coal in China's Decarbonization 145

Generation prices currently contain a range of inefficiencies, deriving from the persistent role of government planning and longer-term scheduling methods. Coal generators have until only very recently received virtually all of their revenues at fixed prices with quantities determined to satisfy "equal shares" and not efficiency principles. This arrangement, quite distinct from typical electricity market designs adopted elsewhere, does not provide efficient incentives to reduce short-run operational costs, which would also naturally benefit low-carbon energy sources with low marginal costs. As long as coal generators see no benefits from markets, such as rewarding increased flexibility, they will naturally oppose any change and will not contribute to a potentially profitable transitional role to balancing intermittent resources.

Spot markets for energy that have sufficient granularity in location and time (ideally, sub-provincial and hourly/sub-hourly, respectively) are a well-accepted basis for accommodating diverse sources of energy and creating incentives for generators to provide more flexibility. Ancillary services, such as reserves, are an increasingly important secondary source of revenue in decarbonizing systems. In China, ancillary services have been uncompensated or compensated at very low levels, with exceptions to this practice being the nonstandard "peaking markets" that take on some aspects of typical energy markets. Transitioning current average tariff-based scheduling dispatch practices plus limited or nonstandard ancillary services toward these two categories of market compensation will generate new profit opportunities for coal plants, even as China increases its share of low-carbon energy. These will help mitigate various challenges facing the economics and politics of China's coal-based system, such as financial health and maintaining employment.

(2) Reform district heating prices and regulation of the sector to promote efficiency and the introduction of new technologies.

Heating prices are currently heavily subsidized and are based on a fixed rate per area. This does not incentivize conservation or end-use efficiency, even if sophisticated thermostats are put in place. On the supply side, the underrecovery of heating costs provides scarce incentives to invest in new technologies that can provide efficiency and flexibility enhancements.

Heating price reform, called for as early as 2003, would accurately meter and charge based on customer usage, as a handful of pilots have now begun doing [120]. Ensuring sufficient supply prices can also incentivize greater cost reductions in producing heat, in particular through optimizing investment and operation of new technologies such as heat pumps and heat storage. These price signals are an important complementary component to the above electricity pricing reforms for the large number of CHP plants, whose inflexibility presents a major roadblock to scaling up renewable energy.

146   *Foundations for a Low-Carbon Energy System in China*

(3) Eliminate local government fiscal and political incentives for continued traditional use of coal.

Local governments derive tangible fiscal differences from various sources of electricity generation, such as reduced tax revenues from renewable energy generation, according to central government policy. They also have political incentives favoring continued coal capacity build-out, such as investment growth targets and the promise of holding onto upstream mining employment. These are, in part, driven by GDP and other macroeconomic indicators used as official advancement criteria.

The central government could provide incentives for renewable energy that do not distort local fiscal conditions, such as setting a consistent local tax rate for all generations while reducing the central tax burden. Furthermore, promotion prospects should not be enhanced by GDP and investment numbers if those investments are inefficient, i.e., building out unnecessary coal infrastructure. Addressing job displacement difficulties with more central funding and regulation – discussed in Section 6.6.3 as a "missing policy debate" – can help mitigate concerns over employment of different energy sources.

(4) Establish consistent transmission and distribution pricing for grid companies that removes bias against new energy sources and promotes least-cost planning.

Current grid company revenue schemes can lead to inefficient dispatch within and between regions – because revenues are based on the difference between average selling and buying prices – and tariffs are based on energy transmitted, which favors the use and expansion of more expensive lines. They also deviate from an efficient systemwide dispatch because of the lack of an efficient market with locational price signals, informing both producers and consumers of the cost of power at any given location on the grid.

Reforming grid revenues toward traditional cost-of-service plus optional performance incentives will ensure that the grid company remains neutral with respect to the markets. It can also lead to better grid planning, such as building lines to renewable resources that can be operated more flexibly.

6.6.3 Socioeconomic Impacts and Missing Policy Debate

Much of what has been covered in this chapter has been discussed and, in some cases, initial implementation has begun. Substantial difficulties remain, but robust policy debates are ongoing. By contrast, a handful of crucial topics are relatively absent from the discourse on climate and the future of coal in China. This section highlights four such topics.

6.6.3.1 Make Transition Plans for Stranded Costs During Electricity Market Introduction

While there is much forward momentum for the introduction of market mechanisms in electricity, high-level guidance on what happens during the transition is relatively sparse. In this absence, localities have tended to deploy familiar annual contracting methods that squeeze generators without providing sufficient revenues for additional services and sidestep the issue of compensation for the cost of the transition.

Ideally, a transition plan should provide explicit guarantees of recovery of some stranded costs for plants built under the legacy system. In the case of coal generation, these should be transparent, time-limited, predictable, and independent of the market. Ad hoc measures, such as those observed in the unpredictable market opening paths of various provinces, should be avoided. Many of the methods that have already been deployed in China for similar purposes, such as generation rights trading, influence market behavior and should also be avoided.

6.6.3.2 Address Distributional Impacts between Provinces with Different Generation and Industrial Mixes

It is well established that larger markets result in greater overall efficiency, while also potentially creating losers. These distributional impacts are perhaps most stark between provinces with vastly different mixes, such as between coal-heavy and renewable energy–heavy provinces, and those with different shares of energy-intensive industry. Given the need for local government buy-in to new market institutions, these distributional impacts represent one of the largest barriers to repurposing investment and creating regional markets. They are also inadequately covered in current policy.

Various mechanisms exist for compensating losses during a market introduction. For example, the market could be cleared and dispatched based on a set of bids or audited costs, and during settlement could incorporate additional transfers based on changes in interprovincial flows. Taxes and other local benefits could also similarly be partially transferred. Whatever the method, it should preserve efficient dispatch across borders.

6.6.3.3 Establish Criteria and Expand Funding to Social Welfare and Job Displacement Assistance

While some high-level policies mention resettlement and social welfare of displaced workers in coal-related sectors, there currently is not an unambiguous set of criteria and payments that workers can depend on, or that local governments can expect from the center. Facing the uncertain prospect of public discontent with displacement programs, conservative local governments may opt for delay.

148   *Foundations for a Low-Carbon Energy System in China*

Given the many differences across firms and provinces, it is unlikely that a single standard would be enough to deal with this issue; instead, it would require a detailed set of conditions and new regulatory powers to oversee. The details of this regulatory regime, as well as the source and size of the funds, should be the subject of a focused policy working group. These could be combined or kept separate from displacement aid for workers lost to automation, a much larger trend affecting coal mining currently.

6.6.3.4 Study and Address Equity Considerations of Coal Power and Industry Relocation

The dominant strategy of reducing air pollution in rich eastern regions is to retire nearby coal plants and coal-using industrial facilities and establish new plants in the center and west of the country. For electric generators, these will largely feed into long-distance lines that serve the east. Based on some social welfare metrics, these investments may be better overall, but they nevertheless create both major infrastructure lock-in as well as sticky equity concerns, given that the populations surrounding the new facilities receive less of the benefit for the increased environmental cost. A policy that enhances large disparities among communities is neither fair nor sustainable in the long run.

A more holistic approach would include, first, much greater coordination among climate change and environmental protection priorities, so that air pollution policies do not run counter to or exacerbate CO_2 reduction policies. The newly created Ministry of Ecology and Environment collects both of these responsibilities, though it is too early to assess its effectiveness at coordination. Second, rigorous population-weighted cost-benefit analyses should be conducted to assess changes in overall welfare as well as on specific demographics. Third, where projects go ahead, communities that bear the burdens of these relocation policies should be appropriately compensated by the beneficiary provinces.

Notes

1 Roughly 86 percent of China's CO_2 emissions are from fossil fuel combustion ("energy-related"), and 13 percent are from industrial processes whose chemical by-products include CO_2 ("process-related"), such as cement production. See J. G. J. Olivier, K. M. Schure, and J. A. H. W. Peters, "Trends in Global CO_2 and Total Greenhouse Gas Emissions: 2017 Report" (The Hague: PBL Netherlands Environmental Assessment Agency, 2017).

2 For example, large coal mining companies can transfer workers to construction work, chemicals plants, even agriculture and tourism on reclaimed land. (Interview with manager in coal mining company, December 2017).

3 For example, assume that there is 100 GW of existing capacity operating at 70 percent capacity factor. A developer is considering a 1 GW project that is slightly less efficient than the existing plants. In a marginal cost-based system, the dispatch would not change, and the new project would have zero percent capacity factor. In an equal shares-based system, all plants, including the new one, would be at 69.3 percent.

From Barrier to Bridge: The Role of Coal in China's Decarbonization   149

4 The 276-working day limitation was put in place by the State Administration of Work Safety for safety reasons in support of capacity reduction policies. See State Administration of Work Safety (SAWS), "Opinion Regarding Supporting Resolving Steel Industry Overcapacity Reduction Problems" (Beijing: State Administration of Work Safety, 2016). Available at: www.mem.gov .cn/gk/gwgg/xgxywj/qt/201604/t20160418_233287.shtml. However, the effect was to dramatically increase coal prices, e.g., by more than 60 percent from the beginning of the year at Qinhuangdao (www.umetal.com). This responded to complaints by coal mines that they were unprofitable at low prices.

5 Interview with respondent in state-owned firm with range of energy investments, November 2016. The specific process of getting generation allocation is sometimes called "grabbing generation" (抢电量), where generation companies will compete for generation with little regard for price (confirmed by respondents in other SOEs).

6 Central government regulatory reports note various instances of dispatch practices that gave preference to certain coal generators over other coal generators as well as renewable energy. See National Energy Administration, "Electricity Dispatch and Market Operations Supervision Report of Shandong and 6 Provinces" (Beijing: National Energy Administration, 2017). Available at: http://zfxxgk.nea.gov.cn/auto92/201703/t20170330_2756.htm.

7 Some government reports claim a fraction of long-distance lines used for transmitting renewable energy, for example, 99 percent in a line connecting Inner Mongolia and Jiangsu. National Energy Administration, "2017 National Renewable Power Development Monitoring and Evaluation Report" (Beijing: National Energy Administration, 2018) People's Republic of China. Available at: http://zfxxgk.nea.gov.cn/auto87/201805/t20180522_3179.htm. This calculation is fraught with assumptions, since specific sources of electricity cannot physically be directed down given lines.

8 There are technical limits on how quickly boilers can be heated once cooled, though these are on the order of eight hours or shorter. Startups incur additional costs in terms of burning more expensive fuel (e.g., oil) and long-term increased maintenance, which represent economic, not technical, reasons for inflexible startup scheduling.

9 Interviews with multiple dispatch operators, 2015–2016.

10 Interviews with grid dispatch and government regulators, July 2015 and July 2018. Over the first two years of the Northeast Grid peak regulation market, the average price reached 0.426 yuan/ kWh. To put it in perspective, this payment is comparable to the benchmark tariff for coal, but compensates plants for *not* generating. Besides encouraging coal plants to ramp down, the market is also supposed to help encourage retrofits to open up more flexibility.

11 Interview with participating researcher, November 2015.

12 Combustion emissions from coal in non-power and heat sectors are 34 percent of the total energy-related emissions. See International Energy Agency, "CO_2 Emissions From Fuel Combustion Highlights 2017" (Paris: International Energy Agency, 2017). The number 42 percent is obtained when considering all CO_2 emissions, including process-related (see Note 1, this chapter).

13 China's EAF efficiencies taken from China Iron and Steel Industry Association, "Iron and Steel Industry Coal Consumption Control Plan and Policy Research." Target of 1,000 million tons from the 13th Five-Year Plan, MIIT, "Iron and Steel Industry Upgrading Plan (2016–2020)." This is the total electrical capacity, assuming all plants are operating.

References

[1] J. G. J. Olivier, K. M. Schure, and J. A. H. W. Peters, "Trends in Global CO_2 and Total Greenhouse Gas Emissions: 2017 Report" (The Hague: PBL Netherlands Environmental Assessment Agency, 2017). Available at: www.pbl.nl/en/publica tions/trends-in-global-co2-and-total-greenhouse-gas-emissions-2017-report.

[2] Olivier et al., "Trends in Global CO_2 and Total Greenhouse Gas Emissions."

[3] H. Rui, R. K. Morse, and G. He, "Developing large coal-power bases in China," in M. C. Thurber and R. K. Morse, eds., *The Global Coal Market: Supplying the Major*

Fuel for Emergine Economies (Cambridge: Cambridge University Press, 2015), pp. 73–122.

[4] B. Wang, "An Imbalanced Development of Coal and Electricity Industries in China," *Energy Policy* **35**(10) (October 2007), pp. 4959–4968.

[5] W. Peng, "The evolution of China's coal institutions," in M. C. Thurber and R. K. Morse, eds., *The Global Coal Market: Supplying the Major Fuel for Emergine Economies* (Cambridge: Cambridge University Press, 2015), pp. 37–72.

[6] University of International Business and Economics and Chinese Academy of Sciences, "Coal Sector Employment Impacts of Capacity Reduction Policies," China Coal Consumption Cap Electricity Sector Research Working Group (Beijing: University of International Business and Economics; Institute for Urban and Environmental Studies, Chinese Academy of Sciences, 2018).

[7] National Bureau of Statistics of China, "Coal mining and dressing," in *China Statistical Yearbook 2016* (Beijing: China Statistics Press, 2016).

[8] L. Zhang, "Electricity pricing in a partial reformed plan system: The case of China," *Energy Policy* **43** (April 2012), pp. 214–225.

[9] Rui et al., "Developing large coal-power bases in China."

[10] D. Fridley and H. Lu, eds., "China Energy Databook V9" (Berkeley: Lawrence Berkeley National Laboratory, 2016). Available at: https://china.lbl.gov/china-energy-databook

[11] National Bureau of Statistics of China, *China Statistical Yearbook 2017* (Beijing: China Statistics Press, 2017).

[12] National Bureau of Statistics of China, "2015 National Input-Output Table" (Beijing: China Statistics Press, 2018).

[13] National Bureau of Statistics of China, "Urban Centralized Heating Statistics" (Beijing: China Statistics Press, 2017).

[14] National Bureau of Statistics of China, *China Statistical Yearbook 2017*, (Beijing: China Statistics Press, 2017).

[15] S. Zhang and X. Qin, "Promoting large and closing small in China's coal power sector 2006–2013: A CO_2 mitigation assessment based on a vintage structure," *Economics of Energy & Environmental Policy* **5**(2) (April 1, 2016), pp. 85–99. Available at: www.iaee.org/en/publications/eeeparticle.aspx?id=130.

[16] China Electricity Council, "Overview of Electric Power Industry (Various: 2003–2016)" (Beijing: China Electricity Council, 2017).

[17] State Council, "Notice of Catalogue of Government Approvals for Investment Projects (2014 Version)," (Beijing: State Council, 2014). Available at: www.gov.cn/zhengce/content/2014-11/18/content_9219.htm.

[18] State Council, "Opinion Regarding Resolving Steel Industry Overcapacity Reduction Problems," (Beijing: State Council, 2016). Available at: www.gov.cn/zhengce/content/2016-02/04/content_5039353.htm.

[19] K. Matus, K. M. Nam, N. E. Selin et al., "Health damages from air pollution in China," *Global Environmental Change-Human and Policy Dimensions* **22**(1) (2012), pp. 55–66.

[20] Y. L. Sun, Z. Wang, P. Fu et al., "Aerosol composition, sources and processes during wintertime in Beijing, China," *Atmospheric Chemistry and Physics* **13**(9) (May 2, 2013), pp. 4577–4592.

[21] National Energy Administration, "Energy Sector Strengthening Air Pollution Prevention Plan" (Beijing: National Energy Administration, 2014). Available at: www.nea.gov.cn/2014-05/16/c_133338463.htm.

[22] State Council, "Action Plan on Prevention and Control of Air Pollution" (Beijing: State Council, 2013). Available at: www.gov.cn/zwgk/2013-09/12/content_2486773.htm.

[23] National Energy Administration, "Energy Sector Strengthening Air Pollution Prevention Plan" (Beijing: National Energy Administration, 2014). Available at: www.nea.gov.cn/2014-05/16/c_133338463.htm.

[24] National Development and Reform Commission, "Notice Regarding Completing 2016 Work on Coal Consumption Reduction and Substitution" (Beijing: National Development and Reform Commission, 2016), Available at: www.ndrc.gov.cn/zcfb/zcfbtz/201607/t20160726_812316.html.

[25] National Development and Reform Commission and National Energy Administration, "13th Five-Year Plan on Energy Development" (Beijing: National Development and Reform Commission, 2016).

[26] Ministry of Human Resources and Social Security (MOHRSS), "Employment and Social Welfare Topic Press Conference," (February 26, 2016). Available at: www.mohrss.gov.cn/zcyjs/gongzuodongtai/201603/t20160310_235121.html.

[27] International Monetary Fund, "People's Republic of China: Financial System Stability Assessment-Press Release and Statement by the Executive Director for People's Republic of China," IMF Staff Country Reports **2017** (358) (December 2017). Available at: http://elibrary.imf.org/view/IMF002/24775-9781484331149/24775-9781484331149/24775-9781484331149.xml.

[28] Ministry of Human Resources and Social Security (MOHRSS), "Notice of Five Departments Regarding 2017 Employment Placement Work During Steel and Coal Industry Capacity Reduction" (Beijing: Ministry of Human Resources and Social Security, 2017). Available at: www.gov.cn/xinwen/2017-03/31/content_5182280.htm.

[29] Interview with manager in coal mining company, December 2017.

[30] "Coal Sector Employment Impacts of Capacity Reduction Policies."

[31] State Council, "Notice Regarding Provisional Guidelines for Encouraging Electricity Investment and Implementing Multiple Electricity Tariffs" (Beijing: State Council, 1985). Available at: http://law.npc.gov.cn/FLFG/flfgByID.action?txtid=2&flfgID=100481&showDetailType=QW.

[32] S. Xu and W. Chen, "The reform of electricity power sector in the PR of China," *Energy Policy* **34**(16) (November 2006), pp. 2455–2465.

[33] J. L. Ma, "On-grid electricity tariffs in China: Development, reform and prospects," *Energy Policy* **39**(5) (2011), pp. 2633–2645. Available at: https://doi.org/10.1016/j.enpol.2011.02.032

[34] Ma, "On-grid electricity tariffs in China."

[35] Guangzhou Committee, *Guangzhou Electricity Sector Annals (1888–2000)* (Guangzhou: Guangzhou Electricity Sector Annals Editorial Committee, 2001).

[36] F. Kahrl, J. H. Williams, and J. Hu, "The political economy of electricity dispatch reform in China," *Energy Policy* **53** (2013), pp. 361–369.

[37] Y. C. Xu, *Sinews of Power: The Politics of the State Grid Corporation of China* (Oxford: Oxford University Press, 2016).

[38] R. M. Wirtshafter and E. Shih, "Decentralization of China's electricity sector: Is small beautiful?," *World Development* **18**(4) (1990), pp. 505–512.

[39] National Bureau of Statistics of China, *China Statistical Yearbook 2017*.

[40] State Administration of Work Safety, "Opinion Regarding Supporting Resolving Steel Industry Overcapacity Reduction Problems" (Beijing: State Administration of Work Safety, 2016). Available at: www.mem.gov.cn/gk/gwgg/xgxywj/qt/201604/t20160418_233287.shtml.

[41] B. Caldecott. G. Dericks, D. J. Tulloch et al., "Stranded Assets and Thermal Coal in China," Working Paper (University of Oxford, 2017).

[42] National Development and Reform Commission and National Energy Administration, "Implementing Plan for Solving Hydropower, Wind and Solar Curtailment" (Beijing: National Development and Reform Commission, 2017). Available at: http://zfxxgk.nea.gov.cn/auto87/201711/t20171113_3056.htm.

[43] Y. Dai, "Who Drives Climate-Relevant Policy Implementation in China?," Working Paper (Sussex, UK: Institute of Development Studies, 2015).

[44] X. Zhao, S. Zhang, Y. Zou et al., "To what extent does wind power deployment affect vested interests? A case study of the Northeast China Grid," *Energy Policy* **63** (December 2013), pp. 814–822.

[45] National Energy Administration, "Electricity Dispatch and Market Operations Supervision Report of Shandong and 6 Provinces" (Beijing: National Energy Administration, 2017). Available at: http://zfxxgk.nea.gov.cn/auto92/201703/t20170330_2756.htm.

[46] "On-grid electricity tariffs in China."

[47] P. L. Joskow, "Incentive regulation in theory and practice: Electricity Distribution and transmission networks," in N. Rose, ed., *Economic Regulation and Its Reform: What Have We Learned?* (University of Chicago Press, 2014), pp. 291–344. Available at: www.nber.org/chapters/c12566.pdf.

[48] J. I. Pérez-Arriaga and C. Meseguer, "Wholesale marginal prices in competitive generation markets," *IEEE Transactions on Power Systems* **12**(2) (1997), pp. 710–717.

[49] National Energy Administration, "Energy Sector Strengthening Air Pollution Prevention Plan" (Beijing: National Energy Administration, 2014). Available at: www.nea.gov.cn/2014-05/16/c_133338463.htm.

[50] "2017 National Renewable Power Development Monitoring and Evaluation Report" (Beijing: National Energy Administration, 2018). Available at: http://zfxxgk.nea.gov.cn/auto87/201805/t20180522_3179.htm.

[51] P. Andrews-Speed, "Reform Postponed: The Evolution of China's Electricity Markets," in F. P. Sioshansi, ed., *Evolution of Global Electricity Markets: New Paradigms, New Challenges, New Approaches* (Waltham: Elsevier, 2013), pp. 531–567.

[52] J. Watson, R. Byrne, D. Ockwell et al., "Lessons from China: Building technological capabilities for low carbon technology transfer and development," *Climatic Change* **131**(3) (2015), pp. 387–399.

[53] M. R. Davidson, "Technology integration in China's electricity system: Central targets and local challenges," in T. G. Rawski and L. Brandt, eds., *Policy, Regulation and Innovation in China's Electricity and Telecom Industries* (Cambridge: Cambridge University Press, 2019), pp. 134–176.

[54] National Development and Reform Commission and National Energy Administration, "13th Five-Year Plan on Electricity Development" (Beijing: National Development and Reform Commission, 2016).

[55] "Cogeneration Management Rules (No. 617)" (Beijing: National Energy Administration, 2016). Available at: www.sdpc.gov.cn/zcfb/zcfbtz/201604/t20160418_798342.html.

[56] M. R. Davidson and I. Pérez-Arriaga, "Modeling unit commitment in political context: Case of China's partially restructured electricity sector," *IEEE Transactions on Power Systems* **33**(5) (2018), pp. 4889–4901.

[57] Danish Energy Agency, "Flexibility in the Power System: Danish and European Experiences," (Copenhagen: Danish Energy Agency, 2015). Available at: https://ens.dk/sites/ens.dk/files/Globalcooperation/flexibility_in_the_power_system_v23-lri.pdf

[58] Agora Energiewende, "Flexibility in Thermal Power Plants" (Berlin: Agora Energiewende, 2017). Available at: www.agora-energiewende.de/en/publications/flexibility-in-thermal-power-plants/

[59] J. Cochran, D. Lew, and N. Kumar, "Flexible Coal: Evolution from Baseload to Peaking Plant" (Golden, CO: National Renewable Energy Laboratory, 2013).

[60] Y. Gu, J. Xu, D. Chen et al., "Overall review of peak shaving for coal-fired power units in China," *Renewable and Sustainable Energy Reviews* **54** (February 2016), pp. 723–731.

[61] R. Sun et al., "Summary of China's conventional coal-fired power plant technologies," *Power and Electricity Engineers* **28** (2013), pp. 28–34.

[62] China Electricity Council, "Status and Prospects for China's Electricity Sector" (Beijing: China Electricity Council, 2015). Available at: www.cec.org.cn/yaowen kuaidi/2015-03-10/134972.html.

[63] Y. Dong, X. Jiang, Z. Liang et al., "Coal power flexibility, energy efficiency and pollutant emissions implications in China: A plant-level analysis based on case units," *Resources, Conservation and Recycling* **134** (July 1, 2018), pp. 184–195.

[64] J. Hu, G. Kwok, W. Xuan et al., "Using natural gas generation to improve power system efficiency in China," *Energy Policy* **60** (September 2013), pp. 116–121.

[65] S. Paltsev and D. Zhang, "Natural gas pricing reform in China: Getting closer to a market system?," *Energy Policy* **86** (2015), pp. 43–56.

[66] National Bureau of Statistics of China, "National Energy Inventory (2000–2014)" (Beijing: China Statistics Press, 2017).

[67] National Development and Reform Commission, "2017 Natural Gas Operation Conditions" (Beijing: National Development and Reform Commission, 2018). Available at: www.ndrc.gov.cn/fzgggz/jjyx/mtzhgl/201801/t20180131_876398.html.

[68] "Energy Sector Strengthening Air Pollution Prevention Plan" (Beijing: National Energy Administration, 2014). Available at: www.nea.gov.cn/2014-05/16/c_133338463.htm.

[69] J. Lin and B. Lin, "Heat tariff and subsidy in China based on heat cost analysis," *Energy Economics* **71** (2018), pp. 411–420. Available at: https://doi.org/10.1016/j.eneco.2018.03.012.

[70] G. Booras, "Engineering and Economic Analysis of an Advanced Ultra-Supercritical Pulverized Coal Power Plant with and without Post-Combustion Carbon Capture" (Palo Alto, CA: Electric Power Research Institute, 2015).

[71] X. Zhang, "Some consideration about the future development strategy of advanced ultra supercritical coal-fired power generation technology," *Engineering Sciences* **15** (4) (2013), pp. 91–95.

[72] Watson et al., "Lessons from China."

[73] Interview with a power plant technology engineer, June 2017.

[74] Agora Energiewende, "Flexibility in Thermal Power Plants" (Berlin: Agora Energiewende, 2017). Available at: www.agora-energiewende.de/en/publications/flexibility-in-thermal-power-plants/

[75] Cochran et al., "Flexible Coal."

[76] S. Korellis, "Coal-Fired Power Plant Heat Rate Improvement Options," *POWER Magazine* (blog), November 1, 2014. Available at: www.powermag.com/coal-fired-power-plant-heat-rate-improvement-options-part-1/.

[77] National Development and Reform Commission and National Energy Administration, "13th Five-Year Plan on Electricity Development."

[78] S. Wang and L. Riemann, "Thermal Power Plant Flexibility" (Paris: Clean Energy Ministerial, 2018). Available at: www.cleanenergyministerial.org/publications-clean-energy-ministerial/thermal-power-plant-flexibility-2018-publication-under-clean.

[79] National Development and Reform Commission and National Energy Administration, "13th Five-Year Plan on Electricity Development."

[80] F. Teng, Q. Liu, A. Gu et al., "Pathways to Deep Decarbonization in China" (Paris: Institute for Sustainable Development and International Relations (IDDRI), 2015). Available at: www.iddri.org/sites/default/files/old/Publications/CHN_DDPP_report .pdf

[81] Global Carbon Capture and Storage Institute, "Large-Scale CCS Facilities," (Docklands, AU: Global Carbon Capture and Storage Institute, August 11, 2018). Available at: www.globalccsinstitute.com/projects/large-scale-ccs-projects.

[82] R. T. Dahowski, C. L. Davidson, X. C. Li et al., "A $70/tCO_2$ greenhouse gas mitigation backstop for China's industrial and electric power sectors: Insights from a comprehensive CCS cost curve," *International Journal of Greenhouse Gas Control* **11** (November 1, 2012), pp. 73–85.

[83] National Academy of Sciences, *Geologic Capture and Sequestration of Carbon: Proceedings of a Workshop* (Washington, DC: National Academies Press, 2018). Available at: www.nap.edu/catalog/25210.

[84] M. T. Craig, H. Zhai, P. Jaramillo et al., "Trade-offs in cost and emission reductions between flexible and normal carbon capture and sequestration under carbon dioxide emission constraints," *International Journal of Greenhouse Gas Control* **66** (November 2017), pp. 25–34.

[85] International Energy Agency, "CO_2 Emissions from Fuel Combustion Highlights 2017" (Paris: International Energy Agency, 2017).

[86] National Bureau of Statistics of China, "National Energy Inventory (2000–2014)" (Beijing: China Statistics Press, 2017).

[87] China Cement Association, "13th Five-Year Plan on the Cement Industry" (Beijing: China Cement Association, 2016).

[88] China Cement Association, "Cement Industry Coal Control Strategy and Implementation Research" (Beijing: China Cement Association, 2017).

[89] China Iron and Steel Association, "Iron and Steel Industry Coal Consumption Control Plan and Policy Research" (Beijing: China Iron and Steel Industry Association, 2017).

[90] M. Åhman, L. J. Nilsson, and B. Johansson, "Global climate policy and deep decarbonization of energy-intensive industries," *Climate Policy* **17**(5) (July 4, 2017), pp. 634–649.

[91] National Bureau of Statistics of China, "Personal coal consumption" (生活消费煤炭消费总量) in "Coal consumption by sector" (Beijing: China Statistics Press, 2016).

[92] K. He and X. Li, "China 'Scattered' Coal Comprehensive Control Survey Report 2018," (Beijing: Natural Resources Defense Council, 2018).

[93] D. Fridley and H. Lu, eds., "China Energy Databook V9" (Berkeley: Lawrence Berkeley National Laboratory, 2016). Available at: https://china.lbl.gov/china-energy-databook

[94] "Energy Sector Strengthening Air Pollution Prevention Plan" (Beijing: National Energy Administration, 2014). Available at: www.nea.gov.cn/2014-05/16/c_133338463.htm.

[95] World Steel Association, *Steel Statistical Yearbook 2017* (Brussels: World Steel Association, 2017).

[96] W. Chen, X. Yin, and D. Ma, "A bottom-up analysis of China's iron and steel industrial energy consumption and CO_2 emissions," *Applied Energy* **136** (December 31, 2014), pp. 1174–1183.

[97] "Sustainable Steel: At the Core of the Green Economy" (Brussels: World Steel Association, 2012). Available at: www.worldsteel.org/en/dam/jcr:5b246502-df29-4d8b-92bb-afb2dc27ed4f/Sustainable-steel XE "steel" -at-the-core-of-a-green-economy.pdf.

[98] K. He and L. Wang, "A review of energy use and energy-efficient technologies for the iron and steel industry," *Renewable and Sustainable Energy Reviews* **70** (April 1, 2017), pp. 1022–1039.

[99] He and Wang, "A review of energy use and energy-efficient technologies."

[100] "A review of energy use and energy-efficient technologies."

[101] Chen et al., "A bottom-up analysis."

[102] China Iron and Steel Association, "Iron and Steel Industry Coal Consumption Control Plan and Policy Research."

[103] Ministry of Industry and Information Technology, "Iron and Steel Industry Upgrading Plan (2016–2020)" (Beijing: Ministry of Industry and Information Technology, 2016). Available at: www.miit.gov.cn/n1146295/n1652858/n1652930/n3757016/c5353943/content.html.

[104] Ministry of Industry and Information Technology, "Iron and Steel Industry Upgrading Plan (2016–2020)."

[105] F. Zhong, "Is It Time for China to Switch to Electric Arc Furnace Steelmaking?," (Blog post: World Steel Association, February 13, 2018). Available at: www.worldsteel.org/media-centre/blog/2018/Is-it-time-for-China-to-switch-to-EAF-steelmaking.html.

[106] Y. Yang, "Scrap steel reuse enters 'Golden Age'," *Economic Daily* (June 5, 2017). Available at: www.gov.cn/xinwen/2017-06/05/content_5199838.htm.

[107] M. Paulus and F. Borggrefe, "The potential of demand-side management in energy-intensive industries for electricity markets in Germany," *Applied Energy*, **88**(2) (February 1, 2011), pp. 432–441. Available at: https://doi.org/10.1016/j.apenergy.2010.03.017

[108] China Iron and Steel Association, "Iron and Steel Industry Coal Consumption Control Plan and Policy Research."

[109] Ministry of Industry and Information Technology, "Iron and Steel Industry Upgrading Plan (2016–2020)."

[110] H. Lund, S. Werner, R. Wiltshire et al., "4th generation district heating (4GDH): Integrating smart thermal grids into future sustainable energy systems," *Energy* **68** (April 15, 2014), pp. 1–11.

[111] X. Chen, C. Kang, M. O'Malley et al., "Increasing the flexibility of combined heat and power for wind power integration in China: Modeling and implications," *IEEE Transactions on Power Systems* **30**(4) (July 2015), pp. 1848–1857.

[112] Paulus and Borggrefe, "The potential of demand-side management."

[113] S. Zhang and X. Qin, "Promoting large and closing small in China's coal power sector 2006–2013: A CO_2 mitigation assessment based on a vintage structure," *Economics of Energy & Environmental Policy* **5**(2) (April 1, 2016), pp. 85–99. Available at: www.iaee.org/en/publications/eeeparticle.aspx?id=130.

[114] Beijing Jiaotong University, "13th Five-Year Building Sector Coal Control Implementing Plan" (Beijing: Beijing Jiaotong University, 2017).

[115] National Bureau of Statistics of China, "2015 National Input-Output Table."

[116] K. Kawase, "China's housing glut casts pall over the economy," *Nikkei Asian Review*, (February 13, 2019). Available at: https://asia.nikkei.com/Spotlight/Cover-Story/China-s-housing-glut-casts-pall-over-the-economy.

[117] T. Huo, W. Cai, H. Ren et al., "China's building stock estimation and energy intensity analysis," *Journal of Cleaner Production* **207** (January 10, 2019), pp. 801–813.

[118] R. K. Morse, V. Rai, and G. He, "The real drivers of carbon capture and storage in China," in M. C. Thurber and R. K. Morse, eds., *The Global Coal Market: Supplying the Major Fuel for Emergine Economies* (Cambridge: Cambridge University Press, 2015), pp. 557–581.

[119] International Energy Agency, "Energy Technology Perspectives 2017" (Paris: International Energy Agency, 2017).

[120] Lin and Lin, "Heat tariff and subsidy in China."

7

Coordinating Strategies to Reduce Air Pollution and Carbon Emissions in China

WEI PENG AND ZHIMIN MAO

7.1 Introduction

The rapid economic growth in China over the past few decades has been fueled by a growing use of energy, especially coal. Such a coal-intensive economic development path not only makes China the world's top carbon emitter, but it also leads to worsening air quality and severe public health risks. Driven by record-high smog events in recent years, the Chinese government has declared war against air pollution and introduced action plans for pollution prevention and control. Since 2013, bringing air quality to healthy levels has been prioritized on the political agenda across all levels of government.

This heavy reliance on coal is a major contributor to both air pollutants and CO_2 emissions. In order to tackle air pollution, the Chinese government has issued plans to curb coal consumption, increase energy efficiency, and encourage new investments in natural gas and renewable energy. These measures aim to lower coal use and can simultaneously reduce the associated emissions of both air pollutants and CO_2. In addition, as the general public acquires more knowledge about the negative impacts of air pollution, the rising awareness of environmental issues could lead to an increasing demand for government actions to tackle other forms of environmental externalities as well. This may include efforts to curb the impact of climate change.

Given the political saliency of air pollution concerns, some strategies that result in near-term reductions in localized air pollution may also bring long-term benefits for combating global climate change. However, air pollution abatement measures are not always aligned with carbon mitigation objectives. For instance, installing sulfur scrubbers on coal power plants, although this can significantly reduce air pollutant emissions, does not reduce carbon emissions.

Therefore, to lay the foundations for long-term decarbonization, policymakers must understand the potential synergies and trade-offs between these two

157

158   *Foundations for a Low-Carbon Energy System in China*

objectives: improving air quality and protecting human health in the near term, and achieving deep decarbonization to tackle climate change in the long term.

7.2 Background

7.2.1 Overview of Air Pollution and Carbon Mitigation Efforts in China

China's major cities have endured high levels of air pollution, which has exacted a heavy toll on human health. While the annual average air pollution levels of Chinese cities have improved steadily in the past decade, cities in northern and eastern China still experience toxic levels of pollution, especially during the winter. According to China's Ministry of Environmental Protection, only 21.6 percent of China's cities at or above prefectural level met national ambient air quality standards in 2015 [1].[1] It was also estimated that 1.2 million deaths in China in 2017 can be attributed to air pollution exposure, making it the fourth-greatest risk factor for mortality and accounting for 12 percent of total national deaths [2].

While the scale of the air pollution challenge is massive, so are China's top-down actions. At the national level, the State Council announced an Action Plan for Air Pollution Prevention and Control in September 2013. The Action Plan set national-level emissions and pollution reduction targets for 2017, as well as more stringent targets for key metropolitan regions. Following the expiration of this earlier plan, in June 2018 the State Council released a three-year action plan for "winning the blue sky war," which set targets for 2020. Most notably, it aims to reduce emissions of sulfur dioxide (SO_2) and nitrogen oxides (NO_x) to at least 15 percent below 2015 levels by 2020. In addition, cities that failed to meet the existing $PM_{2.5}$ standards need to decrease their concentration of $PM_{2.5}$ by at least 18 percent compared with 2015 levels. In 2014, China made the first amendment to its Environmental Protection Law in 25 years. This amendment allowed eligible nongovernmental groups to bring public interest lawsuits against polluters. The government has heightened enforcement, including the removal of limits on fines. Moreover, 15,000 enterprises were required to publish their real-time air pollutant emissions data.

In terms of carbon mitigation, in 2014 China and the United States signed a historic agreement to curb greenhouse gas emissions, and China pledged to peak its carbon emissions by 2030. In its Nationally Determined Contribution (NDC), China also announced that by 2030, it will peak its carbon emissions, lower carbon dioxide emissions per unit of GDP to 60–65 percent below 2005 levels, and increase the share of nonfossil fuels in primary energy consumption to around 20 percent. In 2020, China set a target of carbon neutrality by 2060. Investment in low-carbon energy, especially wind and solar, has increased significantly in the past decades, making China the world's top clean energy investor. To date, China has relied on a mix of policy instruments to tackle carbon emissions, but relies primarily on direct state interventions, such as mandates for energy and technology choices as well as energy efficiency targets. China also launched a national carbon emission trading scheme at the end of 2017, advancing market-based approaches to cut greenhouse gas emissions. The initial trial run focuses only on the electricity sector with an expectation of expanding it to other industries around 2020. (See Chapter 2 for more on the emission trading program.) While the coverage of industries and scale of the mitigation target is not ambitious for now, the process of gradually building up the institutional capacity, such as the monitoring, reporting, and verification system, is crucial for China [3].

7.2.2 Governance Structure for Air Pollution and Climate Issues in China

Until early 2018, conventional air pollution abatement and carbon mitigation historically relied on two largely distinctive bureaucratic lines: air pollution control was mainly under the Ministry of Environmental Protection (MEP) and climate change was the responsibility of the National Development and Reform Commission (NDRC). In March 2018, the National People's Congress passed a plan to form a new Ministry of Ecology and Environment (MEE). The MEE has undertaken most of responsibilities under the former MEP as well as the climate change policy making formerly under NDRC. Such efforts to bring air pollution and carbon mitigation issues under the same regulatory agency create new opportunities for improvements in policy coordination to tackle these two issues in the future.

China's air pollution reduction policy framework is embedded within a governance system unique to China, where five-year plans, national laws and regulations, and political agreements collectively shape the direction of environmental policy. Before the formation of the new MEE, NDRC and MEP, as two ministries under the State Council, shared the responsibilities for air pollution prevention and control efforts at the national and subnational levels. At the planning level, the NDRC led air pollution prevention efforts, while the MEP focused on air pollution reduction. In terms of implementation, the NDRC also assigns tasks to relevant government entities on national air pollution prevention and control strategies.

China's policy framework for carbon mitigation follows a similar top-down system. Before the formation of MEE, NDRC played the most critical role for developing national energy development strategies as well as climate change policies. It was responsible for GHG accounting and led China's efforts in developing a national carbon trading scheme. In addition, the National Energy

160   *Foundations for a Low-Carbon Energy System in China*

Administration, an independent agency within the NDRC, studies and drafts national energy development strategies, which have direct implications for greenhouse gas emissions. MEP was not responsible for regulating carbon emissions, as CO_2 is not considered an air pollutant in China.

The formation of the new Ministry of Ecology and Environment (MEE) could have important implications for China's environmental and climate governance. The State Council presented draft plans to consolidate environmental and climate policymaking under this new ministry. Most notably, MEE has not only taken over all the responsibilities that were previously under MEP, including regulations on air pollution control, but has also undertaken climate change and carbon mitigation policy responsibility formerly under the jurisdiction of the NDRC. Although it is too early to conclude whether the coordination problems between air pollution and climate policies will disappear, this reform moves in the right direction to streamline overlapping functions and to lower the bureaucratic barriers for coordination.

One area of improvement is data collection and monitoring. Previously, data collection and preparation for ambient air pollutants and carbon emissions were conducted by two different entities, i.e., MEP and the National Bureau of Statistics, respectively. While MEP has significantly improved its air pollution monitoring network and associated data quality in recent years, the monitoring of China's carbon emissions and associated data quality has remained subpar. The new ministry provides an opportunity for carbon dioxide and other criteria air pollutants to be monitored under the same data collection and processing framework, which may improve data quality for effective decision-making and implementation.

7.3 Synergies and Trade-offs between Air Pollution and Carbon Mitigation Strategies

The government has increasingly emphasized coordinating strategies to address these two issues. When comparing China's air pollution and climate plans side by side (i.e., the Action Plan on Prevention and Control of Air Pollution and the Nationally Determined Contributions, respectively), one can identify a few common strategies that are included in both plans, such as a shift away from coal to cleaner fuels in the power and residential sectors.

However, some approaches aimed at air pollution control bring no climate benefits. For instance, implementing end-of-pipe controls, such as installing sulfur scrubbers on coal-fired power plants, while it can significantly reduce air pollutant emissions, does not mitigate carbon emissions. Prior studies have also suggested a potential increase in carbon emissions, since these control devices lower the efficiency of power plants, hence increasing the carbon emissions per unit of electric output [4]. Furthermore, some strategies, such as converting coal to gas (i.e., synthetic natural gas), may reduce the air pollution from directly burning coal at the expense of higher life-cycle carbon emissions. Therefore, in this section we provide a few commonly discussed strategies that may lead to synergies or trade-offs between air quality and carbon mitigation objectives.

7.3.1 Examples of Win-Win Policies

7.3.1.1 Carbon Pricing

A price on CO_2 emissions increases the costs of carbon-intensive technologies and makes low-carbon technologies more economically attractive. Since many low-carbon technologies, such as wind and solar energy, also emit no air pollutants, carbon pricing could facilitate a switch in the fuel mix toward cleaner sources, thus bringing air quality and health co-benefits. A prior study quantified the air quality and health benefits of using carbon pricing to help achieve China's pledge of peaking carbon emissions by 2030 [5]. Depending on the economic valuation of the health impacts, the authors of the study found that the health co-benefits, driven by improved air quality, could partially or fully offset the economic costs associated with imposing a carbon price. The scale of benefits would be larger under a more ambitious carbon mitigation target and with a higher price on CO_2. To provide a policy context on carbon pricing, China formally launched its national carbon cap-and-trade system in December 2017. While the first phase of the carbon market only targets the electricity generation sector, it marks the initial step of carbon pricing in China and may contribute to both near-term localized air quality benefits and long-term carbon mitigation goals.

7.3.1.2 Renewable Energy Policies

The production of renewable electricity usually has zero emissions of both conventional air pollutants and CO_2. Given China's transition toward clean energy, continued investments in renewable capacity could help it reduce air pollutants and carbon emissions simultaneously. The magnitudes of air quality and climate benefits will be influenced by the amount of renewables that can be integrated into the power grids, as well as the type and location of power generation being displaced. For instance, to achieve the government's 2030 solar installation target of 400 GW, a study found that deploying distributed PV in eastern China with the help of interprovincial transmission could maximize the potential CO_2 reductions and air quality-related health benefits (4 percent and 1 percent decrease in total national CO_2 emissions and air pollution-related premature deaths, respectively,

162   *Foundations for a Low-Carbon Energy System in China*

compared to a coal-intensive business-as-usual scenario) [6]. Such a deployment strategy results in the largest benefits because it maximizes displacement of the dirtiest coal-fired power plants and minimizes the curtailment of solar-generated-electricity.

7.3.1.3 Energy Efficiency Measures

Improving energy efficiency in the production and demand sectors lowers energy need and associated emissions of air pollutants and CO_2. Energy efficiency improvements are part of China's action plan to curb air pollution. For instance, during the 12th Five-Year Plan, China aimed to lower energy use per unit industrial added value in 2015 by 21 percent from 2010 levels [7]. A study found that for the year 2015, a 10-percent increase in energy efficiency in Chinese industrial sectors, coupled with some end-of-pipe controls, could reduce air pollution-related deaths by 3 percent and carbon emissions by 4 percent nationally [8]. It is challenging to estimate the costs to improve energy efficiency in industrial sectors, and these costs vary greatly among specific industries, depending on their current level of efficiency. Earlier studies have found that adopting cost-effective measures has significant energy savings potential in major Chinese industrial sectors. For instance, in 2030, implementing cost-effective energy efficiency measures in China's cement industry can avoid 17 percent of energy use, leading to a 5 percent, 3 percent, 15 percent, and 12 percent reduction of national total CO_2, PM, SO_2, and NOx emissions, respectively [9]. For the iron and steel industry, it is estimated that cost-effective energy efficiency measures can avoid 22 percent of energy use, hence reducing national total CO_2, PM, SO_2, and NOx emissions by as much as 22 percent, 16 percent, 19 percent, and 2 percent, respectively, in 2030 [10].

7.3.2 Examples of Air Pollution Control Strategies with Potential Climate Penalties

7.3.2.1 Synthetic Natural Gas Development

Switching from coal to gas is a key strategy in China's action plan to curb air pollution. In addition to tapping conventional natural gas resources, China currently plans to expand its coal-based synthetic natural gas (SNG) production. Through 2013, the central government has proved a total capacity of 37.1 billion cubic meters per year (bcm/yr) of SNG production, with another 40 projects being proposed (~200 bcm/yr). The total planned SNG capacity is more than China's total natural gas consumption for 2014. These SNG projects can reduce air pollution by substituting for direct coal use in power, industry, and households.

Coordinating Strategies to Reduce Air Pollution and Carbon Emissions   163

However, these air quality benefits come with a climate penalty (unless carbon capture and storage is applied). One 2017 study estimated that in 2020, using SNG to displace coal in the residential sector could reduce national total air-pollution-related deaths by 2 percent, but would emit 20–40 percent more CO_2 than using conventional natural gas for the same purpose [11]. Therefore, the developments of SNG projects demonstrate potential trade-offs between air pollution and carbon mitigation objectives. Since the SNG production is also water-intensive, it may also intensify water stress concerns, as another sustainability challenge especially critical for the water-scarce northern provinces [12].

7.3.2.2 *Transport and Residential Electrification*

China is already the largest market for electric vehicles (EVs), accounting for more than 40 percent of the EVs sold worldwide in 2016 [13]. It is also a growing market for electric heating devices and cooking stoves, since recent government policies encourage the use of electricity to displace coal and gasoline [14]. Electrifying these end-use sectors can reduce emissions from gasoline and diesel vehicles, as well as from solid fuel used for residential heating and cooking. However, electrification requires generating additional electricity. If electrification is powered by carbon- and coal-intensive electricity, the dominant form currently in use in China, the increase in CO_2 emissions to produce the additional electricity largely offsets any emission reductions achieved in end-use sectors by displacing direct combustion of fossil fuels with electricity. For instance, a 2018 study estimated that by 2030, if the transport or residential sectors were 30 percent electrified, but the electricity were derived from sources as coal-intensive as the current power mix (i.e., 75 percent coal), this would not reduce CO_2 emissions, though it would result in significant air quality and health benefits (a decrease of 41,000–57,000 deaths in China annually) [15]. In comparison, if China rapidly decarbonizes its power sector and maximizes electrification across end-use sectors, these efforts may allow China to significantly reduce its carbon emissions and peak its carbon emissions before 2030 [16], while simultaneously reducing emissions of air pollutants [17].

7.4 Foundations for Long-Term Decarbonization

While the urgency to tackle air pollution could bring some concomitant benefits in reducing carbon emissions, it does not necessarily contribute to long-term decarbonization, for several reasons. First, many air pollution control strategies are not always aligned with carbon mitigation goals, as we discussed thoroughly in Section 7.3. Second, the co-benefits will likely diminish over time as low-cost opportunities are exhausted. Although reducing coal could address both issues, the marginal cost of displacing coal in economic sectors is likely to increase as more and more coal is removed from the energy system. Different options to reduce coal use (e.g., displace inefficient coal units with more efficient ones, improved efficiency, and increase in renewable energy use) are associated with different economic costs. While moderate levels of decarbonization may be possible with low-cost co-control options, deep decarbonization is unlikely to be achieved without turning to higher-cost options (e.g., substantially increasing renewable penetration), which may have large impacts on the economy but few or no air quality co-benefits (e.g., carbon capture and sequestration). In addition, given the high government priority on air pollution reduction, it is likely that air quality will be improved significantly in the coming decade. Such an improvement is essential for protecting human health but will lower the magnitude and value of future air quality co-benefits as the air becomes cleaner. Therefore, despite aligned efforts to mitigate air pollution and carbon emissions in the near term, long-term decarbonization cannot rely exclusively on the actions taken to tackle conventional emissions.

Measures to address air pollution could lay the foundations for long-term decarbonization if they help the institution-building and technology investments in favor of high penetration of low-carbon energy options. For instance, in March 2015, the Chinese government issued a document on "Deepening reform of the power sector" (also known as Document #9). It aims to allow market forces to play a decisive role in the allocation of resources in the power sector, and calls for effective, market-based measures such as electricity pricing, trading mechanisms, and platforms. While the broad principles set forth in this document need to be translated into feasible and well-designed policies, market-oriented efforts for generation, transmission, and distribution could provide an opportunity to encourage clean electricity use and mitigate the emissions of CO_2 and air pollutants from the power sector.

For electricity generation, a transition toward merit order dispatch would give priority to clean generation sources that have low marginal costs as well as low emissions of air pollutants and CO_2. China's present dispatch rules are designed to give thermal power plants guaranteed hours of operation in a year, in order to compensate for their capital and fuel costs. Such a dispatch system does not reflect the marginal costs of electricity production in real-time and leaves limited flexibility to accommodate intermittent renewable generation. Since low-carbon electricity, such as wind and solar, does not require fuel inputs and therefore has near-zero marginal costs, reform in generation pricing and transition toward merit order dispatch could encourage renewable integration and reduce curtailment, leading to co-benefits for both air pollution abatement and carbon mitigation.

Coordinating Strategies to Reduce Air Pollution and Carbon Emissions 165

For transmission and distribution, creating economic incentives for grid companies to integrate renewables and support demand-side management (DSM) could be beneficial for addressing air pollution and climate objectives. Currently, grid companies do not have a strong economic motivation to integrate renewables. Although the Renewable Energy Law requires grid companies to purchase renewable electricity, in reality this regulation has not been strictly enforced. A cost-sharing mechanism that requires grid companies to bear some of the renewable curtailment costs may create incentives for them to pursue possible measures to integrate renewables. In addition, DSM is likely to be enhanced under the ongoing power sector reform, which could improve energy efficiency and reduce the amount of energy production and associated air pollutant and CO_2 emissions.

7.5 Conclusion

In conclusion, air quality concerns can only take China part of the way toward deep decarbonization. In the near term, measures to tackle air pollution (e.g., curbing coal use) could bring some carbon mitigation co-benefits. Continuing the efforts to improve energy efficiency, curb coal consumption, invest in new renewable capacity, and reduce renewable curtailment will contribute to both air quality and climate objectives. There are clear immediate synergies between China's efforts to address these two issues.

However, to lay the foundations for long-term decarbonization, it is critical to leverage these near-term air pollution concerns to incentivize climate-friendly investment and policies. For instance, end-use electrification, independent of the fuel sources, can already reduce air pollutant emissions and health impacts from the transport and residential sectors. However, concurrent efforts to decarbonize the electricity sector are necessary to avoid generating additional electricity and associated CO_2 emissions in order to power the end-use sectors. Emphasizing the near-term air quality co-benefits may also enable the deployments of negative carbon technologies, such as bioenergy with carbon capture and storage capacity, that can reduce ambient air pollution while contributing to negative carbon emissions in the long run [18].

It is also important to further improve the synergy between China's air pollution reduction and carbon mitigation policy framework. The recent formation of the Ministry of Ecology and Environment provides an exciting opportunity to streamline the policy-making process for these two issues. Another area of potential improvement is to encourage market-based incentive policies, such as carbon pricing and market-oriented power sector reform. The Chinese government traditionally relies on command-and-control policies for air pollution reduction, such as mandates that require installing end-of-pipe scrubbers, which lead to no climate benefits. In contrast, market-oriented incentive policies aimed at improving energy and economic efficiency may facilitate a shift toward efficiency improvement measures, as well as actions to increase low-carbon generation and integration. These efforts may lead to co-benefits for both air pollution abatement in the near term and carbon mitigation in the long term.

Notes

1 The compliance of national air quality standard here means meeting the concentration levels of all six air pollutants monitored by the Ambient Air Quality Standard (GB3095–2012), i.e., SO_2, NO_2, PM_{10}, $PM_{2.5}$, O_3, and CO.

References

[1] Ministry of Environmental Protection, "2015 Report on the State of the Environment in China," (Beijing: People's Republic of China, 2016). Available at: http://english .mee.gov.cn/Resources/Reports/soe/Report/201706/P020170614504782926467.pdf

[2] Institute for Health Metrics and Evaluation (IHME), "GB D Compare Data Visualization" (Seattle: Institute for Health Metrics and Evaluation (IHME), University of Washington, 2020). Available at: www.healthdata.org/data-visualiza tion/gbd-compare (Accessed February 27, 2021).

[3] F. Jotzo, V. Karplus, M. Grubb et al., "China's emissions trading takes steps towards big ambitions," *Nature Climate Change* **8** (2018), pp. 265–267.

[4] W. Peng, J. N. Yang, F. Wagner et al., "Substantial air quality and climate co-benefits achievable now with sectoral mitigation strategies in China," *Science of the Total Environment* **598** (2017), pp. 1076–1084.

[5] M. W. Li, D. Zhang, C. T. Li et al., "Air quality co-benefits of carbon pricing in China," *Nature Climate Change* **8**(5) (2018), pp. 398–403.

[6] J. N. Yang, X. Y. Li, W. Peng et al., "Climate, air quality and human health benefits of various solar photovoltaic development scenarios in China in 2030," *Environmental Research Letters* **13**(6) (2018), p. 064002.

[7] State Council, 12th Five-Year Plan for Energy Saving and Emission Reduction (Beijing: People's Republic of China, 2012). Available at: www.gov.cn/zwgk/2012-08/21/content_2207867.htm.

[8] Peng et al., "Substantial air quality and climate co-benefits."

[9] S. Zhang, E. Worrell, and W. Crijns-Graus, "Evaluating co-benefits of energy effi-ciency and air pollution abatement in China's cement industry," *Applied Energy* **147** (2015), pp. 192–213. Available at: http://dx.doi.org/10.1016/j.apenergy.2015.02.081.

[10] S. H. Zhang, E. Worrell, W. Crijns-Graus et al., "Co-benefits of energy efficiency improvement and air pollution abatement in the Chinese iron and steel industry," *Energy* **78** (2014), pp. 333–345, Available at: https://doi.org/10.1016/j.energy.2014 .10.018.

[11] Y. Qin, F. Wagner, N. C. Scovronick et al., "Air quality, health and climate implica-tions of China's synthetic natural gas development," *Proceedings of National Academy of Sciences* **114**(19) (2017), pp. 4887–4892.

[12] Y. Qin, L. Hoglund-Isaksson, E. Byers et al., "The Air, Carbon, Water Synergies and Tradeoffs in China's Natural Gas Industry," *Nature Sustainability* **1** (2018), pp. 505–511.

[13] International Energy Agency, "Global EV Outlook 2017: Two Million and Counting" (Paris: International Energy Agency, 2017). Available at: www.oecd-ilibrary.org/energy/global-ev-outlook-2017_9789264278882-en

[14] National Development and Reform Commission, "Guidance Note on Promoting Electricity to Replace Coal and Gasoline Use" (Beijing: People's Republic of China, 2016). Available at: www.scio.gov.cn/xwfbh/xwbfbh/wqfbh/39595/41802/xgzc41808/Document/1664893/1664893.htm

[15] W. Peng, J. N. Yang, X. Lu et al., "Potential co-benefits of electrification for air quality, health, and CO_2 mitigation in 2030 China," *Applied Energy* **218** (May 2018), pp. 511–519. Available at: https://doi.org/10.1016/j.apenergy.2018.02.048.

[16] Z. Guo P. Liu, L. Ma et al., "Effects of low-carbon technologies and end-use electrification on energy-related greenhouse gases mitigation in China by 2050," *Energies* **8**(7) (2015), pp. 7161–7184.

[17] H. Huo, H. Cai, Q. Zhang et al., "Life-cycle assessment of greenhouse gas and air emissions of electric vehicles: A comparison between China and the U.S.," *Atmospheric Environment* **108** (2015), pp. 107–116.

[18] X. Lu, L. Cao, H. K. Wang et al., "Gasification of coal and biomass as a net carbon-negative power source for environment-friendly electricity generation in China." *Proceedings of the National Academy of Sciences* **116**(17) (April 2019), pp. 8206–8213. Available at: www.pnas.org/content/116/17/8206.short.

8

Conclusion

HENRY LEE AND DANIEL P. SCHRAG

If the world is going to decrease the rate of climate change, China, as the world's largest emitter, must play a major role. Climate science tells us that to prevent the most catastrophic consequences, the world will ultimately have to reduce net emissions to zero. A reduction of this level over several decades will be unprecedented in world history; it took nearly seventy-five years after the invention of the steam engine for coal to surpass wood as the dominant source of energy in Europe and the United States. For a country such as China, with its enormous coal-dependent infrastructure, its large manufacturing base, and its rapid rate of urbanization, transitioning away from fossil fuels will be very challenging.

China has already committed to stabilizing its emissions by 2030, to increasing the percentage of nonfossil-fuel energy to 20 percent, and to reaching carbon neutrality by 2060. The chapters in this book explore how China's actions in the years prior to 2030 will position the country to begin the task of deeper decarbonization post-2030. It also proposes a menu of policy initiatives that will build a programmatic foundation on which China can pursue ever-greater reductions in emissions in the future.

The authors of this volume suggest that if China is to realize carbon neutrality, it will have to embark on three major economic shifts. First, it will have to electrify a significant portion of its economy. Apart from biofuels and, for some uses, hydrogen, all of the technological transitions toward low-carbon energy systems are based on electricity. Thus, a nonfossil-fuel energy system is primarily an electric system. Passenger transportation, now fueled by gasoline and diesel, will likely be powered by electricity; home heating will migrate from fossil fuel-based systems to increasingly more efficient electric heat pumps. Steel, cement, and other heavy manufacturing facilities remain a challenge, but are likely to decarbonize later in the process.

Second, if China is to displace most of the coal capacity in its current electricity generation system, the role of both renewables and nuclear power will have to expand. Because wind and solar both produce power intermittently, a system that depends on these sources will need alternative sources of power that can be used when the sun is not shining or the wind is not blowing, particularly for prolonged stretches of time (i.e., seasonal intermittency). Moreover, as China transitions from an economy focused on heavy manufacturing to one more dependent on service industries, the nature of its electric load will change. Baseload power will become less important and facilities that can follow load will become more important. Hence, as Michael Davidson points out in Chapter 6, in the near and mid-term China must convert coal-fired power plants from being a barrier to increased renewable investment to being a bridge, repurposing its existing coal-based assets to flexible, dispatchable facilities, creating opportunities for greater investment in clean power. It remains to be seen whether nuclear power can serve a similar role, as the economics of this industry make it challenging to use in a dispatchable manner to support deep penetration of wind and solar.

Most importantly, the chapters in this volume argue that, to achieve an electric system that relies on nonfossil energy sources, China will find it increasingly cost-effective to gradually replace its current regulatory system, which is based on government command and control, with one more reliant on market incentives. As Pu Wang points out in Chapter 2, market reforms have many layers of competition at the production level, flexible choice on the consumer side, and accurate price signals that reflect the cost of energy in real time, benefiting both consumers and producers. Markets create greater transparency and predictability, which is likely to stimulate investment in renewables, improve the efficiency of the overall electric grid, and stimulate both consumers and producers to make millions of decisions leading to greater decarbonization of China's economy. Markets are much better at these tasks than command-and-control regulation. Such a market would also increase research and development investment for innovation in energy technologies, which is likely to be important in the overall clean energy transition.

To an extent, China has already started down each of these three paths. In 2018, more electric passenger vehicles were sold in China than in any country in the world, and its government forecasts that by 2030, electric vehicles will comprise 15 percent of China's car fleet, or approximately 80 million electric vehicles. New regulations aimed at both car owners and car producers have been enacted, and China is investing heavily in building the charging infrastructure needed to support this burgeoning industry. The country has installed 180 GW of wind power and is the largest producer and user of solar photovoltaic systems in the world. About 16 percent of China's installed electricity generating capacity is renewable, and that number is growing rapidly. In the case of the iron and steel industry, China is dramatically increasing the efficiency of its production. It is also making a major effort to reduce and eliminate direct burning of coal in rural residential households and small commercial establishments – sectors that consumed almost 90 million tons in 2015. China is building more high-voltage transmission lines than any other nation, and is one of the few countries in which the nuclear power sector continues to expand.

These actions are an impressive start, but the journey to realize ever-greater reductions in emissions will become more difficult and more costly as the less expensive investments – both economic and political – are completed and the more costly options remain. To reduce these costs, China should consider taking certain actions now that will increase the feasibility of this transition.

First, the decisions China makes between 2020 and 2030 will affect the political and economic cost of decarbonizing post-2030. The chapters in this volume provide numerous examples – both positive and negative – of this reality. If China reduces air pollution in its eastern cities by simply moving its coal generation to its western provinces and transporting the power by high-voltage wires to the east, it will have done little to reduce its carbon emissions. Although China's success in improving the efficiency of its present coal fleet has been impressive, it has had the unintended consequence of making its plants less flexible at a time when greater deployment of intermittent renewables requires more flexibility. On a more positive note, development of the best high-speed rail service in the world has resulted in annual decreases in intercity car trips. Hence, for many Chinese car owners, smaller vehicles used for urban transportation are preferable, opening a large and affordable market for electric vehicles (EV) and substantially reducing the range anxiety that constrains EV sales in the United States and Europe.

Second, China has invested heavily in the existing energy system. It cannot walk away from its commitments without a plan to help those displaced by the transition. Several million people are employed in the power sector, many in older and less efficient electricity facilities. A percentage are retired workers, who receive pensions from the companies that own these facilities. Any reform package cannot ignore these people. This concern is particularly acute, since in recent years China has lost over 1.3 million jobs in the coal industry. As Davidson points out in Chapter 6, China does not have a viable social safety net, and thus the threat of higher unemployment is a major concern to provincial leaders. Further, many of the companies in the electric sector are state-owned, often by provincial governments. Profits made by these companies are a key source of revenue for these provinces, which use these funds to meet other social priorities. Finding ways to reduce these fiscal disincentives will be essential for sustaining political support for any clean energy transition in the future. Managing the social dislocations inherent in the transition to a lower-carbon future will be politically and economically challenging, but they cannot be ignored.

Third, markets will matter more for the Chinese energy system in the future than they have in the past. As the costs of the decarbonization initiative increase, the system inefficiencies that are tolerated today will become too expensive and pressure will grow on the government to reduce, if not eliminate, these distortions. Historically, China has been resistant to markets, which are often perceived as unfair and a product of Western economists, who lack an understanding and appreciation of the successes that China has achieved through its centrally-planned system. China will not walk away from many of the factors – such as a strong planning process and a reliance on state-owned companies – that contributed to its successes. But within that structure, China is likely to use market incentives to achieve greater efficiencies, as it accelerates its transition to a lower carbon economy.

The authors of this volume argue that, as China continues to reduce its carbon footprint, it will realize that the cost to the economy of greater use of market mechanisms is significantly less than the cost of relying solely on government contracts, quotas, regulations, and policy mandates. In other words, using command-and-control options to realize a 10–20 percent reduction in carbon emissions may be affordable, but realizing 60–80 percent reductions will be very costly; the only way to reduce these costs will be through the greater use of markets.

Decarbonization will require decisions on investments, operations, and purchases by millions of stakeholders. Whether it be a consumer thinking about how he/she should consume power, an electric distribution company considering greater use of demand-side management options, an investor considering whether to invest in renewable power, or the owner of an existing power plant thinking about whether to allow their facility to be converted to a cycling facility, all of these stakeholders will be influenced by the incentives that they face. As Wang and Davidson point out in Chapters 2 and 6, respectively, the present system pushes companies and individuals toward coal facilities, away from demand management, and to a grid system characterized by large inefficiencies and substantial rigidities. If China wants to reduce its level of carbon emissions, these incentives must change. To achieve this end, China could promulgate a series of regulations directing thousands of stakeholders to make the decisions that the government felt were correct, or it could change the menu of incentives. In reality, it will probably pursue both, but relying only on the first would be unlikely to result in the changes needed in the power sector.

There are three major recommendations that emerge from the chapters in this book. First, we argue that the electrical dispatch system in China must change, replacing the equal-shares system with a system of economic dispatch. Under the former, the grid operator assures each generator that their plant will be dispatched a preset number of hours. The advantage of this system is that it provides the plant owner with a guaranteed revenue stream regardless of how efficient the plant is compared with other facilities on the grid or how much carbon it emits. As Wang and Wei Peng point out in Chapters 2 and 3, respectively, the result is that more coal plants are built than needed, renewable generators often find themselves curtailed off the grid, and dirty plants are often favored over cleaner facilities. When China's electric system was in dire need of more investment, such a dispatch system might have made sense, but in a world in which the value of cleaner power plants is increasing, and the cost of keeping inefficient plants on the system is growing, equal shares dispatch may no longer be economically viable. The more China invests in renewable generation, the greater the cost of this inefficiency. In a world in which power prices are likely to rise, paying for more power capacity than the grid needs will be an increasingly unaffordable scenario.

Second, we recommend that China focus on the challenge of integrating intermittent sources of electricity with dispatchable sources and demand management. China's present system of tariffs reflects the average cost of thermal generation and fails to fully reward plants that have comparatively lower operating costs. Feed-in tariffs (FIT) for renewable generators help correct some, but not all, of these distortions. These tariffs are set through a nontransparent process – the outcome of which is difficult to predict. Thus, investors in new facilities are left trying to guess the future value of their investments. The result is less-than-optimal investment patterns. If China wants to stimulate owners of large, efficient coal facilities to agree to operate below peak outputs and for fewer hours per year in order to be available when renewable power is not, it must find a way to make these investment decisions financially attractive. The more an efficient coal-fired plant is used to follow load, the higher its operating costs. A plant operator will not willingly agree to sell into the load-following market, unless he/she is compensated for this change in operations.

We also recommend that China transition to embracing time-of-day pricing for electricity generation. Economists have long argued that tariffs should be set equal to the cost of power at any given 5- to 30-minute window. Power costs vary throughout the day, as both demand and supply are constantly changing. Most countries, including China, average the cost of power and then set a tariff based on this average. Hence, consumers are overpaying during some parts of the day and underpaying during others. In a world in which people shift their driving to electric vehicles and their heating systems to electric heat pumps, time-of-use pricing becomes even more essential. For example, if all the electric car owners decided to plug their cars into the system at the same time, it would create a surge in demand that the electric system might not be able to handle. If prices vary throughout the day, car owners will strive to charge their vehicles when tariffs are low. But if tariffs remain unchanged regardless of changes in costs, consumers will have no incentive to adjust their consumption patterns. A lower-carbon future will be characterized by intermittent supply and demand patterns which can only be managed through a tariff system that reflects actual costs throughout the day.

Although markets and incentives are important, so too is governance. In Chapter 2, Wang argues that the complexity of China's governance of its power systems is a significant barrier to reform. As mentioned earlier, most of the key segments of China's power industry are owned and operated by the state – either the central or provincial governments; investments are planned and financed by the state; and the state regulates prices and production. Wang argues that these multiple state actors do not have clearly demarked responsibilities, and there is significant duplication. Thus, accountability is blurred and the incentives to optimize the performance of the system are lacking. The National Development and Reform Commission (NDRC) is the lead energy ministry, but its responsibilities in the area of electricity are spread across several departments, and these departments do not seamlessly coordinate their policies and initiatives. Further, the interaction between the Ministries and the state power companies are not always synchronized.

Provincial governments have responsibility for many decisions and have a major stake in the operations of the power assets within their jurisdiction. Many have a conflict of interest, as the tariffs charged to state-owned manufacturing have an impact on provincial revenue streams. When one considers that career promotions within the government are correlated with higher economic growth and lower unemployment figures, decisions around tariffs and investments in electricity generators, transmission, and distribution are of paramount importance to provincial officials. In summary, there are multiple government agencies and jurisdictions who have legal responsibilities for what facilities get built, what the tariff structure will look like, where energy facilities should be sited, and what levels of carbon pollution should be allowed.

To date, China has attempted to resolve this absence of accountability with myriad ad hoc coordinating committees that meet for months at a time. If China is to aggressively pursue a lower-carbon economy, it will need to rationalize its present power structure. Whether this means giving the central government more authority or placing greater responsibilities on the shoulders of local governments is not clear. However, the status quo is untenable in a world of accelerated decarbonization. China's future power structure will continue to rely heavily on state institutions and companies, and the need to find ways to promote greater coordination and more effective operations will become more imperative in the years ahead.

In transitioning away from reliance on fossil fuels, Chinese policymakers will need to make tough decisions, and those decisions will not always be popular.

Transparency will become more important. Citizens will demand to know the costs and risks inherent in these energy programs and projects that their government is asking them to support. Public acceptance will be needed if China is to increase the construction and operation of new nuclear power plants, high-voltage transmission lines, or even large hydroelectric plants. As Matthew Bunn points out in Chapter 4, building public trust is essential for large scale growth in nuclear power – an option that Chinese energy planners believe is essential to developing a low-carbon energy mix. Such trust will only be achieved through government actions at the central and provincial levels to engage the public in an open discussion of the safety, security, and economic risks.

In addition to building public trust and harmonizing the allocation of governance responsibility, China must improve its power planning sector and find ways to integrate market signals into this process. In Chapter 2, Wang provides the example of siting transmission lines in which the construction and operation will be performed by the two state grid companies, but the siting of transmission and the location of future generation will fall within the jurisdiction of provincial governments. Developing a power planning system that could be supported by all the parties at both the provincial and central levels, while simultaneously integrating the use of prices that reflect actual transmission costs, will provide future investors in clean power with greater certainty. This problem is not unique to China, but it is one that cannot be ignored, if the government wishes to pursue a cleaner grid.

Finally, if China is to give a greater sense of urgency to climate and the necessary transition to a lower-carbon economy, China should develop, pass, and implement a climate law. The two greatest emitters of greenhouse gases – the United States and China – have yet to implement a new domestic law or set of laws laying out the major steps that they intend to pursue. Until such laws are put into place, key stakeholders will assume that reducing carbon emissions is a lesser priority and will not plan adequately for the future.

The transition to a decarbonized energy and economic system is one of the most challenging journeys in the history of this planet. It will not be easy and will be fraught with uncertainties and dislocations. The authors of this book have attempted to identify the policy steps that will need to be taken today if China is to successfully navigate this journey. These steps involve changes not only in technology and in economic and energy policies, but also in the operation of basic governance of energy and economic activity. If China implements a solid policy foundation for deep decarbonization, it has the potential to lead the world through the transition to a carbon neutral energy system and realize its 2060 goal of carbon neutrality.

Index

2002 electricity reform. *See* Document No. 5
2015 electricity reforms. *See* Document No. 9
2030, 16, 18, 20, 32, 37, 39, 56, 59, 66, 69, 84, 136
2050, 16, 21, 47, 53, 58, 60, 62, 69, 91, 100, 125

accidents, 12, 67–68, 70–71, 73–75, 78–80, 91–92
    Chernobyl, 12, 66, 74, 76
    Fukushima, 12, 66, 68, 70–73, 75, 78, 87, 95–96,
       98
    Three Mile Island, 74
accountability, 21
ad hoc committees, 22
Air Pollution Action Plan of 2013, 127
Air Pollution Action Plan of 2013, 158
air quality, 134
airlines, 105, 110
airplanes, 117
Ambient air pollution, 166
ancillary services, 34, 135, 141, 143, 145
annual growth, 19
antinuclear advocacy, 73
AP1000, 74, 82–83
apartment buildings, 114, 118
artificial intelligence, 77
authoritarianism, 66, 85

backup, 28, 34–35, 68, 87
banks: central banks, 130
    World Bank, 128
baseload power, 50, 84, 87, 93–94
battery technologies, 54, 137
    flow batteries, 54
Beijing, 22, 26–27, 31, 96–98, 150, 156
    Beijing-Tianjin area, 106
bilateral agreement, 4
Bill Gates, 70, 90, 100, *See* Terrapower
biofuels, 58
Blast Furnace-Basic Oxygen Furnace, 140
Blue Sky War, 158
breed and burn systems, 90

breeder reactors, 67, 88, 90, 93
bribes, 72, 74
budgets, 35, 70, 72, 74
Bureau of Economic Operations, 22
Bureau of Pricing, 22
bureaucracy, 25
buses, 109
business models, 67, 75, 77, 80, 83–84
BYD, 109

cap-and-trade, 28–29, 31–32, 36
capital recovery, 25
carbon capture, 161
carbon intensity, 134
carbon pricing, 28–29
    carbon tax, 28–29
CCUS. *See* carbon capture
central government, 22, 24–25, 29, 31, 35, 43, 46, 124,
      130, 132, 136, 146
charging infrastructure, 13, 108–109, 112, 116, 118,
      169
    garage, 13, 110, 113, 115, 118
    home charging, 113, 115
charging stations. *See* electric vehicles
Chernobyl. *See* accidents
Chifeng, 26–27
Chile, 47, 58, 61
China Demonstration Fast Reactor, 89
China Nuclear Energy Association, 69, 82, 98
China–US bilateral agreement, 1
Chinese Nuclear Energy Association, 12
Chongqing, 26, 31, 42
climate change, 15, 57, 78, 94, 144, 148
coal, 39
    coal mining, 9
    coal prices, 83
    coal-fired power plants, 15–17, 19–20, 22–25, 28,
      32, 34, 36–37, 39, 41, 43, 45, 47–48, 50–53, 57,
      60, 85, 94, 121–125, 127–135, 137–149, 151,
      154

175

176 *Index*

coal (cont.)
  consumption, 31
  deregulation of coal, 22
  local taxes, 131
  reliance on coal, 65
Coal Conference, 123
coastal China, 20, 71, 80
coastal Germany, 47
combustion, 20, 34, 136–137, 139, 148
  internal combustion engines, 108–109
commercial sector, 18
commuting, 103, 109
competitive markets, 21, 31–33, 36, 51, 53, 83, 89, 129
congestion, 34, 53
construction costs, 84, 92
consumer, 28, 36, 137, 140
consumers, 16, 26, 28, 33–34, 51, 53, 56–57, 130, 135, 146
consumption, 15, 19, 28–29, 31–32, 34, 49, 57, 65, 88, 94, 123–125, 127–128, 134, 139, 141, 143
  electricity consumption, 15
contracts, 27, 45, 51, 74, 123–124
conventional generators, 48, 50, 57
cooking, 124, 127, 134, 137
coordination, 21–22, 29, 35, 51, 132, 148
Copenhagen Accord, 4
corruption, 72, 74, 94
  anti-corruption groups, 74
cost allocation, 20, 29, 35
currency exchange rates, 82, 95
curtailment, 25, 29, 39–40, 42, 46–51, 55, 57, 61, 63, 83, 132, 134, 143
cyberwarfare, 77

data collection, 92
deaths. *See* mortality
deep decarbonization, 21, 39, 41, 48, 58, 68, 83, 87, 121
demand centers, 20, 35, 42, 45–47
demand-side management, 23, 41, 55, 57–58
Denmark, 49–50
developing world, 5
diesel fuel, 104, 108, 110, 112, 114–115, 163, 168
direct load control (DLC), 56
dispatch protocol, 7
distributed power, 23
distribution, 62, 146
  costs, 25, 33
  equipment, 115
  networks, 131
  systems, 23
district heating, 57, 122, 124, 133–135, 137, 143, 145
Document No. 5, 32
Document No. 9, 33
dry cask storage, 85

eastern provinces, 20, 43, 45–46, 48
economic dispatch, 24

economic welfare, 25
Electric Arc Furnace, 140, 155
electric grid, 37, 44, 60, 122, 127
electric power sector. *See* electricity sector
electric vehicles, 15, 19, 34, 37, 101, 104, 106–108
  fast-charging stations, 19
electric vehicles, 109
electric vehicles, 114
electricity generation, 16–17, 22, 36–37, 39, 49, 122–123, 127, 134–135, 137, 144, 146
electricity policy, 16, 23, 35
  electricity pricing, 17, 34, 36, 145
electricity production, 17, 28, 36, 50, 90
electricity sector, 15, 31–32, 45, 55, 63, 83, 121, 130, 134, 141
electrification, 15, 19, 39, 51, 65, 122, 127, 139–140, 142–143
  industrial, 6
  transportation, 6
emerging thin film, 58
emissions trading, 31
employment, 24, 122–123, 127, 131, 145–146
  coal sector, 9
  pensions, 170
energy efficiency, 20, 142, 144
energy storage, 15, 41, 54–55, 61, 63
Environmental Protection Law of 2014, 158
equal share dispatch, 23
equal shares dispatch, 24, 28, 36, 51, 128, 148
equal-share dispatch system, 8
ERCOT. *See* United States of America
Europe, 16, 18, 35, 57, 72, 81–82, 134, 143
  European Union, 3
European Pressurized Reactors, *81*

Fast reactors: sodium-cooled fast reactors, 89
fast-charging stations, 15, 19
feed-in tariffs, 28, 31, 36, 42, 81, 83
financing, 66, 82–83, 92, 98
Finland, 81, 98
Five-Year Plans, 159
  12th, 41, 133
  13th, 19–20, 37, 39, 48, 50, 59–61, 127, 136, 140, 142, 149, 151–154, 156
fixed prices, 16, 23, 28, 31, 51, 83, 129, 134, 145
flexibility of systems, 15, 19–20, 28, 34, 45, 47–51, 53, 55, 57, 64, 88, 121–122, 131, 134–136, 142–143, 145, 149
  inflexibilities, 132, 142
fluctuation, 19–20, 55, 133
fluoride high-temperature reactor, 75
France, 50, 81
freight transport, 3, 102, 110
frequency regulation, 135
Fukushima. *See* accidents

Index

garbage. *See* waste

gas-fired plants, 16, 34

gasoline, 104, 108, 111–112, 114–115, 117, 120, 163, 168

GDP, 17, 24, 43, 66, 124, 126, 146

generating capacity, 17, 21, 130, 136

generation capacity, 16, 22

Generation II nuclear reactors, 73, 83–84, 89, 92–93

Generation III nuclear reactors, 84, 89, 92

Germany, 47, 50

global leadership, 20, 35, 52, 86, 144

governance, 5, 16, 21–22, 31, 38, 41

grid companies, 24–26, 32, 36, 45, 51, 56, 130–132, 146

    Southern Grid, 131

    State Grid, 131

gridlock. *See* traffic

ground transportation, 53

Guangdong, 26, 30–31, 33, 130

He Zuoxiu, 73

health, 85, 121, 126, 145

heating prices, 57

heavy industry, 18, 121–122, 127

Hebei, 26–27

Heilongjiang, 26–27, 42

helium, 90

highways, 102, 109, 115

Home Charging, 113

home heating, 9, 168

household, 19, 124, 137, 139

Hubei, 26, 31

hybrid vehicles, 13, 109

hydrogen, 84

hydropower, 16, 20, 45, 48, 50, 58, 128, 131–132

    pumped hydro, 48, 50, 54, 61

ICEs. *See* combustion

incentives. *See* market incentives

income disparities, 9

independent system operators, 33, 36

India, 124

industrial capacity, 67, 86

industrial sector, 18, 137

inflation, 128

infrastructure planning, 16–17, 36–37

Inner Mongolia, 26–27, 30, 40, 42, 149

innovation, 108, 110–111

    automobiles, 104

    in nuclear, 88

    nuclear, 89

    renewable technologies, 169

installed capacity, 39, 53, 81, 86

integration of renewables, 20, 29, 35, 37, 39, 41–42, 46–47, 49–50, 53, 55–60, 67, 135

interconnection, 29, 35, 47, 49, 52

intermittency, 15, 20, 22, 34–35, 40–41, 45, 47, 68, 84, 87, 94, 121, 132, 142, 145

intermittent. *See* intermittency

International Atomic Energy Agency, 71, 94–96, 99

    Integrated Regulatory Review Service, 72, 96

International Energy Agency, 69, *82*

intervention, 22, 25, 34

ISO versus TSO models, 33

Japan, 79, 96, 124

jet fuel, 105

Jilin, 26, 42, 46

light-water reactors, 68–69, 81, 93

liquefied natural gas (LNG), 49, 82, 134

liquid iron, 140, 143

load centers, 16, 20, 35, 132

load profile, 19, 132

loans, 34

local government, 23, 25, 78, 146–147

local governments, 22, 128–131, 147

local protectionism, 25

long-term, 16, 23, 28, 34–36, 41, 45–46, 51, 67, 70, 72–73, 93, 131, 144, 149

    emissions targets, 47

    investments, 88

losses, 23, 25, 33, 53, 75–76, 80, 123, 132, 135, 147

low-carbon development, 17–18

low-carbon policies, 15–16, 35, 37

    carbon pricing, 15, 28, 31, 35, 37, 140

low-carbon technologies, 22–23, 31, 65, 137

marginal costs, 28, 33, 51, 129, 131–132, 135, 145, 148

market incentives, 24

market mechanisms, 31, 34, 37, 147

market reform, 2

market signals, 28, 35–36, 135

markets: electricity markets, 15, 23, 28, 32, 34, 36, 130–131, 145, 147

Massachusetts Institute of Technology (MIT), *84, 89, 99*

merit-based order, 25, 33, 36

metering, 28, 34, 51, 55

middle income trap, 104

military, 76, 86

Ministry of Ecology and Environment, 71, 94, 148

Ministry of Electric Power, 24

Ministry of Environmental Protection, 94, 96

Ministry of Railways, 123

mitigation, 21, 31, 45, 136

molten salt, 75, 90

monopolies, 23, 26, 31, 33, 37, 130–131

morbidity, 11, 107

mortality, 66

    avoided deaths, 163

    pollution-related premature deaths, 158, 161

municipal governments, 24–25

National Development and Reform Commission, 22, 25, 31, 37, 41–42, 56, 58, 60–61, 63, 128, 151–153, 159
National Development and Reform Commission, 41, 56, 58, 60–62, 128, 151–153, 159
National Energy Administration, 22, 38, 40–41, 59–62, 149–150, 152
National Nuclear Safety Administration (NNSA), 71–73, 94, 96
near-term, 34, 41, 43, 45–46, 48, 50–51, 67, 73, 91
  emissions targets, 2, 13
  investments, 34, 88
  policies, 2
NGOs. *See* nongovernmental groups
Ningxia, 26–27, 42, 46
nitrogen oxide, 104, 107, 158, 162
nondiscriminatory, 32–33, 36
nongovernmental groups, 158
northern China, 20, 40, 48, 50, 55, 121–122, 126, 132, 139, 143
northern provinces, 124
NO$_x$. *See* nitrogen oxide
nuclear engineering, 6, 12
Nuclear Power, 95–100
nuclear program, 85
Nuclear Safety Law of 2018, 71–72
Nuclear Safety Plan, 74

offshore wind, 39, 43
oil, 84, 136, 149
on-grid tariffs, 26–28
onshore wind power, 26, 42–43, 60
Open Hearth Furnace, 140
operating costs, 24, 28
operating hours, 24, 32, 45
operational costs, 20, 145
opposition, 20, 35, 78, 92
Organization for Economic Cooperation and Development, 81, 98–99
overinvestment, 24, 128, 139

Paris Agreement, 18, 121
particulate matter, 65–66, 94, 126
passive safety, 66, 75, 77, 80, 84, 86, 90, 92
peak demand. *See* peak load
peak load, 20, 28, 55–56, 142
peak regulation, 135
Pearl River Delta, 106
pebble bed reactors, 69, 89
permits, 126, 128
perverse incentives, 23
petroleum-fueled vehicles, 6
PHS. *See* pumped heat electrical storage
pilots, 23, 31–33, 56, 132, 136, 142, 144–145
pipelines, 134
plutonium, 67, 76–77, 86–87, 89, 93
political resistance, 9, 112
population, 15, 43, 47, 148

portfolio, 21, 28, 31, 36, 55, 58, 94
portfolio standards, 28, 31, 36
primary energy, 18, 58, 140
proliferation, 21, 67, 85, 91, 93–94
protest, 66, 78
provincial governments, 22, 24–25, 43, 122, 128, 132, 145, 147
public charging, 113–114
public health. *See* health
public opinion, 66, 78
  opposition, 21, 35, 69, 78
public trust, 66–67, 73, 79–80, 92
pumped heat electrical storage, 55
purchasing power parity (PPP). *See* currency exchange rates

Qinshan seawall, 71
qu channeng, 126
quotas, 39, 42, 59
  generation quotas, 16, 24, 32–33, 36

radioactivity, 70, 75, 77, 80, 85, 92
rail transport, 123–124
range anxiety, 13, 109, 115, 170
real-time value, 28, 34, 36, 49, 158
Reform and Opening-Up Policy of 1978, 24
regulation, 18, 21–22, 52, 55, 62, 66, 70, 73, 94, 126, 128, 131, 143, 145–146
remote areas, 29, 35, 47
Renewable electricity, 59
renewable energy: renewable energy integration, 28–29, 35, 37
Renewable Energy Law (2005), 41
reprocessing, 67, 77–78, 86–90, 93
  enrichment and reprocessing, *85*
research and development (R&D), 21, 23, 29, 54–55, 58, 70, 81, 90–91, 133, 135–136, 144
reserve capacity, 16, 20, 34
residential sector, 15, 17–18, 20, 27, 34, 49, 135, 139, 143
resource-rich regions, 29, 43, 45–46
retail pricing, 22, 25, 28, 33, 36, 42, 131
  flexible retail pricing, 28, 34
retrofitting, 133, 136, 142
rivers, 20, 48, 78, 81
rural areas, 15, 47, 127, 134, 139
Russia, 74, 94

sabotage, 75–76, 80, 93
safety culture, 71–72, 74
scaling up, 21, 39, 67, 82, 144–145
Scandinavian countries, 50
scrubbers, 157
  end of pipe, 166
  sulfur removal, 11, 160
seasons, 48, 51, 133, 143
  summer, 56
  winter, 48, 57, 133, 135, 143

Index

shandayaxiao, 125
Shandong, 26, 30, 62, 89, 149, 152
    Shidaowan site, 89
Shanghai, 26–27, 30–31, 56, 63
Shenzhen, 31
shortages, 56–57, 122–124, 128
short-term. *See* near-term
Sichuan, 26, 46, 128
siting, 16, 22, 29, 66, 78–80, *81*, 85, 94
small modular reactors, 68, 84
smart technology, 22, 55, 58, 63
social safety net, 127
social welfare, 127, 147–148
solar power, 15, 18, 20, 24–25, 27–29, 37, 39–42,
    44–48, 50, 55, 58, 131–132
South Korea, 104
Southern Power Grid, 25, 29
spot market, 33–34, 132–133, 142, 144
stakeholders, 14, 171, 174
State Council, 33, 41, 60, 71, 73, 78, 150–151
    State Council Research Office, 72
State Grid, 25, 29, 44, 52, 60, 151
State Grid Corporation of China, 29
State Power Corporation, 24, 32
state-owned enterprises, 22, 24, 32, 44, 69, 82–83, 122,
    130–131, 149
    banks, 7
    generation firms, 130
stationary sources, 11, 103, 105, 117
steel, 122–124, 126–127, 136–141, 143
storage technologies, 22, 53–55, 58, 63
stranded costs, 20, 122, 139, 147
structural transition, 18–19
subsidies, 28, 33–34
    cross-subsidies, 27, 34
sulfur, 11, 107, 157–158, 160
supply and demand, 47–48
system stability, 19

tariffs, 35, 42, 131, 145, 149
tax breaks, 34
tax revenue, 80, 146
taxi, 109
technology innovation. *See* innovation
technology lock-in, 25
Terrapower, 70, 90
terrorism, 21, 70, 75–77, 79, 91, 93
Tesla, 114
theft, 75–77, 85, 93
Tianjin, 26, 30–31
Tianshan, 81
Tibet, 26, 123
total capacity, 16–17, 50, 130

traffic, 101, 103–104, 109, 112, 117
transmission lines, 16, 20, 22, 29–30, 33–35, 43, 45,
    52–53, 127, 132
    high-voltage technology, 16, 29–30, 35, 38, 49, 58
    long-distance, 16, 20, 29, 34–35, 43, 45–46, 52, 60,
        127, 148–149
transmission system operators (TSO) model, 33
transparency, 23, 26, 33, 57, 74, 79, 92, 142, 147
transportation, 65, 123–124, 128, 137, 142
trenching, 113
trucks, 101–102, 105, 108, 110, 117

ultra-high-voltage technology, 29–30, 35, 43, 45, 49,
    52, 58
unbundling, 128
United States of America, *16*, *18–19*, 19, *35*, 41,
    49–50, 54, *56*, 56, *61–62*, 63, *70*, 70, *72*, 74–76,
    74, *79*, *81–82*, 84, *85*, *87*, 89–90, 92, 96,
    99–100, 124–125, 137, 139, 158
    Institute of Nuclear Power Operations, 74, 92
    Southwest Power Pool, 47
    town hall meetings, *80*
    Trump administration, 70, 90
    US–China agreement, 1
    US–China trade war, 3
uranium, 75–78, 87–88, 90, 93
urbanization, 15, 50, 122, 124, 137
Urumqi, 26

vertical integration, 23, 128, 135, 144

Wang Yinan. *See* antinuclear advocacy
waste, 57–58, 67, 85, 90–91, 93, 139
    XE "garbage" \t; "*See* waste" garbage
        collection
    waste management, 67, 85, 93
weapons, 73, 75, 77, 85
weather, 19, 24
western provinces, 10, 170
wholesale pricing, 22, 24–26, 32–33, 35–36, 55
wind power, 15, 20, 24–25, 28–29, 35, 39–40, 42, 45,
    47–48, 50, 55, 58, 60, 131
wind production bases, 43
World Association of Nuclear Operators, 71
World Trade Organization, 124

Xi Jinping, 72

Yangtze River Delta, 60, 73
Yunnan, 26, 30, 33, 45–46

zero-emissions targets, 24, 51, 148
Zhejiang, 26, 30, 130